RAILS
IN THE
ROAD

A HISTORY OF TRAMWAYS
IN BRITAIN AND IRELAND

OLIVER GREEN

PEN & SWORD
TRANSPORT

First published in Great Britain in 2016 by
Pen & Sword Transport

An imprint of Pen & Sword Books Ltd
47 Church Street, Barnsley, South Yorkshire S70 2AS

ISBN 978 1 47382 223 8

Pen & Sword Books Ltd incorporates the imprints of Pen & Sword
Archaeology, Atlas, Aviation, Battleground, Discovery, Family History,
History, Maritime, Military, Naval, Politics, Railways, Select, Social History,
Transport, True Crime, and Claymore Press, Frontline Books, Leo Cooper,
Praetorian Press, Remember When, Seaforth Publishing and Wharncliffe.

For a complete list of Pen & Sword titles please contact
Pen & Sword Books Limited
47 Church Street, Barnsley, South Yorkshire S70 2AS England
E-mail: enquiries@pen-and-sword.co.uk
Website: www.pen-and-sword.co.uk

Design and typesetting
by Juliet Arthur, www.stimula.co.uk

Printed and bound in India by Replika Press Pvt. Ltd.

CONTENTS

The greatest horse drawn city. Detail from an atmospheric street scene in Victorian London, looking down Pentonville Road towards the gothic towers of St Pancras station and hotel at sunset. When John O'Connor painted this view in 1884 the horsecar line here had just opened. A woman is signalling with her parasol to stop a tram heading down the hill towards King's Cross, while another car is approaching, assisted on the climb by an extra trace horse. The white horse on the left has helped pull one tram up the hill to the Angel, and is being taken back down by the trace boy in readiness for the next ascent. Museum of London

INSPIRATION AND ACKNOWLEDGEMENTS

Researching and writing *Rails in the Road* has covered an interesting two-year period. When I started work in 2014, the UK's latest tramway was about to open in Scotland. Edinburgh Tram was already years behind schedule, way over budget and considerably scaled back from the original project plans. Two years later, as I finished writing, the full public inquiry into what went wrong there had still not been completed and reported back.

But other light rail infrastructure has continued elsewhere in England and Ireland, with extensions and improvements to the Manchester, Birmingham, Nottingham and Dublin tram schemes making progress. Sheffield has just received Britain's first tram/train for testing. None of these developments are happening fast enough, but neither is it all doom and gloom in the wake of past mistakes and continuing economic uncertainty.

UK light rail is steadily improving and the more I looked at the history of tramways over the last 150 years both in Britain and elsewhere, the more ups and downs came to light. Like most historical narratives, this is not a straightforward story of progress and it would be unwise to predict where we are going next.

Transport policy affects us all and has implications for the environment, town planning, housing provision, air quality and energy use as well as everybody's personal mobility, health and lifestyle. Trams and light rail can play an important part in all of this and understanding their role in the past is essential to help us plan, shape and build our future, particularly in cities.

I would like to thank all those whose knowledge and research have encouraged my thinking about *Rails in the Road*. Early chats with tramway historians Ian Yearsley and Alan Brotchie were particularly helpful in getting me started, and I am also grateful for the wise insights of others who are no longer with us, notably Winstan Bond and John Price. Of authors whose work features in the further reading list, I would particularly recommend John P. McKay's *Tramways and Trolleys*, still the best wide-ranging academic study of tramway development in Europe forty years after publication. The late Theo Barker and Michael Robbins' magisterial two volume *History of London Transport*, long out of print, is also still essential reading. More recently, Michael Corcoran's engaging history of Dublin's trams, *Through Streets Broad and Narrow*, stands out for showing an awareness of the wider social and economic history context so often ignored by specialist tram studies that concentrate obsessively on vehicles and technicalities.

We should all be grateful for the surviving work of the largely anonymous photographers who have recorded the rise and fall of the urban tram. Selecting images to give a broad coverage within the pages of one book has been a demanding but fascinating task. Picture credits have been included wherever possible, and I must apologise in advance for any personal acknowledgements that have been omitted. I am grateful to John Scott Morgan at Pen & Sword Books Ltd for commissioning *Rails in the Road* and to Jodie Butterwood for overseeing editorial and production. My thanks also go to Janet Wood for editing my manuscript so effectively and to the designer, Juliet Arthur, for so creatively marrying the final text and chosen images in the layout of the book.

Now that rails have been back in the streets of some of our cities for twenty-five years, it is surely time for a more detailed study of the impact trams are having second time around and serious consideration of whether the light rail renaissance should be encouraged. This is one for Lord Adonis and his new National Infrastructure Commission, created by the Government in 2015.

Oliver Green
Oxford, March 2016

IMAGE CREDITS

I have used nearly 500 images in this book. Many of these are from my personal collection of early commercial postcards and ephemera, augmented by scans and originals from many other sources, notably the wide-ranging stock of Ray Woodmore (**postcards@raywoodmore.com**).

Seventy images come from the London Transport Museum's extensive digital archive, which can be accessed online at **www.ltmcollection.org**. My thanks to my colleagues there, Caroline Warhurst and Simon Murphy, for making high resolution scans available for publication. These images are identified on individual picture captions as LTM/TfL, and I am grateful to London Transport Museum Director Sam Mullins for permission to use them. As an LTM Research Fellow I am also looking beyond the capital this time.

My thanks to museum sector colleagues elsewhere who have helpfully made high quality images freely available, notably Finbarr Whooley, Director of Content at the Museum of London, Emma Williams and Karl Morgan at Swansea Museum, Laura Waters, Curator of Collections at the National Tramway Museum, Crich and Paul Jarman, Assistant Director of Transport and Industry at Beamish, the Living Museum of the North. Paul's website **beamishtransportonline.co.uk** gives a regular visual update of restoration and development on the museum's working tramline. See also the Crich Tramway Village blog for news of the National Tramway Museum's activities on **www.tramway.co.uk**.

Most of the recent photographs of current light rail operations were taken by me over the last six years (identified on the captions as OG). Special thanks go to photographer Peter Stubbs for letting me use his night shot of Edinburgh trams (see more at **www.edinphoto.org.uk**), to Nottingham City Council for providing images of the excellent NET system and to Oxfordshire County Council for allowing me to show a computer generated future vision of my home city of dreaming spires, traffic free and served by modern trams. If only …

A 1930's London Transport tram stop flag, now in use again at the National Tramway Museum, Crich. OG

THE ROLLER COASTER RIDE 1860-2015

Do trams have a promising future or are they an outdated mode of urban public transport that belongs to the past? There have been passenger tramways in Britain for more than 150 years, but trams have had a roller coaster ride for most of this period. They have been characterised at various times both as a progressive transport success and a long term failure in shaping our urban lifestyle. Their history could be represented on a graph showing early growth under horse and steam power in the late Victorian period, a striking Edwardian electric boom in the early 1900s, a peak in use and development in the 1920s, then a steady decline to virtual extinction in the 1960s. There has been a gradual renaissance of the tram in 'light rail' mode since the 1990s which still looks promising, though progress in the UK is cautious and slow. Will that change?

For such an everyday mode of public transport, trams have always been remarkably controversial, provoking fierce argument and debate about their value and impact on the urban environment. Trams are still remembered with rose-tinted nostalgia by an older generation looking back to an apparently simpler past and revered by those hoping for a greener and more civilised urban future. Proponents and opponents have clashed repeatedly on various grounds

The traditional double-deck British electric tram in its urban habitat. This is Leeds c1914, but the photograph could have been taken in almost any northern industrial town in England.

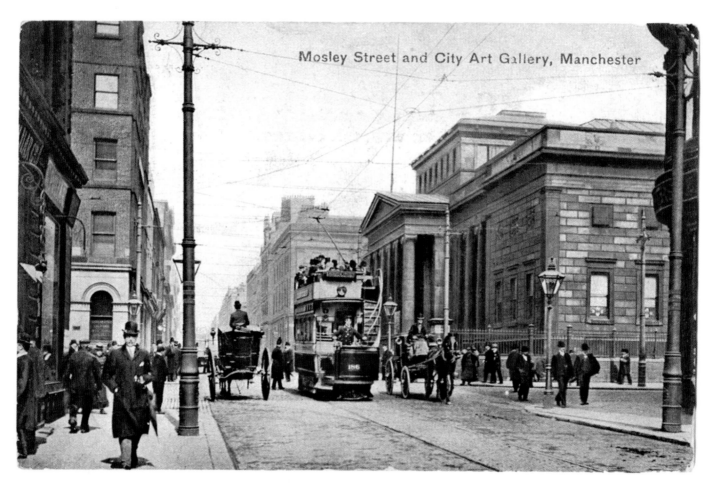

Mosley Street and City Art Gallery, Manchester

Manchester then and now. A postcard view of the City Art Gallery with one of the Corporation's newly introduced electric trams approaching, c1904. Manchester's last tram ran in 1949, or so everyone thought.

which have ranged from cost and practicality to technological development and from vested interests to the wider public and civic benefits. Where are they going next?

The apparent pattern of rise, stagnation, decline and revival has not been consistent across the country. Changing social, economic and political circumstances over the twentieth century have done much to shape and determine local developments in the absence of any national transport strategy set by central government. This is still true today and the invariably tortuous progress of every current project makes any firm prediction about the future role of trams somewhat contentious. The widely reported project management failures and inflated costs of the Edinburgh Tram scheme, currently the subject of a public inquiry, may cast a particularly long shadow over any new

proposals in Scotland. On the other hand, plans to devolve significant responsibilities and budgets from the government in Westminster to new regional city partnerships and the creation of a National Infrastructure Commission in late 2015 should eventually give a major boost to schemes like light rail projects across the UK. We might even get, for the first time in Britain, transport planning which meets both local needs and national priorities, with a much wider distribution than Greater London and a 'northern powerhouse' centred on Manchester.

Light rail must surely now be part of any co-ordinated approach to future infrastructure and land use planning. It makes no sense to continue building new housing and communities where transport and access is based largely around private car ownership. Once they are up and running trams are far more popular, efficient and successful than cheaper bus projects, and the most effective way of getting drivers out of their cars in urban areas. People soon forget about the delays, disruption and inconvenience of the construction period, but big capital projects do require bold thinking, political commitment and long term planning because they are costly and easily delayed, derailed or cancelled in a rapidly changing economic climate.

A century ago, there were electric trams on the streets of nearly every town in the country. The newly built networks were a source of huge local and civic pride, and available to all at affordable fares. Fifty years later the trams had all gone, superseded by buses and cars, but the everyday urban travel experience soon declined rather than improving. Traffic congestion and air pollution got worse everywhere in Britain as various attempts to manage rocketing car use in the city were tried. Encouraging people to use park and ride systems, car sharing, electric vehicles, greener hybrid buses and a resurgence in cycling have all helped, but these measures are all partial solutions. Cars are now widely considered incompatible with civilised city life, but people need to be offered an

The same view of Mosley Street in 2006. Manchester was the first city in the UK to reintroduce street running trams in 1992. This is one of the latest Bombardier Flexity Swift units now used on all Metrolink services.

A modern European tram in a historic Scottish streetscape. This is Edinburgh New Town in 2014, with a sleek Spanish-built CAF articulated unit turning past the National Portrait Gallery into York Place, the current end of the newly opened tram line. Extending the trams from the city to Leith on the Firth of Forth, seen in the distance here, will still take place as originally planned if a suitable funding package can be agreed. OG

attractive and convenient alternative. Light rail, in combination with other public transport modes, can transform urban mobility and improve the quality of town travel for all. Anyone who has spent time in a busy city with modern trams will have experienced this, from Amsterdam to Zurich.

Yet more than twenty years after Manchester first put trams back on British city streets, there are still only ten modern light rail systems in the UK and Ireland. This is in stark contrast to Continental Europe, where in France alone twenty completely new light rail networks have opened since the Millennium and major tramway investment continues in towns and cities from Poland to Portugal. Some of the UK

systems are being expanded and developed, but there are currently no approved plans for any more start-up projects in Britain. Trams will not be seen again soon in Bristol, Glasgow, Leeds or Liverpool, major cities that once had extensive tram networks and had plans for new light rail schemes only a decade ago. All these projects have been shelved or abandoned and no British city seems likely to follow the shining example of Nottingham in making a modern tramway the key feature of its urban transport planning. The idea that we can't afford to build new tram projects is clearly nonsense. If we want sustainable cities in the future, we can't afford not to include trams in the mix, yet still the uncertain roller coaster ride continues…

Chapter 1

HORSE AND RAIL

The passenger carrying tramway was both a very early and a surprisingly late development in Britain. There is a gap of more than fifty years between the introduction of the first recorded passenger service on rails and the opening of the first street railway or tramway in the UK. That original passenger service was started in 1807 on a recently laid mineral plateway in South Wales. It continued to run for up to twenty years but seems to have been a unique operation that was not imitated or developed anywhere else.

The first British tramway designed exclusively for transporting people, and the first to be laid along a street, opened as a trial operation at Birkenhead in 1860. This followed American practice rather than anything pioneered in this country. Indeed it was brought to the UK by an American with the appropriate name of Train. Goods and passenger carrying railways had been opened all over Britain in the interim, but nearly all of them operated on their own separate right of way and they did not run down roads.

The street railway, or tramway, providing the equivalent of a timetabled bus service on rails and sharing road space with other traffic, was an exclusively North American development that was brought to the UK from the US. After Train's short-lived experiments here, the American style of urban street railway, first seen in New York City in 1832, was only gradually introduced to Britain's towns and cities on a permanent basis in the 1870s and '80s.

The first public railway in the UK to be authorised by Act of Parliament had been the Surrey Iron, opened in 1804 alongside the River Wandle between Croydon and Wandsworth, then just outside London. This was a horse-drawn goods plateway which never carried passengers. Two years later a similar operation incorporated as the 'Oystermouth Railway or Tramroad' opened in South Wales along the coast of the Gower peninsula between Swansea and Oystermouth, a distance of about 5 miles. At the time there was no road link along the Gower and all minerals mined or quarried in the area had to be transported across Swansea Bay by boat.

The 'tramroad' was authorised 'for the passage of Wagons and other Carriages', but its main purpose was to carry coal, limestone and iron ore on payment of a toll. The line was constructed as a plateway with track made up from short cast iron angle sections laid on granite blocks. The small open wagons, known locally as trams, were pulled by horses,

Drawing by Miss J. Alford, who sketched the Oystermouth Tramway car during her holiday in South Wales in 1819. This is thought to be the second tramcar used on the world's first passenger carrying line at Swansea from c1815. A reconstruction of the vehicle based on this sketch is on display at Swansea Museum.
Swansea Museum

either individually or coupled together in a short train. Two years earlier the inventive Cornish engineer Richard Trevithick had demonstrated the first steam railway locomotive on another Welsh industrial tramroad at Merthyr Tydfil, some 30 miles away. This was a successful trial, but it did not lead to any further developments with steam locomotion and there were no early attempts to use mechanical power on the Oystermouth line.

Goods operation on the tramroad using horse power began sometime in 1806. Benjamin French, one of the tramroad's directors, was then authorised to start a passenger service on the line in addition to freight. French offered the company £20 a year in lieu of tolls 'for permission to run a wagon or waggons on the Tram Road for one year from 25 March next *for the conveyance of passengers*'. He provided a suitable vehicle, which can be considered the first ever passenger tramcar, although at the time it was described as a carriage, and was more like a stagecoach on rails. Services duly commenced in March 1807, making this the earliest known date for the conveyance passengers by rail . It was evidently quite a successful venture as a year later French was being charged an additional £5 for the passenger contract. The fee had gone up to £25.

An early journey on the tramroad was described with great enthusiasm by Miss Elizabeth Isabella Spence, author of 'novels and accounts of travel,' in a letter to the Dowager Countess of Winterton dated 3 August 1808. She wrote excitedly from Swansea that:

I never spent an afternoon with more delight than the former one in exploring the romantic scenery of Oystermouth. I was conveyed there in a carriage of a singular construction, built for the convenience of parties, who go hence to Oystermouth to spend the day. The car contains

twelve persons and is constructed chiefly of iron, its four wheels run on an iron railway by the aid of one horse, and is an easy and light vehicle.[1]

A few years later Richard Ayton was rather less enamoured of the passenger tramway in his *Voyage round Great Britain undertaken in the Year 1813*. He describes the Oystermouth tramcar as:

A singular kind of vehicle…it is a very long carriage, supported on four low iron wheels, carries sixteen persons, exclusive of the driver, is drawn by one horse, and rolls over an iron railroad at the rate of five miles an hour, and with the noise of twenty sledge hammers in full play. The passage is only four miles, but it is quite sufficient to make one reel from the car at the journey's end, in a state of dizziness and confusion of the senses that it is well if he recovers in a week.

Ayton may not have enjoyed the experience, but it was apparent that the tramroad had become more profitable as a leisure line for wealthy tourists paying a shilling a time than for its original purpose of mineral transport. Sometime in the late 1820s a turnpike road was constructed alongside the tramway, and this appears to have killed off the passenger business once a more comfortable road coach operation was started along the new highway.

It is not clear how long the freight operation limped on, but the plateway had become derelict by the 1850s, when part of it was relaid as a conventional standard gauge railway to carry coal to Swansea from a local colliery. George Byng Morris, the son of one of the original proprietors, then reintroduced a horse-drawn passenger service in 1860 between Swansea and Oystermouth. In the same year George Francis Train opened what he and most historians since have considered

Passenger car used on the relaid Oystermouth Railway in the 1860s, a curious mixture of horse tram, stagecoach and railway carriage. This oil painting with Swansea Bay in the background is attributed to John Joseph Hughes.
Swansea Museum

to be the first proper street railway in Britain, at Birkenhead on the Wirral.

It was of course a complete coincidence that these two services should open (and re-open) in the same year and it does seem surprising that there had been no other regular passenger tramway services running anywhere in the UK over the previous thirty years. By 1860 more than 10,000 route miles of railway had opened all over the country, mostly with both passenger and freight services available. However, the steam-hauled passenger traffic by train was nearly all *between*

towns and cities. Rail transport was not developed on city streets.

A few examples have been found of horse-drawn operation of passenger cars on short rail lines in the 1830s, such as the Elgin Railway in Fife, Scotland. Arguably there is little distinction between a light railway and a tramway in such cases. However, there does not seem to have been any attempt at this time to lay rails in the streets of an urban area of Britain in order to provide regular passenger transport within a town. By coincidence, shortly after the Oystermouth Tramroad had effectively had its original passenger business destroyed by the arrival of a smooth macadamed turnpike road alongside it in the 1820s, the poor state of the streets in rapidly expanding New York City helped to create the right conditions for the first street railway to be introduced on the other side of the Atlantic.

New York, New York

Some towns and cities in Europe and North America were becoming sufficiently prosperous in the 1820s and '30s to create a market for short distance passenger transport on urban streets. The middle-class residents of London and Paris were now able to hire the latest fashionable two-seater cabs (cabriolets) rather than walk in town, and large box-like coaches carrying up to twelve or fourteen passengers began operating on fixed routes and schedules across both cities. These 'omnibuses', the name

meaning 'for all' in Latin, appeared in quick succession in Paris (1828), London (1829) and New York (1830).

While the European city streets were generally well made up and paved, the main roads of New York were poor and could become a quagmire in winter. It was logical to suggest running coaches on rails in the road which would give passengers a smoother ride through the streets and make more efficient use of horse power than an omnibus. Nobody had ever proposed this in a European city, but the idea did take off in booming New York, where the population of Manhattan alone had nearly doubled in the 1820s.

The relatively spacious urban grid layout of New York's streets made the prospect of rails in the road much less threatening to the state and city authorities than they might have been in the crowded, medieval heart of the City of London or Paris. Accordingly, when the

The first London omnibus, introduced between Paddington and the Bank by George Shillibeer in 1829. He copied the idea of a scheduled urban coach service from what he had seen in Paris. New York then followed in 1830, and two years later the Manhattan omnibuses faced competition from the world's first street railway.

London Transport Museum/TfL

New York & Harlem Railroad Company was established in 1831 it was able to secure official sanction to build the first railway in Manhattan right on the city streets. The agreed route was from City Hall uptown and along the Bowery and 4th Avenue to the Harlem River, a distance of about 8 miles. The section in Lower Manhattan, which was already built up, was laid entirely on the streets and opened for business in 1832. The full length of line to Harlem, which involved excavating a deep cutting and tunnel in Upper Manhattan, then still in open country, was completed in 1838.

Once the Harlem River had been bridged, the line was linked with another to become the first long distance railroad from New York City, running into New York State and eventually reaching Albany, the State Capital, some 150 miles away. The original section in Manhattan doubled as both a local horsecar line and the first railroad access to the city from upstate. This dual role was effectively forced on the company by the restrictions in its charter, as after a number of boiler explosions on early steam engines, locomotives were banned from the downtown streets of New York City. The carriages of all arriving trains had to be uncoupled at 27th Street and pulled individually by teams of horses along the street railway through Lower Manhattan to the City Hall terminus.

This arrangement continued at least until the opening of a full off-street railroad depot on 27th Street in the 1850s. On the lower street section of line a local service, the first urban tramway, was also in operation using smaller horsecars of a completely different design to the larger long distance railroad cars. The American streetcar was emerging as a distinct type of vehicle offering a new mode of urban transport in direct competition with the city omnibuses. One of the first suppliers of both vehicle types was Irish-American

coachbuilder John Stephenson, whose New York City workshops later became the largest builder of horsecars in the world, exporting to Europe, South America and Australia.[3]

All this was a complete contrast to the way in which railways were first introduced to European cities in the 1830s. In London all railways were kept off the streets from the start, and under the terms of its Act of Parliament each line that approached the capital had to acquire and construct its own right of way. In town this usually meant brick arches above or a cutting below street level as they approached the centre, and a final terminus outside the City of London and Westminster boundaries.

The first passenger railway to arrive in the metropolis, the London & Greenwich, opened in 1836, terminating just south of the river in Southwark, close to London Bridge. The following year the London & Birmingham opened the first terminus for trains from the north at Euston Square, more than a mile from the City. These and subsequent lines were grade separated and rails in the road would not have been countenanced anywhere in the capital. Onward journeys to the centre of town had to be made by cab, omnibus or on foot. It

City line horsecar of the New York & Harlem Railroad passing the Astor Place Theatre in Lower Manhattan. From *Views of New York* by Henry Hoff, 1850.
New York Public Library

An invitation to the opening of the London & Greenwich, the first passenger railway in the capital, December 1836. No street running was allowed and the line was carried on a brick viaduct all the way to the terminus at London Bridge. LTM/TfL

was not until the 1860s that rail access to the City and Westminster was opened up by new bridges over the Thames and the construction of the Metropolitan Railway, the world's first underground line. None of these new transport developments were street railways.

Charles Dickens was fascinated by the many contrasts with London when he first visited New York in 1841, and commented in particular on Manhattan's unique street railway with its horsecars in his *American Notes*:

> *Again across Broadway, and so –*
> *passing from the many-coloured*
> *crowd and glittering shops – into*
> *another long main street, the Bowery.*
> *A railroad yonder, see, where two*
> *stout horses trot along, drawing a*
> *score or two of people and a great*
> *wooden ark with ease.*[4]

Further horsecar lines were to be developed on the streets of Manhattan, but not until the early 1850s. Initially the only other US city to follow New York's example with a street railway was New Orleans in 1834. When five additional lines were laid in Manhattan twenty years later, new horsecar routes also opened in Boston (1856) and Philadelphia (1857).

Then, in quick succession, before the end of the decade, horsecars came to Baltimore, Cincinnati, Pittsburgh and Chicago, all in operation before any street railways were operating in Britain.

Alphonse Loubat, a French-born wine merchant who had prospered after emigrating to New York in the 1820s, brought the idea of urban street railways across the Atlantic when he returned to France in 1852. It is often claimed that Loubat was an engineer and had personally devised the grooved wrought iron rails used on the New York tramways in the early 1850s. Recent research suggests that he probably had no direct involvement with the New York lines, though he was certainly inspired by their example.[5]

Loubat took out patents for tram rails in France which were very similar to the Second and Eighth Avenue Railroads in Manhattan, but this did not mean he designed them personally. As an entrepreneur he was responsible in 1853 for promoting and laying the first Parisian *Chemin de fer Americain*, as the urban tramway became known in France. Unfortunately, his street railway in Paris was not a great financial success. Within two years he had been persuaded to sell out to the newly formed *Compagnie Générale des Omnibus de Paris*, which consolidated most of the city's omnibus operators into a single company and was given authority to run nearly all public street transport in Paris. Loubat's tramway survived, but only became profitable some years later under the new management when it was extended.

A similar large omnibus company was proposed soon afterwards for London, and was initially registered in Paris under its French title, only becoming anglicised as the London General Omnibus Company in 1856. The LGOC did not secure complete dominance of city transport operation like its French equivalent, but it quickly acquired more than 70 per cent of the existing omnibuses in London. The General got off to a rocky financial start but was to remain the city's main bus operator right up to the creation of London Transport in 1933.

It was associates of the LGOC who made the first serious attempt to introduce street tramways in England. In 1857 a Bill was presented to Parliament for authorisation of a tramway running from the fashionable western suburb of Notting Hill through central London via Oxford Street to the Bank. The LGOC, already struggling to develop their newly acquired omnibus operations, clearly underestimated the antagonism that a street railway proposal might face. Their Bill was defeated in 1858, largely because of the implacable opposition in parliament of the influential Sir Benjamin Hall MP, whose carriage wheels had been badly damaged more than once when crossing colliery tramroads in his South Wales constituency. It was the first of many battles that proposals for street tramways would provoke and which delayed their adoption in Britain.

Train to England
According to his colourful but unreliable autobiography, George Francis Train first thought about bringing the American street railway to England after making a business trip to Philadelphia in 1858:

> *I observed the network of Street Railways in that city which then, perhaps, had the most perfect system of surface transportation in the world. I was struck with the idea of the great convenience these railways must be to business men and to all workers, and wondered why London, with so many more persons, had never had recourse to a street railway….I stored the idea up in my mind, intending to utilise it some day, when I returned to England.*[6]

Like Loubat, Train was not an engineer, but he was a persuasive businessman who had travelled the world in his twenties as an agent for his uncle's shipping company. He was very much an ideas man but also an irrepressible self-publicist, later running for US President and claiming to be the model for Jules Verne's globetrotting character Phileas Fogg in his novel *Around the World in 80 Days*, published in 1873.

When the 29-year-old American sailed into Liverpool in 1859 to pursue his street railway plans, Train already had extensive, though variable, experience as a trader in Europe, Australia and the Far East. He had decided to target Liverpool with his plans before London because:

> *… I had long been associated with it and because, as it was the leading seaport of the world, I had a false idea that it was progressive…now, when I proposed the laying of a street railway, I found the leading men of the city just as narrow and just as hopelessly behind the times as they had been in the matter of improving shipping facilities. They would not consider the proposition at all.*[7]

Guided five-wheel road/rail omnibus using Haworth's 'patent perambulating principle' at the entrance to Peel Park, Salford, 1861. This experimental system did not develop into a full street railway operation and the rails in the road were removed after a few years' use.
Salford Museum & Art Gallery

Launch of the first street railway in England at Birkenhead, 30 August 1860. Promoter G.F. Train, with arm outstretched, is at top left. The boy with a cap at the other end of the top deck is James Clifton Robinson, later to become a successful tramway entrepreneur himself.

In fact a London engineer and inventor, William Curtis, was given permission in the same year to run his patented 'railway omnibus' on part of the existing Line of Docks goods railway system in Liverpool in 1859. But as this was not on newly laid street track it does not qualify to beat Train in the street railway stakes. The vehicle Curtis had designed was a convertible road/rail vehicle rather than a tramcar. It had moveable wheel flanges, enabling it to run both on rails and, with an adjustment, on a flat road surface. This sounds ingenious if it allowed a quick and easy changeover, but Curtis' system may not have been entirely practical and was not developed further.

Two years later another hybrid road/rail system devised by John Haworth was tried out in Salford by omnibus proprietor John Greenwood. Haworth's 'patent perambulating principle' involved laying a length of track in the road with a third, grooved middle rail which could be used to guide standard omnibuses on the street when they were fitted with a small extra central wheel. This omnibus/tram experiment continued on a short stretch of line for about five years, but never amounted to a full street railway operation.[8]

Train, meanwhile, had turned his attention to Birkenhead, just across the Mersey from Liverpool. He took the idea of a US-style street railway to shipbuilder John Laird, chairman of the town Commissioners, the local body responsible for the town's streets. Laird and his colleagues were persuaded to allow Train to install a short temporary tramway on just over a mile of roadway between the Woodside Ferry and Birkenhead Park. It was duly laid in only six weeks. On 30 August 1860, with full American razzmatazz, a colourful decorated horsecar and a lavish inaugural banquet, Train was ready to launch the first street railway in England.

George F. Train had great flair for publicity and promotion, announcing in the Liverpool papers that he had invited not only Queen Victoria and Prince Albert, but most of the crowned heads of Europe to the opening, together with 'Her Majesty's Ministers, several of the Nobility, Members of Parliament and members of the leading Corporations in the Kingdom'. Few of these grandees actually attended, but it was a suitably grand event. More than 300 guests came to the party and Train followed up by having printed and distributed a booklet recording every speech and toast (there were eleven of them), which fills more than 100 pages.[9] He even included some of the less than flattering press reports of his campaign, including this piece by the anonymous 'lounger at the clubs' from the *Illustrated Times* of 8 September:

Mr Train, the inaugurator of Street Railways at Birkenhead, is a very different man to what you would judge him to be if you knew him only from his speeches and books. His speeches are the most extraordinary orations that have been uttered since the first spouter mounted his stump. There are some good things in them, but these are few and far between, like plums in a parish Christmas pudding. On the whole, they are the most extravagant, bombastic, egotistic, windy utterances that ever mortal man delivered. Judging from these, you would hardly decide that he is a farseeing, sagacious, hard-working practical man; but that is what he really is…His 'Herculean idea' as he calls it, is to develop Street Railways in every great city and town in England, and he has certainly made a commencement.

Train's flamboyant manner no doubt alienated as many reserved British listeners

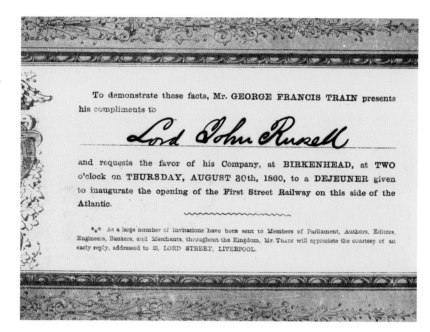

and readers as he convinced, making it difficult to decide whether ultimately he advanced or delayed the permanent adoption of tramways in Britain.

By the time the pioneer Birkenhead line had opened, Train was trying his luck in London. In 1860 there was no single authority in a position to authorise tramways across the capital and Train made a series of separate applications to local vestries, district boards of work and turnpike commissioners to lay short demonstration lines in different parts of the city. He knew it would not be straightforward, but this scattergun approach was risky. Train might have done better to target working- and middle-class areas where there would have been less opposition from wealthy carriage-owning citizens who would not wish for or need to use trams.

He made a second mistake by insisting on using his patented step rail, which protruded above the road surface and was considered a potential risk to other road users. Similar track had been used without problems in the streets of Philadelphia, but American experience cut no ice in London. The perceived threat of the edge rails to other traffic allowed the

Invitation sent to Lord John Russell, British Foreign Secretary, for the Birkenhead inauguration in August 1860. He was one of several government ministers invited by Train to his tramway launch party, but the only Russell who attended was a journalist from the Liverpool *Daily Post*.
LTM/TfL

THE IMPROVED STREET RAILWAY CARRIAGE.
PATENTED BY GEORGE FRANCIS TRAIN.

An artist's impression of Train's first proposed street railway in London from Bayswater to Marble Arch. This was part of his submission to get Board of Trade approval in 1860. It was authorised as a 'temporary concession' and opened in March 1861 but never had a double-deck car as shown here.
LTM/TfL

carriage owning residents and the omnibus operators to form an unlikely alliance against Train's plans.

In the end just three of Train's short trial lines in London were approved as 'temporary concessions' and opened separately in 1861. They ran from Notting Hill along Bayswater Road to Marble Arch, down Victoria Street to Westminster and from the south end of Westminster Bridge to Kennington Gate. All three aroused fierce criticism and had to be removed after only a few months, but not before Train had managed to convince a good many people of the merits of his tramcars, which were considerably larger and more comfortable to ride in than a standard London omnibus. Ever the salesman, Train just kept on pressing his case. As he expressed it on the invitation to a 'Yankee breakfast' launch for his third London line 'I cannot think that anyone

would wish to throw any impediment in the way of introducing so great a luxury as THE PEOPLE'S CARRIAGE.'

Possibly realising that there was little benefit in promoting the street railway in England as something essentially American, even Train began suggesting that his tramcars were entirely British. In fact it seems likely that all his original cars were imported from Philadelphia, possibly with final assembly in the UK. Even 150 years later it is difficult to be certain of all the facts surrounding Train's tramway schemes, and recent research has revealed yet more information which contradicts much of his own and subsequent myth-making.[10]

As economic historian Theo Barker has pointed out, the unsuitability of Train's edge rail, allied to the man's own bombastic manner 'prejudiced tramway promotion in London for several years to come, and it may have been to some extent responsible for keeping the tramcar permanently out of most of the West End',[11] Barker quotes a contemporary Victorian civil engineer who felt certain that Train's 'highly objectionable and futile' schemes and approach had 'contributed more than any other cause to bringing public misconception, disfavour and discredit, upon the Tramway question as applied to London streets'.[12]

The indefatigable Train got local permission to open street tramways in Darlington and the Potteries (from Hanley to Burslem) in 1862, but failed to get them built in seven or eight more towns where he made applications, including Birmingham, Cork, Dublin and Glasgow. By the end of the year he had left England, returning to the US to pursue other projects including the construction of the first transcontinental railroad, the Union Pacific. Train remained convinced that the antagonism he had met in England, and especially his failure in London, was driven by the prejudice of the upper-class establishment rather than any rational, practical or even personal objections to him. In particular, he cited the strong British sympathy with the Confederate cause in the American Civil War that he had encountered as a vocal supporter of the Union when that conflict broke out in 1861.

Local authorities in Britain were only empowered to authorise temporary street tramways at this time, and even that could be challenged in the courts, as Train

'The People' tramcar used on Train's second short demonstration line in London, opened along Victoria Street, Westminster, in April 1861. His trams were a hit with the public but less popular with the competition and other road users, whose complaints led to their removal in 1862. LTM/TfL

had discovered to his cost in London. Some influential figures opposed to his tramway plans, including omnibus proprietors worried about potential competition, had pressed for Train to be prosecuted. Two of his three London lines had already been removed when early in 1862 Train was indicted over the third for 'conspiracy and for causing a public nuisance in the Kennington Road by laying down iron rails thereon and thereby impeding the passage of, and inconveniencing, the public.'

His case was heard before a jury at the Surrey county court at Kingston-upon-Thames, where a petition of more than 11,000 names was submitted in his defence. It made no difference. He was found guilty, fined £500 and ordered to remove the track of his remaining Surrey Side Street Railway immediately. When he refused, the Sheriff of Surrey sent in a gang of workmen to do the job.

The magistrates had ruled that it was illegal to lay track in the street without Parliamentary authority because it interfered with the rights of the general public to use the highway. For a permanent and fully legal street tramway operation an Act of Parliament was necessary, they claimed, as was already required for a railway. Train had neither the time, money nor inclination to go through this long and expensive bureaucratic rigmarole. He decided to move on, defeated by vested interests and legal process even though his tram trials had been quite a success both financially and with the general public.

Following Train

Other tramway promoters were more persistent, but only a handful of proposals got through the tortuous parliamentary route to the statute book during the 1860s. In 1863 the Landport & Southsea Tramway Company became the first in Britain to open a line along a public highway with both the approval of the local town council (in this case Portsmouth) and full Parliamentary authority. It ran for just over a mile from Portsmouth Town railway station to Clarence Pier at Southsea, primarily to provide a link between the train and the Isle of Wight steamer service.

Although the tramway was laid in the street, there was no ambition to make it a new town transport service, which probably accounts for its rapid path to

Ryde Pier tramway on the Isle of Wight, opened in 1864. This view from the pier head towards the town shows the double-deck passenger horsecars introduced in the 1870s, with luggage vans on the right.

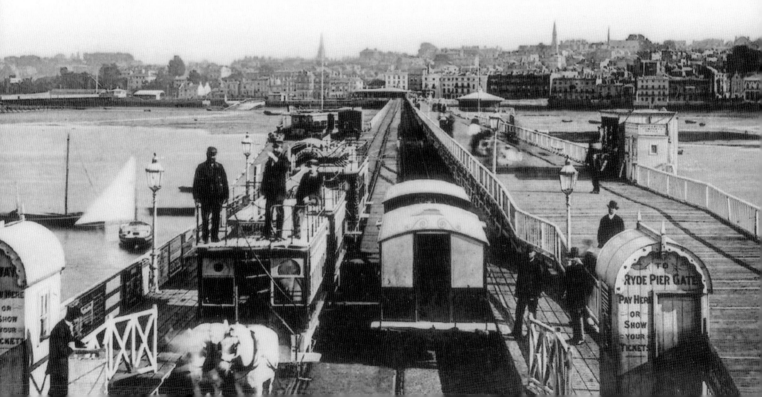

approval without opposition. Over on the Isle of Wight, at the Southsea steamers' destination point, another tramway opened in 1864 along Ryde Pier. This carried passengers and their luggage from the paddle steamers to the shore and was extended in 1871 to reach the island's nearest railway station in the town. One of the early horsecars built locally for this line is thought to be the oldest surviving tramcar in Britain, now preserved in Hull's Streetlife Museum.

The two short tramways at either end of the Solent crossing had a specialised role and purpose. Other larger schemes planned at this time were more ambitious and required closer consideration because they were more contentious and faced opposition. The 1860s was also another boom period for big railway projects in Britain, especially in London, which looked more promising and profitable to investors than the less familiar proposition of urban tramways.

The result was that tram schemes made slow progress. By the end of the decade only one street tramway in Liverpool and three in London had been authorised by Parliament and were able to lay their tracks and begin public services. By then there was a growing backlog of schemes from around the country waiting to come before Parliament and a clear need to streamline the system of approval.

The Tramways Act of 1870 established a set of procedures and regulations to be met before a street tramway service could be introduced anywhere in Great Britain except Ireland (still part of the UK at this time), where it did not apply. Responsibility for considering and supervising tramway schemes was given to the Board of Trade, which could authorise them on the government's behalf under what was termed a Provisional Order. These Orders were only given to proposals which met a demanding set of conditions, the first being the consent of

The Ryde Pier tramcar now in Hull's Streetlife Museum. It is thought to be the oldest surviving horsecar in Britain, built in 1871 but altered and reconstructed during its long working life of over fifty years.
Hull Museums

the local authorities involved, and still had to be ratified by Act of Parliament. The administrative process was speeded up and made less costly for promoters, though hardly less complicated.

The government was unwilling to formally delegate responsibility for tramways to local authorities, many of which were still fragmented and poorly organised at this time, particularly in the larger towns and cities where most tramway schemes were being prepared. The national politicians wanted to retain ultimate authority and control, but still encourage local, independently run tramway operations to work within a regulatory framework.

The upshot was that the 1870 Act was a classic compromise. It gave local authorities the power to build but not actually operate street tramways. The operating contract could be awarded to an independent company for a maximum of twenty-one years after which the council had the right to purchase the tramway company and all its assets at their scrap value.

The Act also specified general rules of construction and operation: rails flush with the road surface, animal power unless otherwise specified, maintenance by the company of the road surface between the rails and for an additional eighteen inches outside the track. The scene was set for years of argument and dispute about the detail. Some of these

A contemporary lithograph showing one of the first London horsecars introduced in 1870 outside St Mark's Church, Kennington. Early double-deck trams had back-to-back 'knifeboard' seating outside, accessed by precarious ladders at either end which were later replaced by staircases. LTM/TfL

clauses were to have major and unforeseen consequences later on in the 1890s, when the leases would come up just as large scale modernisation and electrification were being considered. At the same time many new and growing local authorities would, by then, seize the opportunity to exercise some municipal muscle in urban transport planning and civic expansion.

London and beyond

From 1870 onwards, horse tramways authorised by Parliament began to appear all over the country, though there was no consistent pattern to their development. Local circumstances and market conditions varied considerably. In London the three initial tramways opened in 1870/1 quickly attracted a remarkably large traffic. The North Metropolitan Company, for instance, carried more than a million passengers on its Bow to Whitechapel route in its first six months of operation. This new line in the East End was providing working-class Londoners with the first means of city

transport that they could afford and at times that enabled them to ride rather than walk to work.

Omnibuses had always catered almost exclusively for the middle classes, with high fares and a late start in the morning, often after 8:00 am. The trams, by contrast, were now often obliged to provide cheap early morning workmen's fares and weekday services were usually running by 5:00 am. All three London tram companies had agreed to charge no more than a penny a mile, and as the tramcars were twice the size and capacity of an omnibus, they could still make a good profit with low fares. It was the start of an urban transport revolution.

The London omnibus operators soon dropped their opposition to tramways and quietly came to new accommodations with them which suited both parties, almost making them partners rather than rivals. The LGOC, London's principal bus company, became the main supplier of horses to the North Metropolitan

Tramways and there were soon shared stabling arrangements between the companies. They also agreed to service changes so that omnibuses and trams were not in direct competition on the same streets. Tramlines appeared along most of London's inner suburban main roads, but the fierce opposition that Train had encountered to trams in the City and West End remained. When the new tramway companies tried to penetrate the busy central area there was the same unrelenting hostility, and these districts were to remain tram free and bus dominated into the twentieth century.

After just six years' operation the London tramways were carrying almost as many people as the LGOC omnibuses, with each mode recording just under 50m passengers in 1875.[13] The overall market for urban transport was clearly expanding anyway as London's population grew, but the tram companies catered for a much wider cross section of society than the omnibus, while carefully avoiding some of the affluent west London suburbs like Notting Hill and Kensington where Train had faced such antagonism.

Trams *did* serve many middle-class neighbourhoods, but they soon became associated with and increasingly dependent on working-class custom. This could even be presented by the companies as providing a social benefit. In 1884 the chairman of the London Tramways could claim that:

> We have relieved London of an immense number of poor people by carrying them out to the suburbs… building has been going on very largely on our line of roads in south London…the principal centre of our population is along the Old Kent Road and out by Walworth to Camberwell.[14]

Of course the same suggestion about the social benefits of tramways could be inverted and used as an argument for

An illustration from *The Graphic* depicting middle-class Londoners comfortably seated in a spacious new Brixton and Kennington tram, 1870. Cars were soon crowded with travellers of all classes, and the American expression 'straphanger' for standing passengers quickly crossed the Atlantic. LTM/TfL

Horse trams leaving the Westminster Bridge Road terminus for south London c1885. Trams could not cross the bridge and passengers heading for Westminster had to get off here and walk or change on to an omnibus to complete their journey to central London. LTM/TfL

Trams in Mare Street, Hackney, near the North London Railway station, c1890. Presumably taken on a Sunday morning as this normally busy high street is empty and the shops are shuttered. LTM/TfL

The Old Kent Road in south London with a Greenwich tram approaching, c1885. Drivers of other vehicles often locked one wheel into a tram rail groove to keep their horse on track, as demonstrated by the cart in the foreground. LTM/TfL

limiting their spread into 'respectable' areas of town. When the London Street Tramways Company tried to get permission in 1882 to extend its line up Haverstock Hill to Hampstead Village, a committee of local residents drew up a 'memorial' of objections with which to petition Parliament. Their most revealing point was the assertion that:

> It is a well-known fact that, wherever trams are permitted in the suburbs, the result is the gradual decline of the neighbourhood in residential and commercial importance, as witness Islington, Brixton and Clapham, in the last named of which many houses are deserted and will remain so. Trams will vulgarise Hampstead and lower its tone as a superior residential suburb.

The local worthies of Hampstead won the day and the north London 'village' remained in lofty isolation from rail transport until the arrival of the Tube in 1907.

Outside London, horse tramway proposals were rapidly authorised and built under the 1870 Act in Birmingham, Edinburgh, Glasgow, Leeds and Plymouth, but other planned developments across the country were still often held up or delayed by local disputes. The pace of tramway adoption varied considerably in different towns, and successful development was never certain. Local conditions and circumstances could vary whatever rules and procedures were determined at Westminster, and friction between promoters, managers and shareholders could sometimes affect a project's take-off or failure. In the early days this was unknown territory for all concerned.

Ireland was not covered by the 1870 Act, but similar legislation was needed before trams could be introduced in towns. Licensed street tramways were opened in all three of Ireland's main urban centres in

Clapham High Street in the 1880s, showing how much larger a double-deck tram was when compared with a standard 26-seat London omnibus (left). As the tram ran on smooth iron rails rather than a rough road surface, a pair of horses could manage twice the weight. LTM/TfL

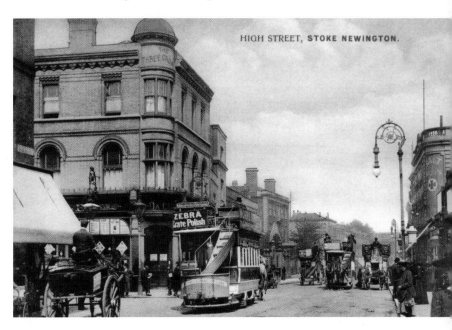

Two trams in the middle of the road and two omnibuses on the outside squeezing past each other in Stoke Newington High Street, north London, c1900.

1872, though with very different results. Trams quickly became a popular success in Dublin and Belfast, with services progressively extended across both cities. In Cork, where tramlines were laid in the

Belfast Street Tramways began operations in 1872 and had over 100 cars in service by 1900. This postcard shows horse trams in Donegal Place in the city centre soon after the turn of the century, just before electrification in 1902.

A horsecar owned by the short lived Cork Tramways Company at the city's Victoria Quay, 1874. A year later the company was closed down and its six trams were snapped up by the Dublin United Tramways. There were then no trams in Cork until a new all-electric network opened in 1898.

street primarily to link the town's separate railway stations, relations between the London-based tram company, the different railway companies and the city corporation soon deteriorated badly. Within three years of opening the tram service was closed down and the company wound up 'amid much bitterness', one of the shortest lived urban street railways anywhere.[15] Cork's six horsecars were immediately snapped up by the Dublin Tramways Company, whose much larger operation was already carrying 6 million passengers a year by 1875 and making healthy profits.[16]

Managing the brief rise and fall of the Cork Tramways Company was an early setback in the career of James Clifton Robinson, later to be known as 'the tramway king'. After Cork's collapse, he worked on several new tramway projects in Britain and the USA before returning to the UK well equipped to champion both cable and electric systems in the 1890s, including major new projects for Bristol, Dublin and west London. As always, a great deal seemed to depend both on particular local situations and the personalities and skills of the leading individuals involved with a project. Robinson, who had first worked for Train as a boy of fourteen in Birkenhead, clearly learned some hard lessons in what can go wrong before he achieved success and a knighthood much later in life.

In England, the Liverpool Tramways Company was the first to be authorised under its own Act of Parliament in 1868 and started services a year later before the General Tramways Act had been passed. The company had the benefit of American advice from some of Train's former associates, which might have given it a head start, but here too there was a rapid descent into expensive litigation with the local omnibus lobby. This soon ate up profits and, it seems, delayed the company's progress and development.[17]

By the mid-1870s the main tram and omnibus companies in Liverpool had

decided to merge and pool resources, but disputes continued with other bus operators and there were soon bitter legal battles with the local authority over road and track maintenance. Eventually in 1897 Liverpool Corporation, which had laid the rails, exercised its right to purchase outright the tram operating company, and began to electrify the whole system. Thirty years of acrimonious disputes and poor management of transport services on Merseyside finally came to an end. In this case, the corporation takeover and a

Four staff and just two passengers on the Chapeltown service of the Leeds Tramway Company, probably just before the takeover by Leeds Corporation, who bought the whole concern for £112,225 in 1894.

pioneer electrification scheme saved the day, though it did not end the arguments.

It was a different story across the Pennines in Leeds, where the first horse tramway services were established in 1870 by the Busby brothers, William and Daniel, two sharp operators who had long experience of running omnibuses in Liverpool. They were deeply involved in the unresolved transport disputes in their home town but had far greater success elsewhere, starting with an entrepreneurial plan to run trams in Leeds, the first in Yorkshire.

Unlike many other promoters, the Busbys clearly understood how to work the complex new procedures under the 1870 Act. In Leeds they moved fast and impressed the local authority and business rivals alike with their scheme. The brothers beat off three other bids to the Corporation to win a concession to build and operate five tramway routes in the city, paid the council £1,000 and offered compensation to the existing omnibus operators before they had even prepared their objections to this potential competition on the streets.

The first public tram services were ready for opening in September 1871. A few months later the Busbys formally set up the Leeds Tramway Company (LTC) in 1872 to run the new operation and brought in William Turton as one of its directors. Turton was already a successful hay, corn and coal merchant in Leeds, providing horse fodder and running some of the city's existing local omnibus services. He was also a city councillor on the corporation's Highways Committee, and despite what would now no doubt be considered a conflict of interest, was clearly able to facilitate tramway development in a town where he had growing civic and business influence.

Later, as chairman of the LTC, Turton was closely involved in the transfer of the company to municipal ownership in the 1890s. Relationships between the different parties involved in tramway promotion, management and ownership in Leeds were not always smooth, but never seem to have descended to the level of dispute and legal wrangling that characterised Cork, Liverpool and many other cities in the horse tram era.

William Turton and Daniel Busby established a very successful informal partnership, becoming closely involved with tramway promotion in major towns all over the North and Midlands including Sheffield, Leicester, Nottingham, Blackburn, Manchester & Salford, Newcastle and Bradford. Turton's story is particularly interesting and well told in a recent biography by his great grandson.[18] He is probably unique as an early tramway entrepreneur who was quietly successful at bringing the new transport mode to more English cities

This horse's head still presides over the entrance to William Turton's former warehouse and provender store in the Calls, central Leeds. It was built in 1876 when Turton had become chairman of the Leeds Tramway Company. OG

than the noisy Train had failed in, yet he is almost a forgotten figure.

Turton's riverside warehouse and wharf in the centre of Leeds, once the heart of his urban horse transport and supplies business, have been given listed building protection and converted into residential apartments. The warehouse now carries a commemorative blue plaque and still sports a sculpted horse's head over the main carriage entrance, an appropriate reminder of the importance of horse power and logistics in the Victorian city.

The tram makers

Although the pattern of development was patchy, the horse-drawn street tramway was generally a late Victorian success story in Britain's towns and cities. By 1878, 237 miles of line were in operation. Twenty years later this figure had quadrupled to 938.[19] This was close to the peak mileage for horse traction. In the early 1890s services were provided by at least 100 separate tram companies in the British Isles, roughly the maximum number before the twenty-one year leases

set under the 1870 Tramways Act began to expire and municipal takeovers of many undertakings began.

In 1884/5 the *Railway & Tramway Express* published a series of articles describing in some detail the operation of the leading horse tram companies then operating in the big cities of England, Scotland and Ireland. There are some curious omissions (nothing on Birmingham, Belfast or Leeds), but the chosen systems give a revealing insight into the state of the nation's urban tramways only fifteen years after they began operating. The anonymous author is clearly very well informed about the tramway business, highly opinionated and surprisingly critical of certain practices and individuals, especially where a company had been secretive or unco-operative with the press on his visit. Two of the London systems are described, together with operations in Bristol, Dublin, Edinburgh, Glasgow, Liverpool, Manchester, Nottingham and Sheffield.[20]

The Glasgow Tramway and Omnibus Company is praised as one of the largest

Sheffield Tramways Company's newly acquired horsecar 33 at the Albert Road terminus in Heeley, c1877. The scene features a loud display of commercial advertising on tram and billboard by the new Lewis's general store, promoting its tea and gas mantles.

Trouble with mules. Following advice from New York, Glasgow and London operators tried using mules instead of horses in the late 1880s. It was not a success and the experiment was quickly abandoned in both cities. This illustration is from *Tramway Car Sketches* by 'JN', published in Glasgow in 1889.

and best, having astutely bought out most of the omnibus competition. In 1884 they had 1,030 staff, 233 tramcars and 24 omnibuses. This required a stud of over 2,500 animals, kept at ten stables and depots across the city. The animal total included some 250 mules, acquired on the advice of a New Yorker on the board of directors who insisted that they would be cheaper, sturdier and more resilient than horses. According to another source, Glasgow's experience was that mules had all those qualities but were 'an unmitigated nuisance to handle. They were taciturn, truculent, headstrong, bad tempered and resentful beasts and very difficult to curb.'[21] The London Tramways Company had similar problems with mules and also abandoned their experiments with alternative animal power.

Glasgow was one of the first companies to adopt the bell punch ticketing system, later to become almost universal on trams and buses in Britain well into the twentieth century, but still novel in the 1880s. This system, with the accompanying waybill, allowed the management to keep the first reliable check on takings recorded against

tickets issued. It became difficult, though not impossible for conductors, or anyone else, to fiddle the figures:

The entire clerical duties in connection with the issue of tickets are performed with great regularity and accuracy by female clerks, who make the boxes ready for each depot, with a complete supply of every requisite for the next day's working for the whole of the Cars from that particular depot, everything being provided in duplicate for alternate days.

The company employed fifteen women in the ticket department and twenty-eight in the cash offices, an unusually high female presence at the time as the larger North Metropolitan in London had only eleven women on its books, and Dublin had none at all. Glasgow was clearly run as a tight ship financially, but it was also quite socially progressive: 'We must not omit to mention the four tenements of very superior dwelling houses for workmen at Scotstoun…this is quite a novel idea for Tramway Companies in providing accommodation for their workmen.'

The second Scottish company reviewed, the Edinburgh Street Tramways, was also praised for its staff facilities:

…a very excellent institution that ought to be copied by every Tramway and Omnibus Company in the Kingdom, viz: a kitchen and dining room for the men where cheap, and well cooked food can be obtained at a trifling cost. The company provides the rooms, coals and gas and a female cooks the food, who carries it on as a speculation on her own behalf – of course under the supervision of the Company….The benefit of having a warm and comfortable place to sit down in, after cold, wet and weary journeys, and of being able to get something warm to eat, cannot be over-estimated.

This was another rare provision at a time when tram crews generally worked up to sixteen hours a day six days a week, often with no proper rest or comfort breaks. Edinburgh even had a Sick and Benefit Society 'which is doing good service amongst the men'. In London the North Metropolitan also started a provident society soon afterwards in 1889. Staff paid 6d a week into this to provide their families with some insurance and social security, but their contributions came out of wages that had not increased in the fifteen years since the company started up.

Tramway staff were not well paid and the companies were hardly benevolent. Jobs were insecure, with fines or even dismissal for quite minor rule breaking. Perks and benefits were few, and in the

1880s tram crews were not provided with uniforms or given any kind of weather protection. The indoor staff, whether in clerical office jobs or the workshops, often had better physical working conditions, but were less well paid unless they had a particular craft skill such as being a carpenter or blacksmith. It was early days for organised labour to make a difference, but the newly formed Amalgamated

A North Metropolitan tram at Edmonton in north London about to set off for Finsbury Park c1895. By this date most trams had forward facing 'garden seats' on the upper deck and a uniformed conductor issuing tickets with a bell punch, as seen here. The NMT cap badge dates from about 1900. LTM/TfL

Omnibus & Tram Workers' Union began to build up its membership in the early 1890s.

Horse power

The horses were far more valuable to a tramway company than its staff, and actually worked shorter hours than the men on the trams. It made financial sense to look after the most costly of a company's assets and keep them in good condition, while most of the unskilled men were dispensable

and easily replaced. There was always a large turnover of labour, especially in London. During 1891, for example, the North Metropolitan Tramways, which employed 1,800 men, dismissed conductors at an average rate of five a week and drivers at the rate of two a week. [22]

Horses, on the other hand, were chosen carefully and generally well looked after. The working life of a tram horse was short and tough, on average only four years to the omnibus horse's five, according to contemporary estimates. [23] It was not unusual to see a horse collapse and even die in harness on the streets, but a good tram company did not want to see its reputation sullied by being taken to court for animal cruelty. To keep a tramcar in service for a working day, covering around sixty-five miles, required ten horses working in relays. That is five pairs, each pair working around fourteen miles per day.

Spare horses were required to cover sickness and accidents as well as a stock of extra animals to assist on gradients, known as trace or tip horses. Hill climbs

Stablemen and horses outside the Southampton Tramways Company's main depot in Portswood, 1892. By this time the company owned around 200 horses. The company's elaborate decorative device was carried on the side of every tramcar in the fleet.

Tram panel Southampton Museums

normally involved hitching a trace horse to the harnessed pair for just one difficult section of route, but sometimes involved running a car over the whole line with a team of three or even four horses. Any town that developed a network of tramways over hilly terrain, such as Bristol, Liverpool or Sheffield, would need an average of up to twelve horses per tramcar, including single-deck one-horse cars to run on lightly used routes.

There were reckoned to be over 9,000 tram horses working in the British Isles in 1878. By 1890 there were more than that in London alone (just under 10,000) and the number for the whole country, including Ireland, had trebled. In that year the tramway companies spent nearly £830,000 on buying replacement horses, nearly as much as their working expenditure covering fodder and care. Annual costs could vary considerably because there were unpredictable risks such as a sharp rise in the cost of feed following a poor harvest or

an outbreak of serious disease in the stables such as equine influenza or 'pinkeye'.

Initially, the tramcars used in the UK were either American imports from various manufacturers in the New York and Philadelphia areas or British built, but following similar designs to those of experienced US makers like John Stephenson. Some established railway

An Aberdeen District Tramways horsecar. This was the most northerly tramway in Scotland, first opened in 1874, and ran a unique sledge service in snowy winters. The company was purchased by the council in 1898 for electrification, the last horse tram running in 1902.

A Bristol horse tram with two trace horses being harnessed in front of the main pair in anticipation of difficulties on the city's steep hills in wet weather, c1890.

Driver and conductor taking the horses 'round the car' in Glasgow. The drawbar was re-attached at the other end of the tram for the return journey. Another scene from *Tramway Car Sketches* by 'JN', 1889.

carriage builders diversified into tram building while other coachbuilders were set up to supply the sudden new market for tramcars in the 1870s, notably in the Birmingham and Manchester areas. A few major operators, such as the North Metropolitan Tramways in London and the Manchester Carriage and Tramways Company, set up workshops to build their own trams rather than buying them in. Small tramway schemes sometimes used local coachworks to either build one-off vehicles or to assemble trams from parts supplied by one of the main companies.

By far the largest car builder and supplier in the UK was the Starbuck Car and Wagon Company, first established in Birkenhead by George Starbuck in 1862. He was one of G.F. Train's American associates who stayed on in Britain when Train returned to the USA. When the first tramways in Salford and Manchester were opened in the late 1870s, initial operation was with a fleet of bought-in Starbuck cars, but the Manchester Carriage Company soon adapted its existing omnibus works in Pendleton, Salford, to build and repair tramcars. John Eades, the works manager, who was an experienced coachbuilder, came up with his own innovations, notably an ingenious reversible tramcar with bodywork which could revolve on its own underframe, a design he patented in 1877.

The Eades reversible was a single-ended tram with only one staircase, and

An Eades reversible car being turned on the spot by the horses themselves in Chesterfield, a rarely photographed procedure, c1890.

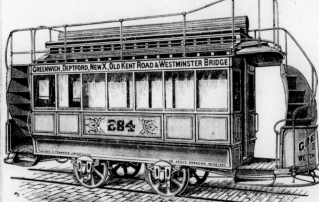

JOHN STEPHENSON COMPANY, LIM.,
NEW YORK, U.S.A.

TRAMWAY CARS.

LIGHT.

ELEGANT.

DURABLE.

Every Description.

Best Materials.

Minimum Prices.

LIGHT.

ELEGANT.

DURABLE.

Orders Quickly Filled.

Careful attention to Shipments.

All Climates Suited.

GREENWICH, DEPTFORD, NEW X, OLD KENT ROAD & WESTMINSTER BRIDGE

284

JOHN STEPHENSON COMPANY, LIM.,
New York, Etats-Unis.

OMNIBUS POUR TRAMWAYS.
Légers, élégants et durables.

Faits dans toutes les façons,
Construits des meilleurs matériaux et
Aux prix les plus modérés.
On exécute les commandes promptement.
On donne des soins spéciaux à l'exportation.
Ces omnibus s'adaptent à tous les climats.

John Stephenson Company, Lim.,
New York, Vereinigte Staaten.

Pferdebahnwagen.
Leicht. Elegant. Haltbar.

Von jeder Art.
Aus besten Materialien hergestellt, zu den
Mässigsten Preisen.
Bestellungen werden rasch ausgeführt.
Besondere Sorgfalt bei Aufträgen für Ausfuhr.
Für jedes Klima geeignet.

JOHN STEPHENSON COMPANY, LIM.,
Nueva York, Estados Unidos.

COCHES DE TRANVIA.
Ligeros. Elegantes. Duraderos.

De toda clase.
Materiales de 1ª calidad.
Precios módicos hasta no más.
Se ejecutan pedidos con prontitud.
Esmero especial para exportación.
Los productos de la Cª se adaptan á cada clima.

was shorter and lighter than the standard Starbuck cars. Instead of unhitching the horses at the end of the line and walking them round with the drawbar for re-attachment at the other end of the tram, the driver got the horses to turn the car themselves. The tram body was unlatched from the truck and the horses simply circled on the spot, turning the tram round as they did so, a much easier manoeuvre. Eades reversible cars were soon in considerable demand from other British cities, with more than 500 built in the Manchester area. Some had to be supplied under licence by other coachbuilders as the Pendleton works found it could not build them fast enough.

There were clearly various agreements and even partnerships between at least some of the Victorian horsecar builders in Britain, though as few records survive it is not easy to confirm exactly what these relationships were. [24] Perhaps the most surprising fact is that even when British horsecar builders had become well established, John Stephenson was still able to build and supply top quality tramcars for Britain from the USA at competitive prices. They remained in demand from UK operators despite the cost of shipping the cars across the Atlantic in knocked down form. The South London Tramways horsecar now on display in the London Transport Museum has all four of its metal axle boxes clearly stamped John Stephenson, New York. This hardy all-American import of the 1880s was one of nearly 300 Stephenson cars that trundled

A John Stephenson company trade advertisement, c1880. Around 300 horsecars like the one shown were shipped across the Atlantic from New York to London. LTM/TfL

Toast-Rack Tramcar, Hythe.

An 1897 open 'Toast rack' car for summer use on the Folkestone, Hythe & Sandgate Tramway in Kent, c1910. The service was run by the South Eastern & Chatham Railway, who finally closed it down in 1921.

through the streets of London on a daily basis for over twenty years.

After about 1895 very few new horsecars were built as systems were mechanised, but a surprising number lasted well into the twentieth century working as trailer cars on both steam and electric tramways. Most of them were redundant and sold off in the early 1900s but then had a second life grounded as outbuildings and storage sheds, or even re-used as cheap homes. None were preserved at the time, but decades later a handful were rediscovered around the country and have been restored for museum display and occasional operation, including one of the Eades reversible cars. [25]

It was often the smaller horsecar systems that were among the last survivors, where the high capital cost of

electrification could not be justified or was locally controversial. This was the case in both Oxford and Cambridge where no agreement could be reached between the respective city councils and tram companies about modernising their ageing horsecar lines at the start of the twentieth century. The worn out horse trams in both university towns were eventually replaced by motor buses rather than electric trams just before the outbreak of the First World War in 1914.

A few of the minor horsecar operations survived into the twenties as leisure attractions, mostly in seaside resorts. The last remaining horsecar service in mainland England ran along the promenade at Morecambe in Lancashire, originally opened in 1887 and finally closed down in 1926. A year later the Pwllheli &

Both Oxford and Cambridge had notoriously decrepit horse tram systems which were never modernised. This card was posted in 1905, nearly ten years before the company system in Oxford was eventually closed and replaced by motor buses.

Llanbedrog Tramway, by then the only surviving horse tram line in Wales, succumbed. This had been built in 1897 by Solomon Andrews, an entrepreneur who ran cabs and omnibuses in Cardiff and expanded his business interests into tramways and property in several Welsh towns. His Pwllheli horsecar operation, cheaply built to carry summer trippers and holidaymakers visiting the town rather

Last day of the Cambridge horse trams, 18 February 1914. The single horse was presumably not expected to move such a heavily overloaded car.

MORECAMBE, WEST END.

The last remaining horsecar service in mainland England casts a long shadow on an almost deserted seafront at Morecambe. It survived until 1926.

An open car carrying holidaymakers on the Pwllheli & Llanbedrog Tramway in the early 1920s. By then this was the last horse line in Wales, closed down in 1927.

HORSE VAN (G.N.RLY) FINTONA.

'Dick' the horse with the Fintona van in the early 1950s. Ireland's last horse tram is now on display in the Ulster Folk and Transport Museum at Cultra, County Down.

than local residents, closed permanently after part of its track was washed away in a violent storm in October 1927.

Over in Northern Ireland a horsecar built in Birmingham in 1883 provided the sole passenger service on a short branch line linking the small town of Fintona with Fintona Junction, the nearest station on the railway through County Tyrone. The Fintona 'van', as the tram was always known in the town, was in daily service, hauled by a single horse, until as late as 1957. By the time the line closed, the van and its regular horse, 'Dick' (the horse was occasionally changed but its name was always Dick), had become minor celebrities. The van, but not Dick, is now preserved on static display in the Ulster Folk and Transport Museum at Cultra, County Down. [26]

Traditional horse trams are still running along the front at Douglas, Isle of

DOUGLAS CORPORATION TRANSPORT

Traditional horsecars still run during the summer season along the seafront at Douglas, Isle of Man. A note on the reverse of this postcard dated July 1950 reads 'Went on these on quite a few occasions with Tony and the rest. I always had a smashing time.'

Most redundant horse trams were sold and found new uses. This West London car became a feed store on a country estate, still carrying a sticker announcing transfers to the Central London Railway at Shepherd's Bush. As the Tube opened in 1900 and electric trams arrived in 1901 this dates its disposal quite precisely. LTM/TfL

A few old horsecars continued in active use for many years. This train on the North Devon mineral railway photographed in 1931 includes former North Metropolitan horsecars which had been displaced by electrification in London twenty-five years earlier! LTM/TfL

Man, where they are a unique surviving feature of a traditional Victorian seaside experience. The Douglas Bay line was opened during the first British tramway boom in 1876 and ran daily in the summer season with few breaks or interruptions until 2015, making it the oldest continuously operated horse tramway in the world. In early 2016 Douglas Borough Council decided to close the heavily subsidised service as an economy measure and announced plans to sell off all its tramway assets. The Manx Government has stepped in to take over and run the whole operation, as it did with the island's heritage steam and electric railways, but the future looks uncertain for the famous Douglas horse trams. [27]

Chapter 2

STEAM AND CABLE

Costly though horse power was, it still allowed most British tramway companies to make good profits throughout the 1870s and '80s. In the early years there was little incentive to look for alternatives to the horse or to invest in new sources of motive power that had not yet been tried out. At the same time the limitations of horse power were becoming all too apparent. Most city systems had reached their maximum growth by the late 1880s and could not expand beyond the horse's physical capacity even though the passenger market was clearly there as the urban areas grew.

There was also a rather obvious environmental issue, particularly in the big cities. Michael Corcoran, historian of the Dublin tramways, has quantified the amount of ordure on the streets with a simple calculation based on the number of horses owned by the Dublin United Tramways. At its peak of activity in the early 1890s, the company owned just over 1,500 horses. Each horse produced a minimum of 14lbs of manure every day, a total of nearly ten tons dumped straight on to the streets. In Corcoran's words: 'As the tram horses were a minority of Dublin's total equine population, the dirt, the stench and the danger to public health can be easily imagined.'[1]

The issue was of course even greater in a bigger city like London, but it was not widely perceived as a problem at the time. Victorians of all backgrounds were used to an urban environment dominated by horses, and there were few expectations of change in this area even towards the end of the nineteenth

A stereoscopic view of Dublin in 1896, with horse trams and carts on O'Connell Bridge. The Dublin United Tramways owned over 1,500 horses at this time, shortly before electrification.

The horse-drawn city could be grim in winter. This evocative study of steaming car horses, mud and snow outside the old Astor House Hotel in New York was captured by photographer Alfred Stieglitz in 1893, just before mechanised trams replaced horsecars.

Horse trams were easily derailed if dirt was allowed to build up in the grooves of the track. This meant regular scraping out of the rails was necessary, one of many unpleasant jobs on the trams. A street scene in south London in the 1890s.

National Tramway Museum

century. Innovation and mechanisation on the tramways would remain in the experimental realms of eccentric inventors unless it could be shown to be both practical and economically viable.

Steam traction was an obvious possibility, and had long been used on railways of course, but its application on urban streets remained problematic. Early road steam carriages tried out by Walter Hancock and others back in the 1830s had failed, and the Locomotives Act of 1865 limited any mechanically propelled road vehicles to 3km/h (2mph) in towns and 6km/h (4mph) elsewhere. As a further precaution against accidents, the Act also required a man with a red flag to walk fifty yards in front of any mechanical vehicle using a public road. Neither the law nor the Board of Trade encouraged risk taking or innovation.

These strict conditions were not relaxed until 1896, and it was early trials with steam trams in the late 1870s that began to finally open up Britain's roads to mechanical traction. A combined steam engine and tramcar designed by John Grantham was demonstrated in London in 1873 and later ran on the roadside Wantage Tramway in Berkshire from 1876, thought to be the first use of a steam tram in passenger service in the UK. Other self-propelled engine and tramcar combinations were tried out in Sheffield, Dublin and Portsmouth but without lasting results.

Stringent regulations governing steam tram operation on public roads were drawn up by the Board of Trade in 1875. Engines could not emit visible steam or smoke, should be free from noise and all fire and machinery had to be fully enclosed. The main concern here was clearly not operational safety or even the convenience of passengers but a continuing worry by the authorities that steam on the streets could frighten the horses and potentially cause traffic chaos

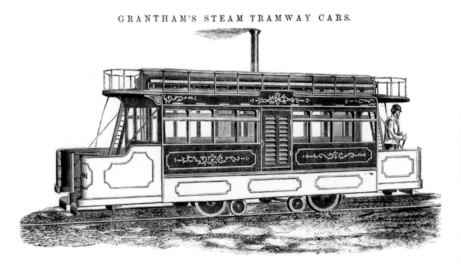

GRANTHAM'S STEAM TRAMWAY CARS.

or accidents on a busy high road. This was understandable when nearly all other road traffic was horse drawn, but it does seem unduly cautious and restrictive. In practice, as one tram writer has observed, before long 'it was common for some of the regulations to be more honoured in the breach than the observance.'[2]

Steam tram development moved on after 1875 from self-propelled vehicles like Grantham's to the separate steam engine or 'dummy' and trailer car arrangement which became standard. One of the first manufacturers in the field was Merryweather & Sons, a London company that specialised in building fire engines and pumps. By the late 1870s Merryweather were making more steam trams for export than the UK market and had supplied nearly fifty of their locomotives to work on the streets of Paris. Similar tram engines were developed by other British suppliers including Kitson and Thomas Green, both in Leeds, the Falcon Works at Loughborough, and Beyer Peacock of Manchester.

In 1876 the Vale of Clyde Tramways in Govan, Glasgow, became the first company to introduce steam operation on urban streets. By the early 1880s various experiments around the country had turned into a major boom, with some fifty British tramways opting for steam to

John Grantham's combined steam engine and tramcar, demonstrated in London in 1873 and first put into passenger service on the Wantage Tramway in 1876.

The roadside Wantage Tramway near Grove in rural Berkshire, c1911, with a typical train of antiquated rolling stock dating back more than thirty years. Tram engine no.4 was built in 1877, and the trailers are adapted horse tramcars from 1875 and 1890. The passenger ticket carries advertising from a range of local businesses.

replace horse traction. These developments fall into two basic categories. The majority were urban street systems, where steam powered trams were an entirely new phenomenon. Others were largely rural roadside lines, which although they were called tramways, could equally be characterised as light railways and were more like country branch lines.

The town lines all used boxed-in, purpose-built tram engines to meet the new Board of Trade regulations, while the isolated rural lines usually made do with small standard or adapted railway locomotives. The handful of little country

tramways were hopelessly uneconomic from the start, even though they ran combined passenger and goods services. They could sometimes only afford to use second hand rolling stock and by the turn of the century had already acquired an air of dereliction because after the initial outlay for opening they were rarely invested in again.

The Wantage and Wotton Tramways are characteristic of this, lingering on as underused branches off full scale railways until final closure to passengers between the wars (in 1925 and 1935 respectively). By this time both had become charming anachronisms, virtually unchanged in decades, and with no apparent commercial future even for goods traffic. The Wisbech & Upwell Tramway in East Anglia is another curiosity, originally built in 1883 by the Great Eastern Railway (GER) alongside country roads. It was mainly for agricultural traffic, though it did also run passenger services on the line until 1927. Here a busy goods operation with steam tram engines continued right into the British Railways era, and it had the distinction of becoming BR's first exclusively diesel powered line in 1952. Final closure was in 1966, when it had become the last rural tramway in England. None of the distinctive box-like GER steam tram engines built for this line survive, but they have achieved lasting recognition as the model for Toby the Tram Engine in the Reverend W. Awdry's popular children's railway stories.

The original passenger trailers used with steam engines on tramways were often former horsecars. Running two or more of them coupled together in a train was not generally permitted, and most of the urban operations used high capacity double-deck cars to take full advantage of the locomotives' pulling power. Quirkiest of

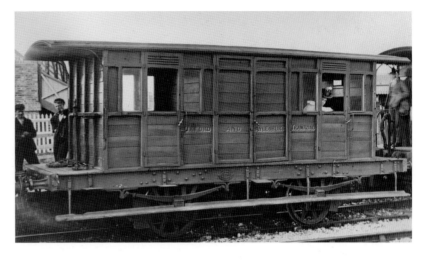

them all was the Wolverton & Stony Stratford Tramway in Buckinghamshire. It was built in 1887 to link the town of Stony Stratford to a station on the main London and Birmingham railway, but was used mainly to transport employees to and from the London & North Western Railway's works at Wolverton.

Unusually, the line was a combination of rural roadside and urban street tramway, for which the company optimistically

The Oxford and Aylesbury Tramroad was the company name adopted by the Wotton Tramway near Aylesbury in the 1890s, reflecting ambition not reality. This ageing tramcar/coach will carry its single passenger the 6 miles from Quainton Road junction to Brill, but the line would never reach Oxford. LTM/TfL

A mixed goods and passenger train on the Wisbech & Upwell Tramway in Cambridgeshire, c1925. Passenger services ended in 1927, but the steam tram engines operated a freight service until the 1950s.

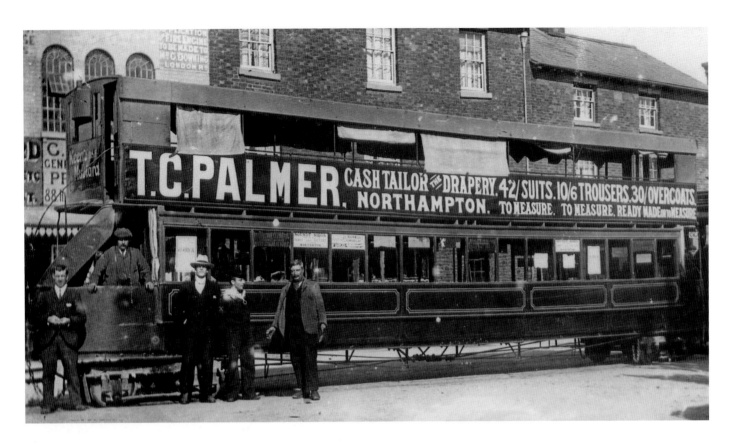

One of the enormous 100-seat double-deck trailer cars pulled by steam engines on the Wolverton & Stony Stratford Tramway, c1910. At the time these were the largest tramcars in the country and would have been far too heavy for horses to manage.

In 1881 the newly formed Blackburn & Over Darwen Tramways Co was the first in the country to start with steam traction only. It began operations with Kitson tram engines and double-deck trailers fitted with partial top covers for smoke protection, as seen here.

ordered enormous 100-seat double-deck trailer cars. At 13.4m (44ft) these were almost certainly the largest tramcars in the country, far bigger than the generally meagre, and later diminishing, traffic required. The LNWR took over its operation in 1920 but when the service was suspended during the General Strike in May 1926, the line never re-opened. One of the monster trailer cars can still be seen today, impressively reconstructed by Milton Keynes Museum.

Steam trams were not a great success in Britain, although most of the

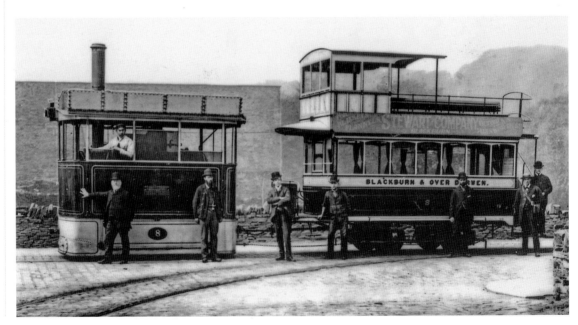

operations started in the 1880s continued for about twenty years. Meeting the strict Board of Trade rules proved difficult, and steam trams were never popular with passengers because of the smoke and dirt, which was almost impossible to control. Some operators found the steam engines unreliable or unsuitable because the heavy locomotives damaged lightweight track, which was not always reconstructed and strengthened when horse working ended. Steam operation on former horse lines in north London seemed particularly prone to breakdown and only lasted from 1885 to 1891, when horsecar operation was brought back. No other company in the metropolis took up the challenge, and the steam tram experiment in London was quickly branded a failure by the local press.

Steam operation fared better in other towns, particularly in the industrial districts of the West Midlands and the north of England. In Birmingham and the Black Country seven separate companies

Steam tram locomotive and trailer in Leeds, c1885. Engine no.12 was built locally by Thomas Green & Son. To meet the strict conditions for street working it has a 'skirt' enclosing the wheels and a set of pipes on the roof which reduced emissions by condensing exhaust steam.

The Swansea and Mumbles Railway used conventional steam tank engines and horse tramcar-style passenger cars coupled together to form tram/trains in the holiday season. The line was eventually electrified and equipped with very large double-deck electric cars in 1927.

A rusting and dilapidated steam tram engine with a sagging trailer car, both clearly overdue for replacement at Barrow-in-Furness, c1910.

'The old and the new'. A commercial postcard showing an ageing MBRO steam tram at the Heywood cemetery terminus in 1905, with a new tram beyond on Rochdale Corporation's first electric route, which opened along the Bury Road in 1902.

The panel on the side of the trailer car reads 'the last steam tram to leave Rochdale, May 8 1905'. This group shot at the depot marked the final demise of the Manchester, Bury, Rochdale & Oldham Steam Tramways system, which at its peak had routes covering over 30 miles of south Lancashire.

The Lover's Lament. A mock elegiac postcard with sentimental verses marking the end of Birmingham's steam trams in 1906.

introduced steam trams on routes which criss-crossed an extensive industrialised region with considerable traffic potential and continued in operation until the early 1900s. The largest single system to develop was the Manchester, Bury, Rochdale and Oldham (MBRO) Steam Tramways Company, which eventually had a fleet of ninety-one locomotives. Its network covered nearly 31 route miles across and between the industrial towns of south Lancashire.

The practical problems associated with steam operation on city streets were never fully resolved, though arguably more damaging was the reputation for dubious business practice that tarnished the steam tram companies' image. The principal villain of the piece was one Henry Osborne O'Hagan, a successful but dodgy London financier who became the most prominent promoter of steam tram projects around the country in the 1880s, including the Birmingham and MBRO companies.

O'Hagan was the George Hudson of steam tramways, though unlike Hudson's notorious early railway

The Lover's Lament
AT THE LOSS OF THE
Old Steam Trams,
Electrocuted Dec. 31st. 1906.

'Twas NOT SWEET OF OLD, as our love we told
On the top of the Old Steam Car,
When a wand'ring breeze, made us cough and sneeze,
With a smell, like rotten eggs and Tar!

But the lights were low, and the pace was slow,
And the corner seats were cosy,
And many a Miss has received a kiss
On the top of the Car
From Perry Barr
Or the Tram that came from Moseley!

Yes, the Electric Car, can go very far,
In a very short space of time.
But that dazzling light, is FAR too bright
So each loving pair, have a stony air
Of not being aware, that each other is there
And gone are their joys sublime!

No, the fact that these Cars are painted blue
And are awfully, terribly, painfully new,
And the fact there is plenty of elbow room,
Will never make up for that friendly gloom
And the joys so sweet,
Of the corner seat
ON THE TOP OF THE OLD STEAM CAR.   F.S.R.

SCOTT RUSSELL & CO., B'HAM. SCOTT SERIES.

A steam tramway system opened in Accrington, Lancs, in 1884. It was closed down in 1907 when its 21-year lease from the council ended and the corporation started running its own electric services. The change prompted production of this local *in memoriam* postcard.

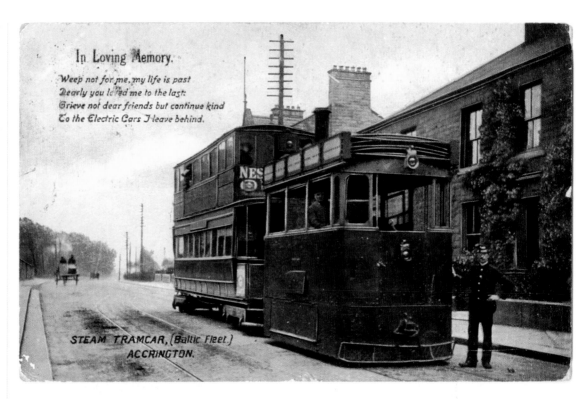

In Loving Memory.

Weep not for me, my life is past
Dearly you loved me to the last:
Grieve not dear friends but continue kind
To the Electric Cars I leave behind.

STEAM TRAMCAR, (Baltic Fleet.) ACCRINGTON.

schemes of the 1840s, O'Hagan's shady business methods were never fully exposed at the time. He later freely admitted in his autobiography that he had often secured contracts with local authorities in the 1880s through bribery and corruption of local councillors and officials.[3] O'Hagan's grandly titled City of London Contract Corporation, through which he set up lucrative agreements to build and operate steam tramways for more than a dozen local authorities, was little more than a front. He and his fellow directors made substantial profits from both ratepayers and passengers, but did not invest properly in their equipment and operations or provide a decent service. When the local authorities eventually acquired the steam tram companies as their leases expired in the 1900s they inherited almost worthless and worn out assets.[4]

Gripping the cable

An ingenious alternative method of harnessing steam power for tramways was developed in the USA in the early 1870s and brought to England a decade later just as conventional steam tram systems were booming. Andrew Smith Hallidie was a British-born engineer who emigrated to the United States and developed a successful wire rope manufacturing business for mining operations in California. He was also the promoter of the first practical passenger cable car system, the Clay Street Hill Railroad in San Francisco. This opened in 1873 using Hallidie's cable to haul passenger cars up the steep hills of the city, where conventional horsecar operation was almost impossible.

The principle of the cable tram system was simple. A stationary steam engine drove a winding drum with a continuously moving endless wire cable. This ran through a shallow tunnel or conduit between the tram rails. Individual tramcars could be attached to or disconnected from the moving cable by a control device known as the grip, which passed below the tram through a central slot rail in the street surface to the underground cable. The tramcars all

End Of Accrington's "Baltic Fleet" July 1907.

Accrington's 'Baltic Fleet' being broken up in July 1907. The nickname for the old steam trams was an ironic reference to the ageing Russian naval fleet which had accidentally sunk three British fishing vessels in the North Sea in 1905. The Russian warships were heading for the Far East, where they were routed in battle by the modernised Japanese Navy, ending the brief Russo-Japanese War.

moved at the constant speed of the cable when attached to it and stopped when the driver (the gripman) released the grip and applied the brakes. Operation was usually with two-car trains consisting of a 'dummy' or grip car and passenger trailer. Each route had to have a separate cable linked back to the winding house through sub-surface pulleys and sheaves.

The cable car principle was not adopted anywhere in the USA beyond San Francisco for nearly ten years. A development of the Hallidie system was applied in Dunedin, New Zealand, in 1881, but the real boost to cable came a year later with the introduction of the same technology to the much larger and rapidly growing mid-western city of Chicago, Illinois. The Chicago City Railway, opened in 1882, was a convincing demonstration that a cable system could be an efficient way to mechanise mass urban street transport even in a completely flat city. By 1890, when cable car transport was at its brief zenith in the

Brochure design for the opening of the Highgate Hill Tramway in north London, the first cable line in Europe, 1884. LTM/TfL

THE FIRST Cable Tramway IN Europe 1884

Postcard of Highgate Hill in 1906 with two trams passing each other halfway up the steep incline. These double-deck cable cars were introduced after the line's reconstruction in the 1890s. In 1909 the LCC bought out the struggling private company and rebuilt the line again as part of its conduit electric system.

Driving car used on London's second cable line between Streatham and Kennington. The trailer cars were standard horse trams which continued under animal power beyond Kennington to Westminster Bridge. The gripman in this 1894 photograph is Charles Grover, who later became an inspector on the trams and finally retired from London Transport in 1938. LTM/TfL

USA, there were 283 miles of urban cable track including lines in New York, Los Angeles and Washington DC, carrying between them 373m passengers a year. [5]

Hallidie's patent cable system was first used in Europe on the extremely steep 1 in 11 grade of Highgate Hill in north London, where a cable line from the Archway Tavern at the bottom up to Highgate village was opened by the Lord Mayor of London in 1884. According to J. Bucknall Smith, the engineer who managed its construction, the route was chosen primarily to demonstrate the system rather than for its traffic potential. If so, it did not produce many other customers or orders in Britain.

The Highgate Hill Tramway was certainly not profitable in itself and the operation was bankrupt within five years. A successor company took over but after a serious accident with a runaway car in 1892, the line had to be closed down and substantially rebuilt with a new continuous cable and safety braking system. Re-opening after a five-year closure, the new

operation only lasted for twelve years before being taken over by the London County Council and reconstructed again as part of the LCC's electric network.

Only one other cable system was installed in London when the original horsecar line of 1870 running south from Westminster Bridge to Brixton was extended southwards up the long hill to Streatham as a cable operation in 1892. Unlike the isolated Highgate Hill line this soon carried very heavy traffic, as passengers could travel right through on both the cable and horse-powered sections of the route without leaving their seats. Tramcars were cable-hauled using grippers from Streatham through Brixton to Kennington, where horses were attached to continue on to Westminster Bridge and vice versa.

The arrangement worked well enough, but by this time cable technology had already been overtaken by advances in electric traction across the Atlantic. There were to be no further cable schemes in the capital above or below ground. London's

Edinburgh & District company cable car on the Murrayfield line, c1895, with uniformed gripman and conductor. The cable grip release lever and the brake mechanism, which resembles a ship's wheel, are on the right of the boarding platform.

first deep level tube, the City & South London Railway, had originally been designed for cable operation but took the leap of pioneering electric traction underground before the line was opened in 1890. The Glasgow underground, which followed in 1896, was cable-powered when it opened, but was eventually electrified in 1927.

The only city in Britain to adopt cable traction for its street tramways on a large scale was Edinburgh. Horse trams had been operating on a growing network of routes here by the Edinburgh Street Tramways Company, which also ran omnibuses, since 1871. However, the hilly terrain of the city's northern districts were proving almost impossible to serve with either type of horse-drawn vehicle. Even the addition of up to three trace horses to make a team of five on a standard omnibus proved inadequate on some of the steeper

roads. Steam traction was tried on one route in 1881 but abandoned within a year.

The Hallidie cable system appeared to be an ideal solution to Edinburgh's gradient problem, though the street pattern and terrain was to prove far more challenging than San Francisco's spacious grid layout. The Edinburgh Northern Tramways Company was formed in 1884, construction began in 1885 and the first cable line, covering just 1.5 miles from Hanover Street in the New Town to Goldenacre, was finally opened in 1888. A second cable line to Stockbridge, slightly shorter but including an even steeper hill climb, followed in 1890. Both routes offered a reliable five-minute service which replaced far less frequent and more difficult to operate omnibus services. Cable cars could be run at more than twice the speed of horse trams or buses, initially at a constant 7mph in Edinburgh but later at

Cable cars in Waterloo Place, Edinburgh, on a postcard sent to New Zealand in 1915. A century later a short section of cable track, including the centre slot rail, survives at this point in the middle of the road (opposite). Both views are looking east towards Calton Hill. OG

G. P. O. and Waterloo Place, Edinburgh.

between 8 and 12mph on different routes, and of course they could take any incline in their stride. Fixed stopping points, never used for horse trams, were introduced for the first time on the cable routes.

During the 1890s Edinburgh City Corporation acquired both the horse and cable tram companies as their leases ended, though not without lengthy dispute about the purchase price. Plans were drawn up by the local authority to create a comprehensive cable network across the whole urban area, but the traditional animosity between the City Corporation and neighbouring Leith Town Council made agreement about cross-border operation impossible. The upshot was that the cables never reached Leith, but by 1902 Edinburgh had a cable tram network covering 36 miles of urban roadway, the biggest in the country by far, and the fourth largest in the world.

It was, as D.L.G. Hunter describes it in his history of Edinburgh's transport 'a marvel of mechanical ingenuity' with its complex invisible system of underground pulleys and cables. This undeniably impressive work of engineering was run with considerable skill, but maintenance was expensive and difficult. If a cable failed, jammed or got tangled it could bring a whole route to a halt for several hours of repair work. By the time the Edinburgh system reached its maximum extent at the turn of the century, the cable car was already an outmoded technology.

The neighbouring burghs of Musselburgh and Leith, which had both shunned the cable, proudly introduced their own electric tram services in 1904/5 leaving passengers from the city to change cars at the boundary. Edinburgh opened its first electric route in 1910 and only finally began the conversion of its entire cable system to electric working after the First World War. The changeover, completed in 1922/3, was overseen by a new general manager still in his twenties. This was R. Stuart Pilcher, who

A lament for the only cable car line in Birmingham, which ran from the city centre to Handsworth, published as a local card when electric trams were introduced in 1911.

A cable car on the short but very steep line in Matlock, Derbyshire, opened in 1893 to serve Smedley's hydro hotel and the upper part of town on Matlock Bank.

Crown Square in Matlock, with the cable car line running up the hill beyond, c1905. The elaborate shelter on the left was moved to the town gardens nearby when the tramway closed. The cable winding house and depot at the top of the hill is now a garage.

Crown Square, Matlock

The Promenade, Douglas, I.O.M.

arrived from Aberdeen in 1919 and later moved on to Manchester, where he initiated the replacement of electric trams by buses in the 1930s. In Edinburgh all that remains to be seen on the street from the cable era is a short section of track with the conduit slot in Waterloo Place and a surviving cable pulley unit at the former Henderson Row depot in Stockbridge.[6]

There were very few other cable tramway installations in the UK. In Birmingham the original horse tram line from Colmore Row in the city centre to the original city boundary at Hockley Brook was extended to Handsworth and converted to cable rather than steam traction in 1888. The cable cars on this route outlasted steam in Birmingham by five years and were finally replaced by electric trams in 1911.

At Matlock in Derbyshire, a short but extremely steep cable tramway opened in 1893 from Crown Square up the I in 5 hill to Matlock Bank, where Smedley's, the inland resort's largest health hydro hotel, overlooked the town. The tramway was privately funded by Sir George Newnes, born in Matlock Bath, who had made a fortune as the publisher of the popular newspaper *Tit-Bits* and *The Strand Magazine*, where Conan Doyle's Sherlock Holmes stories first appeared. Sir George donated the tramway to his home town in 1898, but within a few years Matlock Urban District Council found the operating and maintenance costs outstripping the meagre income from fares (2d up the hill, 1d down). From 1917 onwards, deficits were up to £1,000 a year and in 1927 the tramway was closed down.[7]

A cable tramway in Douglas, Isle of Man, closed two years later after a similar lifespan to the Matlock line. Built in 1896 to link upper Douglas with the

The Promenade at Douglas, Isle of Man, c1905, with a cable car at the terminus of the Upper Douglas line (left) and an empty horsecar on the seafront. By 1929 the cable line had closed, but the horse trams continued to run round the bay from here and connected with the Manx Electric Railway at Derby Castle.

A 1930's postcard of the panoramic Welsh mountain view from the summit of the Great Orme at Llandudno, with the cable tramway terminus in the foreground. The tourist line is still in operation and celebrated its centenary in 2002.

VIEW FROM SUMMIT, GREAT ORME, LLANDUDNO.

W. 1703.

The Victorian funicular cliff lift at Saltburn-by-the-Sea, North Yorkshire, designed and installed by George Croydon Marks in 1884. It is the oldest water balanced lift still in operation in the UK and has been carefully refurbished in recent years, together with the original pleasure pier buildings.

seafront below, this line was planned to connect at both ends with the flat horse tram route along the town promenade. As a financial investment the Upper Douglas Tramway was a disaster and the original promoters were bankrupt within four years. Douglas Corporation bought the cable line in 1901 along with the horsecar operation but like Matlock soon found the deficit growing annually. Neither tramway covered its running costs even as a seasonal operation for holiday visitors and the much heavier maintenance demands of the cable line sealed its fate. Only the horsecars were still running after 1929 and the rest of the town was served by buses.[8]

A cable car ride can still be experienced in Llandudno, north Wales, where the Great Orme Tramway was opened in 1902 as a tourist attraction, carrying visitors 1.6km (1 mile) up from the town to the Summit Hotel and panoramic views of the Welsh mountains from the top of the Great Orme. This is the only cable-hauled tramway still operating on British public roads, with its lower section laid in the street. Unlike the Hallidie and similar gripper systems, this is a funicular railway where two cars are permanently attached to the cable and counterbalance each other with one going up as the other descends.

Although it is partly a street railway, the Great Orme Tramway works on the same principle as an inclined plane or cliff railway. These became popular at Victorian seaside resorts following a pioneer installation at Scarborough South Cliff in 1875, which is still in operation. One of the early pioneers of funicular railway technology was George Croydon Marks, who worked on cliff lifts at Saltburn, Bridgnorth, Lynton & Lynmouth and the Clifton Rocks Railway in Bristol as well as the Matlock Cable Tramway, each of which had financial assistance from Sir George Newnes. Today there are still thirteen late Victorian and Edwardian

funiculars running in Britain, all of them refurbished but still using some of their original equipment.[9]

In the air
There was one final remote application of steam power to tramways which avoided bringing smoke and fire to the streets. This was an ingenious compressed air system devised by Louis Mekarski in France, and used successfully from 1879 in the city of Nantes, as well as on some lines in Paris. A British trial was carried out in 1880 with two Mekarski engines on the Wantage Tramway.

The compressed air trams were apparently quite successful, although

The West Hill Cliff Railway funicular at Hastings, opened in 1891. Originally powered by a gas engine, it was converted to electric power in 1971 and fully refurbished for its centenary in 1991.

A Mekarski compressed air tram built in 1879 for the urban system in Nantes, France and similar to the engines tried out on the Wantage Tramway in 1880. This may be the only surviving example of a compressed air tram, now in the AMTUIR museum collection in Paris. A century later Nantes became the first French city to reintroduce trams in 1985.

rather more machinery was installed than was necessary for the comparatively light passenger work on this country line. The experiment included using *two* stationary steam engines to work the special compressor pumps which charged the reservoir air tanks on each tram. Large and costly coal supplies were needed at the depot to provide power for the compressors, almost *five times* the amount of coal normally used for steam locomotive operation. Even then the system was not entirely reliable and at Wantage they experienced difficulties maintaining sufficient air pressure for a return journey on the short 2 mile tramway.

Nevertheless George Stevenson, engineer to the Tramway Company, was clearly very taken with the system. He described compressed air as 'a very beautiful power, clean and noiseless,

with probably less wear and tear than steam…for street traffic I should think it must be unequalled.'[10]

Just before the trials ended there was an unfortunate accident when the two tram engines were involved in a collision. It was nothing to do with the compressed air system, but the high cost of coal had already tipped the balance against Wantage adopting the Mekarski system. After going on show at Victoria Station in London for three days in February 1881, the trams were shipped back to France. Compressed air was clearly not the answer, and no other British tramway experimented with it. There were further experiments in the 1880s with compressed air trams developed by British engineers in London and Liverpool, but it was effectively a dead-end technology for locomotion.

Chapter 3

GOING ELECTRIC

In the early 1880s the future route of tram mechanisation remained uncertain everywhere, but developments in Germany gave a strong indication that the answer might come through harnessing the power of electricity for transport. In May 1881 the world's first electric street tramway to offer a public service opened at Lichterfelde, a suburb of Berlin. It was built and equipped by the Siemens & Halske Company, whose founder Werner von Siemens had long been experimenting with dynamos as electrical generators for industry.

Siemens had first demonstrated the potential of electric traction two years earlier at a Berlin Trade Exhibition where he had set up a miniature electric railway circuit in the grounds. A tiny locomotive powered by a 2hp dynamo picked up current from a central third rail and pulled three open trailers seating eighteen passengers. Some 86,000 visitors experienced a ride on the Siemens electric railway in Berlin, and it was exhibited again at an International Electric Exhibition at the Crystal Palace in Sydenham, south London, in 1881/2. Sensing a potential new product market, Siemens and Halske took over an old 2.5km horse tramway at Lichterfelde for full scale development and testing of their electrical equipment.

An electric motor was mounted under the floor of a converted horsecar with a belt drive link to one of the wheel axles. Direct current supply at 180 volts was picked up through one rail and returned to the other. It was quite a crude and potentially dangerous installation (with a risk of electric shocks), but it did work successfully in rather irregular passenger service. Having shown that electric traction was possible, the Siemens engineers turned their attention to improving current collection methods with safer and more efficient pick-up arrangements.

Meanwhile other individuals were experimenting with electric traction, though without the resources of a large manufacturing company like Siemens & Halske behind them. An impoverished Austrian inventor called Henry Bock Binko, who was living and working in England, devised and patented an electric railway similar to the Siemens design which he exhibited at the Crystal Palace in 1882. Two years later he installed an improved version at the International Forestry Exhibition in Edinburgh, where his electric locomotive *Ohm* pulled three carriages on a demonstration circuit.

Knowing that the Prince and Princess of Wales (the future King Edward VII and Queen Alexandra) were to visit in August 1884, Binko had a special car constructed by Edinburgh coachbuilders John Hislop and Son for the royal party to use on their

The world's first electric tram in passenger service. It was a converted horsecar equipped by Siemens & Halske and first operated at Lichterfelde, near Berlin, in May 1881.

The International Forestry Exhibition held at Edinburgh in 1884, where Henry Bock Binko operated his electric railway in the grounds of Donaldson's School. On the last day of the show Binko ran an electrified horse tram along the street outside to Haymarket railway station.

City of Edinburgh Council

exhibition tour. A week later the royal carriage, carrying the royal insignia and named *Alexandra*, was made available to Prime Minister William Gladstone on *his* official visit. The *Scotsman* newspaper reported that:

> Mr Binko explained the workings of the elegant electric car and…before leaving on the return train the company were photographed by Mr Moffat of Princes Street, and Miss Binko presented Mrs Catherine Gladstone with an electric bouquet, Mrs Laura Binko a similar one to Countess Rosebery, and Mr Binko illustrated the effect of the tiny incandescent lamps among the flowers.[1]

Despite this enviable publicity through royal and celebrity visits, Binko's electric railway came to nothing. He was already seriously in debt and a month later was declared bankrupt, with his railway put up for sale by his creditors. On the last day of the Edinburgh Exhibition, 11 October 1884, Binko gave a final demonstration of his system's potential. He fitted the electrical equipment from his exhibition railway into an ordinary horsecar and ran it along the street from the exhibition gates to the

Haymarket railway station, a distance of about 700 yards. The tramcar picked up the current via a wheeled collector running along two lines of copper plate laid between the tracks.

It worked as a one-off trial, but was completely unsuitable for wider use on street tramways with its dangerously exposed live electrics. Binko had succeeded in running the first street tramcar in the UK to be supplied with electricity from a stationary source. Sadly, his ingenuity took him no further. The man who might have brought electrification to the streets of the Scottish capital became a forgotten footnote of history.

The first electric tram to be demonstrated in London carried its own power source. This was a battery powered car fitted out by another Austro-Hungarian émigré engineer working in England, Anthony Reckenzaun. Trials were held in suburban Leytonstone in 1882 and again at Gunnersbury, in west London, a year later. The experiments were conducted using converted horsecars, and on both occasions the accumulator tram ended up ignominiously towed away by a team of horses. Reckenzaun worked for the Electrical Power Storage Company, and had more success with the development of light

1. The Car.—2. **The Interior of the Car, With One of the Cushions Removed to Show the Accumulators.**—3. The Starting and Reversing Handles.

THE NEW ELECTRIC TRAMCAR AT KEW BRIDGE

electric launches driven by storage batteries, which became very popular at this time for leisure trips on rivers and lakes.

The North Metropolitan Tramways in London later ran five larger and more powerful battery trams for a four-year trial period from 1889 to 1893. Ten accumulator trams also ran on the Bristol Road line in Birmingham from 1890, but battery electric power was not adopted on a large scale anywhere in Britain. The lead-acid accumulators were heavy and could not provide enough power over time or distance. The trams were also very slow and unpopular with passengers because the batteries, which were under the seats, tended to give off acrid fumes which filled the inside of the car. As a

means of supplying electrical power for mass transit, batteries were simply not fit for purpose, although accumulators were later used to provide back-up or supplementary power in some city centre tram routes in Continental Europe where overhead wires were banned.

On Brighton Beach

Brighton-born engineer and inventor Magnus Volk pioneered electric traction in England with a reliable direct external power supply. Having successfully introduced electric lighting to the Royal Pavilion in April 1883, Volk was given permission by Brighton Corporation to lay a short miniature railway along the beach, which he opened to the public just

Anthony Reckenzaun's battery tram tried out at Kew Bridge, London, in 1883, showing the accumulators under the seats and the control equipment. This was another converted horsecar, powered by fifty batteries, said to be capable of working the vehicle, fully loaded, for seven hours. LTM/TfL

An Edwardian postcard of Volk's Electric Railway, opened in August 1883. The railway is still running on Brighton Beach today on a slightly different alignment.

Volk's Electric Railway, Brighton.

four months later. His little tramcars used Siemens motors and at first worked on the same two-rail power supply with positive and negative running rails used in Germany, soon modified to third rail supply to avoid current leakage. Volk promoted his railway as 'the first public electric conveyance in the United Kingdom' and it has continued in operation to this day, with an extended and re-laid line.

Volk's electric traction work did not progress from his beach railway to developing full scale street tramways as might have been expected. Instead, he was drawn back to seaside novelty entertainment with his next big project, the bizarre but grandly named Brighton and Rottingdean Seashore Electric Tramroad. The extraordinary vehicle Volk designed for this venture, named the *Pioneer*, was more accurately described as a moving pier than a tram. It featured a large ship-like passenger saloon standing on a platform deck supported by four braced steel legs 7.3m (24ft) above the

ground. The whole structure weighed 50 tons and was designed to carry 150 passengers along the shoreline parallel to, but further seaward from, Volk's electric railway. It ran on specially constructed twin tracks from a jetty by the aquarium in Kemptown nearly 3 miles (4.7km) east to another jetty at Rottingdean. The rails were completely submerged at high tide making it, as Volk's advertising poster announced 'a sea voyage on wheels'. Its only resemblance to a tramway was the overhead electric power supply.

The 'Daddy Long-legs', as it soon became known when it first appeared in 1896, was briefly quite an attraction for visitors to Brighton. It was almost certainly unique in the world and even the correspondent of the *New York Herald*, jaded by successive amusement park sensations at Coney Island, was obliged to admit that 'mechanically, and as a seashore novelty, (it) beats anything yet done by us inventive Yanks.'

But Volk's creation was just that: inventive but neither practical nor robust.

In December 1896, only a week after the grand opening ceremony, the *Pioneer* was blown over and almost wrecked in a violent storm that destroyed the old Brighton chain pier nearby. The damage was repaired for the following summer, but *Pioneer* only operated sporadically for another three years before new sea defences had to be built which forced the line's closure. Tramcar, rails and landing piers were all removed by scrap merchants in 1910, but at low tide some of the concrete blocks which supported the track can still be seen on the beach more than a century later.[2]

Irish Pioneers

In September 1883, one month after the public opening of Volk's original railway, the initial section of a line described by the contemporary *Railway Times* as 'the first long electric tramway in the world' was opened on the coast of Ulster by the Lord Lieutenant of Ireland. This was the Giant's Causeway, Portrush and Bush Valley Tramway, a far more ambitious project than Volk's. It was designed to use hydro-electric power generated nearby, and initially used a direct supply through the running rails. This was found to cause current leakage, so before the public opening the tramway was fitted with a separate, raised conductor rail for current supply, the first to use such a system. A second system change, to an overhead wire supply, had to be made after the unfortunate death in 1895 of a cyclist who came into contact with the live rail. The original electrical system was devised by the Antrim bothers William and Anthony Traill, who worked closely with Sir William Siemens (the German-born anglicised brother of Werner) and his British Siemens Company on the electrical equipment.

On the opening day, according to one observer: 'Vast numbers of people congregated at both ends of the system and along the entire coast road and were amazed to witness tramcars moving steadily and slowly along without visible means of propulsion.'

No doubt they were even more surprised to see that the inaugural tram was driven by a woman. Miss Jeannie Richardson had been deputed by William Traill to take charge of the car for the official run, and was almost certainly the world's first female tram driver, if only for a day.[3]

Two more innovative electric railways opened in the British Isles in 1885. The first was another Irish line, the Bessbrook and Newry Tramway, which despite its title was more like a light railway, running mainly

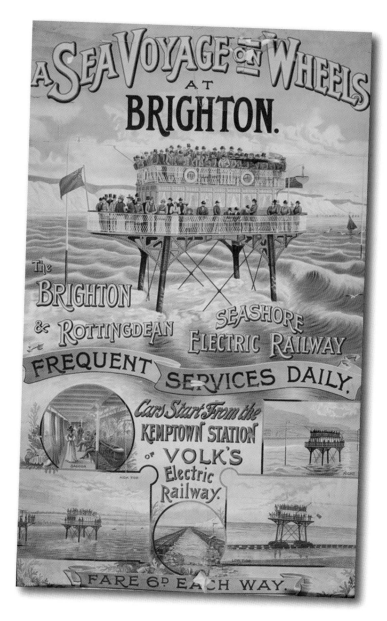

Poster advertising Volk's ambitious second scheme, the Brighton & Rottingdean Seashore Electric Tramroad, opened in 1896 but closed after a three-year battle against the elements. Volk was eventually defeated by the power of the sea.
Brighton Museums

The pioneering Giant's Causeway, Portrush and Bush Valley electric line in County Antrim, Northern Ireland, opened in September 1883. This postcard shows the spectacular view of the coastline and Dunluce Castle from the tram. The raised electric conductor rail can be seen on the right.

Lawrence, Publisher, Dublin.

Dunluce Castle,   Co. ANTRIM.

We passed this Castle ruins on the way from the Causeway to Port Bush. JCG.

on its own right of way. Originally intended for steam operation, this too became an electric project, planned and engineered by Dr Edward Hopkinson of Salford electrical engineers Mather & Platt. Hopkinson used a central conductor rail for power supply, apart from a long crossing over a public road near Bessbrook, where for safety reasons an overhead wire was used for the first time. The directors of London's first Tube line, the City & South London, were so impressed with Hopkinson's installation that they abandoned their plans for cable traction and engaged him to equip what became, in 1890, the world's first underground electric railway.

Blackpool First

The second innovation that year was an electric tramway along nearly 2 miles of the seafront at Blackpool, a location guaranteed to get exposure in every way. This was an early example of partnership between inventive private enterprise and a fledgling local authority struggling to manage a town in rapid transition from fashionable watering place to mass working-class holiday resort. The scale and speed of development was quite different to Brighton, or indeed any other holiday town in Britain, and there was a close relationship between novelty, entertainment and a growing seaside leisure industry.

In January 1885 the *Blackpool Herald* made a well observed assessment and prediction of the way things were going:

Blackpool is becoming a place where the people expect to have a jolly care-for-nothing sort of scamper, rather than to avail themselves of the benefit of the sea breezes… During the best months of the year the town is deluged by the lower classes, and it would be unreasonable to expect the higher grades of society to mix with them.

An electric tramway looked like something that would be seen as an innovative and progressive feature by everyone visiting the town. Blackpool Corporation decided to go into partnership with an inventor from Halifax, Michael Holroyd Smith, who had demonstrated an electric railway in the grounds of the new Winter Gardens in 1884. The council would lay the foundations and track, with a channel underneath, while a new company created by Holroyd Smith would install a copper conductor rail to carry the electric current through the conduit. In appearance, with no visible power supply, it resembled a cable car system.

Addressing the crowd gathered for the ceremonial start of construction work on 13 March 1885, where he laid the first rail, Alderman McNaughton, Chairman of the Transport Committee, said it was fortuitous that Blackpool had delayed building a tramway. Otherwise, as he pointed out, they would have had horses or steam 'instead of nature's most wonderful, immense and mysterious agency – electricity'. Electrical engineer Holroyd Smith then attached an insulator to the rail, explained its purpose and announced to the crowd:

'This little act is important because … this line will be the first in the world to be worked safely in the public street by electricity.'

On 29 September 1885, just six months after construction had started, a public service was inaugurated. It was a triple win for Blackpool: the first electric street tramway in Britain, the first to be built by a local authority (although leased initially to a private operator) and the first to be powered through a sub-surface conductor rail laid below and between the tracks.

Each tramcar on Holroyd Smith's line picked up its power with a 'plough' which ran through a central slot rail flush with the road surface like a cable line and made contact with the electrified conductor rail just below the street. It was visually neat, but the system proved particularly unsuited to Blackpool. The shallow conduit regularly became clogged with seawater in stormy weather, windblown sand from the beach and even, in the holiday season, children's hoops. Kids quickly discovered that if the circular metal toy that they rolled along the street was dropped into the conduit slot it could cause a spectacular short

10028   STORM AT BLACKPOOL.   ROTARY PHOTO, E.C.

Heavy waves often battered the seafront at Blackpool, flooding the original conduit power supply for the trams. The system was replaced with overhead wires in 1899, as shown in this postcard from the early 1900s. The real surprise is that the conduit system survived these regular washouts for nearly fifteen years.

circuit that brought every tram to a standstill! Despite these local difficulties, conduit operation continued in Blackpool until 1899, when the overhead wire system was adopted instead.[4]

Curiously enough, when Blackpool abandoned the pioneering Holroyd Smith conduit after more than a decade's intensive operation, this was still some months before a similar, though admittedly more robust, conduit system was chosen as the means to electrify most of London's tramways. The London County Council ignored the experience of what it no doubt considered a vulgar northern holiday resort and became the only authority in Britain to emulate New York and Washington with an absurdly expensive and over-engineered sub-surface power supply.

Ultimately Blackpool was to become as synonymous with its seafront electric trams as its seasonal electric illuminations, and the great British tramway survivor. Decades later, it was the only street system in the UK to continue in operation as every other tram network closed in the 1950s and early 60s. Blackpool would not only celebrate its working centenary in 1985 but join the other 'second generation' tram systems with its transformation into a modern light rail operation in the twenty-first century.

Electric streets

The early progress with electric tramways in Britain and Germany was overtaken in the late 1880s by developments in the USA. Here a dramatic breakthrough came in the work of electrical engineer Frank Julian Sprague, who designed a complete electric streetcar system for the city of Richmond, Virginia, in 1887/8. When it opened this was the largest electric tramway network in the world, running over 12 miles of track. Sprague equipped each of his cars with two electric motors, a controller at either end of the vehicle and a roof-mounted, spring-loaded pole with a swivel head that picked up current from a single overhead wire. Unlike any other system yet devised, the

A calmer summer's day on the south promenade at Blackpool looking north towards the Tower. The large 'Dreadnought' tramcars, with their twin staircases at either end for rapid loading, were first introduced in 1900.

REAL PHOTO SERIES NO. 10.   BLACKPOOL PROMENADE SOUTH.

Richmond network could be reliably operated with all thirty, soon rising to forty, electric cars 'notching up' to full power through Sprague's controllers at the same time.

Sprague's successful Richmond installation marked a seminal moment in the development of the electric tram. It heralded the transition of electric traction from a period of trial and experiment to successful commercial application in the US. This started with Boston, Massachusetts, a much larger city than Richmond, where a group of horse-drawn streetcar companies had just been consolidated in 1888 into the West End Street Railway Company, which was closely linked to suburban property development. The WESRC was already planning wholesale mechanisation with a cable system when its president, Henry M. Whitney, was invited to Richmond by Sprague to see his electric line in action. The story goes that Whitney decided there and then to abandon cable and go electric, although the main contract beneficiaries were Sprague's rival companies, and he himself soon got out of the streetcar business. Overhead electric projects using variants of Sprague's system quickly took off in towns all over the US.[5] The electric streetcar boom that followed was astonishingly fast, and has been described by a leading American historian as 'one of the most rapidly accepted innovations in the history of technology'.[6]

By 1890 just over 900 miles of street railway had been electrified in the US, about a sixth of the total. Three years later there were 12,200 miles of street railway in American cities, 60 per cent of them using electric cars. The whole electrical industry in the US was soon consolidated into a few giant companies: Sprague sold out to Edison General Electric, which in turn merged with Thomson-Houston to create the giant General Electric Company (GE). GE and the Westinghouse Electric &

An experimental electric tram operated briefly on the streets of Northfleet, Kent and was featured in the *Illustrated London News* in April 1889. It ran on the 'Series' system, picking up power from an electric current supply fed from underneath one of the running rails.
LTM/TfL

Manufacturing Company, formed in 1886, became the two great corporate rivals for the rapidly spreading electrification of urban America in the 1890s. As the domestic market became saturated they looked overseas and pressed hard for orders in Europe through newly formed associate and subsidiary companies such as British Thomson-Houston. Meanwhile the thousands of new electric streetcars in town and country soon became known to most Americans as 'trolleys' after the little pick-up wheel on the end of the pole that ran under the wire and powered the electric motors.[7]

The future may have looked electric in US cities, but the introduction of electric street railways on the new American model was much slower in Britain, where the vehicles remained resolutely called trams. Predictably, the overhead wire with trolley-wheel connection was first introduced to England by another US engineer, William Graff-Baker of the Thomson-Houston International Company of America. Graff-Baker led a pioneering project to electrify the Roundhay Park tramway in Leeds. The track had been laid by Leeds Corporation in 1889 as a suburban extension of the city's existing tramway network, and was originally expected to be steam operated by the Leeds Tramway Company.

However, the short lease on offer from the council was not attractive and the company declined. Instead the Corporation agreed a showpiece deal with Thomson-Houston to supply, install and operate a complete American electric system with its own power station and to run it as a five-year contract. Accordingly, when the Roundhay Park line was officially inaugurated on 29 October 1891, it became the first overhead trolley-wire street tramway in the British Isles, and indeed the whole of Europe.

However, the Roundhay Park line did not spark an electric boom in the UK, as the American suppliers must have hoped, and Leeds Corporation was in no rush to extend what they still viewed as an interesting but strictly limited demonstration. There would be no further electrification in Leeds until after the corporation had taken over all the other horse and steam lines in the city. In fact the council ended its contract with Thomson-Houston in 1896 and only then began planning to extend its own future tramway electrification and operation.

The next UK conversions to electric traction were two existing steam lines of the South Staffordshire Tramways (SST) in Walsall, which were electrified by a local firm, the Electric Construction Corporation of Wolverhampton, and opened on 1 January 1893. Company and contractor soon fell out when the ECC was forced to go to court to get paid for its work and had to sell its interest in the tramway to the newly formed British Electric Traction (BET) Company, which became owner and operator in 1897. In less than a decade BET, established by Emile Garcke in 1895, would become the largest private owner of electric tramways in the UK.[8]

At the same time a much longer and completely new operation was under construction on the Isle of Man. The Manx Electric Railway (as it later became) is a rural tramway similar in nature to the inter-

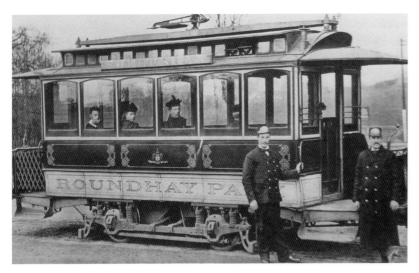

An American Thomson-Houston equipped electric car on the Roundhay Park Tramway in Leeds, the first overhead trolley wire street tramway in Europe, opened in 1891.

urban electric lines then being built in the USA. It covers 17 miles of the island's east coast between Douglas and Ramsey, mostly running alongside the main road, and was opened in stages in 1893/4. A year later a linked enterprise, the Snaefell Mountain Tramway/Railway (both names were used in the early days), was opened from a joint station at Laxey to the summit of the island's highest mountain. The electrical engineering of the whole Manx system was in the hands of Edward Hopkinson, with equipment supplied by his company Mather & Platt, which had acquired the British rights to the Edison dynamo. It was all essentially American-style equipment adapted, improved and manufactured in Salford to the specification of Hopkinson's elder brother John, who was head of Mather & Platt's electrical engineering department as well as being a consultant to the English Edison Company.

The original tramcars for the Isle of Man lines were supplied by G.F. Milnes of Birkenhead, the successor firm to horsecar builders Starbuck. These early electric cars

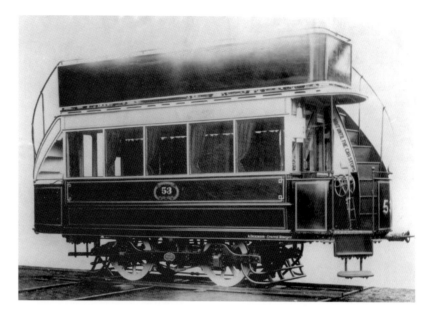

have a very American appearance, with long open saloons and clerestory roofs. The wooden bodies were carried on a large swivelling bogie truck at either end of the car. Amazingly, nearly all the original rolling stock from the 1890s survives, and most of it is still used. The Manx Electric is the only substantial early electric system that still runs public

Two steam lines of the South Staffordshire Tramways in Walsall were the first to be electrified by a UK company, the Electric Construction Corporation of Wolverhampton, and opened on 1 January 1893. No.53 is one of the small original electric cars used by the SST.

Tram Station at Derby Castle, Queens Promenade, Douglas, I. o. M.

The Douglas terminus of the Manx Electric Railway in a coloured postcard sent in 1904, when the line had been open for ten years. The open-sided Milnes tramcar dates from 1898 and is still in service today, but the ornate canopy was unfortunately demolished in 1980.

Laxey station, where the Manx Electric Railway (centre) meets the Snaefell Mountain Railway (left). The SMR was built and opened in just seven months in 1895. Tram no.1 is one of the six original Milnes single-deck saloon cars, which remain fully operational on the Isle of Man today. The station has hardly changed.

services in Britain today, a fully operational veteran that 120 years ago represented cutting edge technology.[9]

Wiring the towns

The slow progress of tram electrification in Britain at this time had more to do with finance and local authority powers than technical tardiness. The new technology was now readily available in reliable, mass-produced form, whether imported or licensed from the USA. However, the planning and legal controls set by Parliament in 1870 for urban horse tramways in the UK were still inhibiting new developments in a changing world twenty-five years later. The relationship between private companies and municipal authorities was also very different from the unrestricted free market approach that generally prevailed in the US.

The Manx Electric Railway was an untypical halfway house between the two. It was originally promoted by a banker, a retired stockbroker and a former railway engineer with a keen eye on the potential for estate development and tourism on the island. The project still had to be approved and overseen by Tynwald, the Manx parliament, but state regulation of private enterprise in the Isle of Man was fairly light touch. It was, however, a very long way from the free-for-all which took place in most US towns and cities during the so-called Gilded Age.

In a discussion at the Institution of Civil Engineers in 1893, the battery electric expert Anthony Reckenzaun pointed out the contrast between British and American developments:

Electric traction in the United States is encouraged primarily by estate agents and speculators…the estates were worth very little – probably they were only agricultural or waste land – but they have been developed by those means. The profit derived by the speculation has in many instances more than paid for the electrical street railway.[10]

Special issue of *The Tramway & Railway World* featuring the Tramways and Light Railways Exhibition at the Agricultural Hall in Islington, London, July 1900. This show had a major influence on electric tramway development in the UK, and was attended by managers and councillors from all over the country.

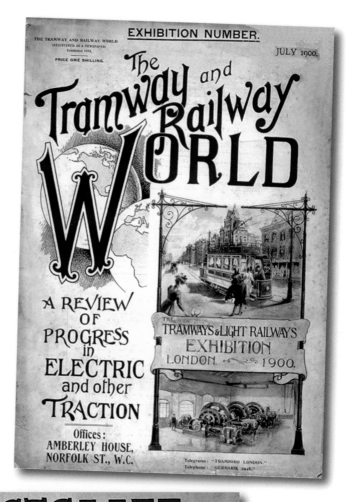

In the US the growth of 'streetcar suburbs' was a new phenomenon, where speculative vacant site sales took place linked to new electric tramways projected to run out into open countryside where house building could take off.[11] Nothing comparable seemed likely in Britain or Ireland in the 1890s, where suburban growth on the edge of towns and cities was much slower anyway and only really developed in the early twentieth century. However, this was not the main factor holding back electric tramway promotion at this time.

Theo Barker has given a convincing explanation of the particular

Advertising for the Westcliff Park Estate near Southend-on-Sea, 1901. It was the closest that UK developers got to the sales promotion style already successful for 'streetcar suburbs' in the US. Electric trams began running in Southend in July 1901.

circumstances which delayed electrification in the UK:

> The British were slow to follow America's example partly because many tramway companies, whose 21-year leases from local authorities were about to end, were reluctant to indulge in capital expenditure of any sort…. (while) many local authorities were keen to acquire, electrify and work the tramways themselves. These authorities worked through committees of elected representatives who, not well versed in the new technology, had to seek outside advice and took time to make up their minds.[12]

This led to a varying pace of electrification in different areas of the country, sometimes led by a well organised and persuasive private company which came to a working agreement with the local council, but more often driven by a local authority that wanted to increase its direct control over a new public service that could give it more power, influence and a financial contribution to the rates. Inevitably, this

was part of a wider debate at the turn of the century about how far 'municipalisation' and local government power should be released or restrained in British society.

Electric trams were suddenly at the heart of this. Local power dynamics will always vary, but it is interesting to compare the different ways in which electric trams arrived in the only four major cities to introduce them on a significant scale before the end of the nineteenth century. The first two were through private promotion: Bristol (1895) and Dublin (1896/7), while the next pair were examples of early municipal drive: Glasgow and Liverpool (both 1898).

Bristol

The first British city to develop an extensive electric tram network was Bristol, and here the initiative came entirely from private enterprise and not from the local authority. It was largely driven by two ambitious individuals who had first met in the mid-1870s and were to become two of the most influential and entrepreneurial figures in tramway promotion: George

George White's Bristol Tramways & Carriage Company, created in 1887, dominated first horse drawn and then electric transport in the city. James Clifton Robinson planned the electrification of the entire tram network between 1895 and 1900. This postcard shows electric cars at the Zetland Road junction outside the company's Bishopston depot, c1901.

White and James Clifton Robinson, both later to be knighted for their services in the early 1900s.

White was a lawyer and stockbroker with considerable finance and business acumen who acted as secretary and adviser to the Bristol Tramway Company and a number of others. He was particularly good at winding up failed companies and restructuring them into more efficient and profitable businesses. Robinson first met him in 1875 when he became manager of the Bristol operation after the collapse of the Cork Tramway in Ireland. They became lifelong friends and business associates, working together on a succession of projects that each became involved with in Britain, Ireland and the USA. White was the legal and financial fixer, and Robinson the flamboyant front man.

In 1887 White engineered the merger of local horse tram and cab operating companies in his hometown to form the Bristol Tramways & Carriage Company, of which he became managing director. This soon became part of the larger Imperial Tramways Company, which owned horse tram networks in Dublin, Gloucester, Reading, and other towns. White was the majority shareholder and effectively controlled the whole group.

Robinson, meanwhile, whose career path had taken him to Edinburgh, London and Los Angeles to work on cable schemes, had become one of the most knowledgeable and outspoken British advocates of tram system building and mechanisation. Returning to Bristol after valuable experience with new developments elsewhere, Robinson became expert consultant and engineer to the Bristol Tramways with a brief to modernise the horsecar system he and White had first worked on nearly twenty years earlier. He now had the considerable advantage of being up to date with the latest technological developments in the USA which most British tram companies and their managers knew very little about.

Robinson's report to the chairman and directors in December 1893 confirmed that although the Bristol operation was achieving a 'fairly satisfactory result' relative to others in the UK:

When a comparison is made with the use of tramways in America, in cities of lesser importance than Bristol, it is clear that an immense field remains for cultivation by means of extensions between the city and its suburbs. But to enable the Company to exploit the necessary lines for creating that traffic and developing it, some less expensive method than horse traction must be sought, and this I am able with perfect confidence to say has been found in the recent advance of electric power.[13]

He recommended initial electrification of an extended 4-mile route running eastwards from Old Market in the city centre through St George to the suburb of Kingswood. It required complete reconstruction of the track, converting the old horsecar stables into a power station, providing electrical supply through overhead wires suspended from

A smartly turned out crew on the Staple Hill route in Bristol. Tram 161 was supplied by the American Car Company in 1898. All Bristol trams were similar open-top double deckers and were never modernised or fitted with top covers before the system was closed down from 1938 onwards.

218 Tramway Centre, Bristol

The triangular Tramway Centre at Broad Quay, Bristol, where all the city's electric tram routes converged, c1910. The half-timbered building in the centre with a large three-faced clock housed the tram company offices. Building and clock survive, but no longer have a transport function.

bracketed standards in the street and, of course, a fleet of new electric cars.

It must have felt like a daunting leap in the dark for the directors, but Robinson reassured them that 'even upon a very low and conservative view of traffic possibilities it shows a satisfactory return on the capital invested.' He was also able to persuade local councillors of the benefits of electric trams that 'the public will greatly appreciate', but that would not cost the local authorities a penny. Once the first line was up and running he was convinced that 'at no far distant date, the Corporation will suggest the extension of the use of Electric Traction to other districts of Bristol.'

Robinson's scheme was approved and just under two years later, on 14 October 1895, the Kingswood line was opened with due ceremony and a trip up and down the line for some 200 guests conveyed in eight new electric cars. Company directors, investors and

councillors could all bask in the reflected glory of an innovation for Bristol that was ahead of the whole country.

There was luncheon afterwards in the Assembly Room of the Grand Hotel in the city centre with copious toasts and mutual admiration between the distinguished guests. George White, as Managing Director of the tram company, was loudly applauded when he said that 'Bristolians have before them one of the most convincing proofs of the marvellous process of scientific evolution through which they are passing.'

He went on to boast of the £330,000 that had been spent in capital outlay over the previous twenty years (all, presumably, by his company) and that now they were carrying 15m passengers a year and 'showing a condition of vigorous growth' with the electrification scheme.

One of the councillors responded that their trip down the line on the open top of a tram had been an excellent opportunity to inspect the overhead wiring installation that some people were worrying about and 'to judge the extent to which the standards and branches could be deemed objectionable'. He had found them to be about as decorative and ornamental as in reason they could be. 'In fact', he concluded amid laughter, 'they made the wooden telegraph poles look even more wretched than before!'[14]

While the invited guests tucked into their luncheon, out east down the line the company had arranged other festivities including a free 'meat dinner' for 1,200 aged and deserving poor in the districts of Kingswood and St George. Factories and schools closed at midday and, as dusk descended on the celebrations, there were illuminations and fireworks. White and Robinson were always good at public relations and press publicity. Everything looked extremely promising and as the *Railway World* commented guardedly in its November edition '...nothing but unreasonable prejudice now stands in the way of progress.'[15]

Bristol's first electric trams were an immediate popular success and plans were soon prepared for further

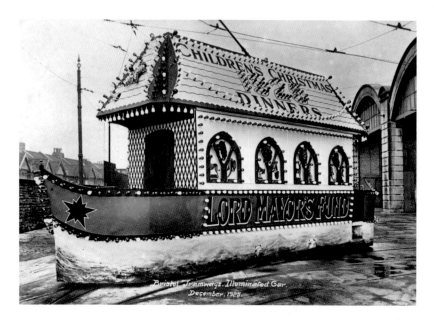

Bristol Tramways. Illuminated Car. December, 1925.

electrification. All did not go quite as smoothly as Robinson had suggested when there was a major dispute over who should supply the electric power for the enlarged system. The corporation was building a new power station for the city, and wanted to supply the trams as well so that it could charge the company for electricity. Robinson, meanwhile, had brought in a leading American expert, Horace Field Parshall, to design a complete system of power generation and supply for the trams alone which the company believed would be far more economic (and profitable) for them to use. There was stalemate for two years until the corporation relented. A new Act of Parliament was obtained in 1898 allowing the company to proceed with all its extension plans and, most importantly, its own central power supply from a single large generating station.[16]

Existing horse tram lines throughout the city were re-laid, electrified and extended to cover hilly parts of town and outer suburbs and villages that the horsecars had never been able to reach. By December 1900, when the last horse trams were withdrawn, Bristol had a complete electric network in operation running out in every direction from a triangular hub

Bristol Tramways car decorated and lit up to raise money for the Lord Mayor's Fund, 1925. The elaborate design was changed for each year's charity appeal at the company's Brislington works, seen on the right, where the whole tram fleet was maintained.

The Bristol Tramways power station at Counterslip in the city centre, seen here in 2014, awaiting conversion into luxury apartments as part of the Finzells Reach development. The original architect in 1900 was William Curtis Green, who was also responsible for the LUT generating station in Chiswick and thirty years later for the Dorchester Hotel in London. OG

on Broad Quay, which became known as Tramway Centre. By this date Bristol Tramways had also developed an impressive architect designed infrastructure, including an unusually elegant generating station at Counterslip in the city centre opposite the corporation's own electric power house and an extensive modern depot and works complex on the edge of town at Brislington, all of which survive today as listed buildings with new uses.

Bristol's new electric network was privately built with the slightly grudging agreement of the local authority and the confident expectation by the company that it could thrive as a profitable, independently run operation. In practice, being first in the electric field was to prove a disadvantage for Bristol Tramways. The battle with the corporation over competitive power generation and the subsequent threat hanging over the company of a council takeover, as the terms of their lease allowed, tended to inhibit further capital development or renewal plans after 1900. As a result Bristol was almost unique in never modernising its original electric tramway system. The company was still running a fleet of antiquated open top cars in 1937 when the council finally purchased the system and began replacing the trams with buses.

Dublin

As the first significant urban electrification in the UK was taking place relatively smoothly in Bristol, Dublin became what one historian has described as 'a notable battleground' in the electric tram saga:

In the capital of an agricultural country there were sure to be powerful vested interests ranged against it…The electricity versus horse controversy was exploited skilfully by the inevitable coalition

Newly introduced electric trams on four tracks over the O'Connell Bridge in Dublin, c1902. The main tram terminus for the city was at the Nelson Pillar in the centre of O'Connell Street (then called Sackville Street), seen in the distance.

Bank of Ireland, Dublin

opposed to electrification. Manipulating public opinion shamelessly, in the process they battened on to people's legitimate fears…Passions were stirred and the level of debate rapidly descended to widespread mud-slinging.[17]

But despite this fierce controversy and overheated debate, a start to electrification was to be achieved in Dublin well before any other comparable British[18] city apart from Bristol. It was no coincidence that early progress in Ireland was again down to the persuasive influence of James Clifton Robinson.

Within the city the Dublin United Tramways Company (DUTC), created in 1881, had a comfortable and profitable monopoly of horse tram operation, but a fractious relationship with the corporation. When the DUTC directors

first proposed electrification in the early 1890s it sparked an unexpected level of political and civic controversy in Dublin that would continue for years to come. Clifton Robinson's involvement came about almost as a flanking movement from the outside after he became manager of the suburban Dublin Southern District Tramways (DSDT) in 1892. He had, of course, worked in Ireland before during his first time as a tramways manager in Cork from 1873-4. The tramway company there had failed but in that short period Clifton Robinson had met, charmed and married Miss Mary Edith Martin of Blackrock, County Cork, who became an essential partner in his later rise to success in the tramway business.

The Dublin Southern was part of George White's Imperial Tramways group and ran two ramshackle horse lines outside the city in the coastal towns of

A Dublin United electric car outside the Bank of Ireland on College Green, c1904.

Tram coming, Howth at Dollymount, Dublin.

A postcard view of the Clontarf & Hill of Howth Tramroad at Dollymount, where it ran along the northern shore of Dublin Bay. The line opened in 1900 and was taken over by Dublin United Tramways in 1907. Trams ran right through to the Nelson Pillar over the DUT system.

Dublin Bay. Appointed on behalf of the parent company, Robinson arrived in Dublin and soon came up with an ambitious modernisation scheme in partnership with the British Thompson-Houston company. He planned to link, rebuild and electrify the DSDT's out of town lines and then extend the system right into the centre of Dublin.

While the wider debate on electric trams being allowed within the city boundaries continued, Robinson's suburban scheme for the Dublin Southern was approved and constructed very rapidly in 1895-6. The electric line from the city boundary south east to Dalkey was ceremonially opened on 16 May 1896 by the Lord Mayor of Dublin, who agreed to 'drive' the first car. This was quite a coup in itself as the mayor was known to be an outspoken opponent of electric

trams, claiming that they would destroy the livelihood of Irish farmers who supplied horses and feed for the city's transport services.

In fact the successful opening of the Dalkey line was an important step in unlocking the DUTC's stalled plans for electric trams in the city and countering the corporation's continued obstruction. Within weeks the powerful Dublin United Tramways had agreed a takeover deal for Robinson's upstart DSTC, which was sold on to them by Imperial Tramways. Shortly afterwards the DUTC's own electrification programme was finally approved by the corporation and got under way in 1897. On 19 March 1898 the first electric car arrived at the Nelson Pillar in Sackville (now O'Connell) Street at the heart of the city, and by 1901 the last horsecars in Dublin had been replaced. An independent electric line running north east from the edge of the Dublin United system out to the Howth peninsula opened in 1900 and was taken over as another addition to the city network in 1907. The whole operation stayed in private hands with no municipal control from Dublin Corporation either before or after the Easter Rising of 1916, the War of Independence (1919-21) and the creation of the Irish Free State in 1922.

Back at the turn of the century, the American *Street Railway Journal* could hardly have been more complimentary about the Dublin United Tramway's electrification achievement. On 5 May 1900, it began a review of Dublin's large new Ringsend power station, built for the DUTC by Thomson-Houston, with these words: 'The Dublin United Tramways Company may well be congratulated upon the practical completion of its magnificent system of electric tramways, which may safely be said to be the most extensive and most complete in the British Isles.'[19]

The Dublin United's new trams were set to play a major part in the growth of the twentieth-century city, while company chairman William Martin Murphy became a key if controversial figure in city business, politics and labour relations. Electric trams were an everyday presence in the urban lives evoked by James Joyce in *Dubliners*, his book of short stories published in 1914.[20] More specifically, the DUTC system, management and staff were to be closely involved in a decade of tumultuous events in Dublin which began with a bitter labour dispute, strike and lock-out on the trams in 1913. Chairman Murphy was also head of the employers' organisation, which was resolutely opposed to trades unions, and fighting another battle with the newspaper he owned, the *Irish Independent*. The events are too complex to even summarise here,

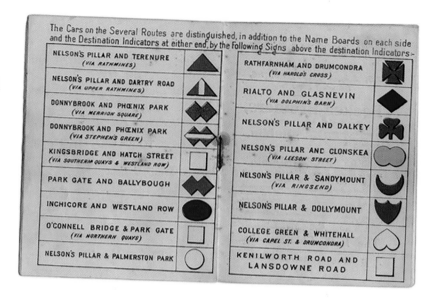

but suffice it to say that there is no other city in the world whose tramways became so intimately associated with social and political changes that shaped a nation's future.[21]

Glasgow

Glasgow was the first local authority in Britain to exercise its right to take over the privately run tramways in its area as soon as their twenty-one-year leases ran out. The city's boundaries were enlarged in 1891 and the old Town Council became the Corporation of Glasgow, a much larger authority determined to take full control of municipal transport as well as other services in the growing city. Relations with the private Glasgow Tramways Company which ran the extensive horse car network in the city had deteriorated sharply since its heyday in the early 1880s. By the early 1890s, as the end of the company's twenty-one year operating lease approached, there were testy discussions of terms for a council buy-out or even a lease extension. Negotiations came to nothing, and as the clash became the talk of the town, the dispute reached a bitter stalemate.

Early in 1894 the new Corporation tramways department set up workshops at Coplawhill to construct as quickly as

A page from the *Dublin United Tramways Guide*, c1910. Routes are identified by symbols rather than numbers.

The Glasgow Corporation stables at Coplawhill, in the late 1890s. By this time the council owned nine depots, some 3500 horses and about 250 newly built horse cars, many of which were soon to be motorised rather than replaced when the system was electrified.

Glasgow Museums

possible its own fleet of horsecars and a new depot. At midnight on 30 June 1894, when the lease expired, the GTC withdrew its tram service and its trams. Next morning the corporation started its own service with its own newly built cars, facing down the competition on the streets from the private company's large fleet of omnibuses. In its battle with the company's buses, Glasgow Corporation slashed tram fares, including the provision of early morning workmen's tickets, and also improved staff working conditions with free uniforms, shorter working hours and better pay.

This was a winning combination. By the second year of municipal ownership Glasgow Corporation Tramways were carrying 60 per cent more passengers than in the last year of private operation, and the opposition withdrew its bus service. The corporation also found they were running the tram service at a substantial and growing profit despite the fare reductions, and could write off their initial investment in replacement horsecars. It put the corporation in a powerful position to plan for the future development of services and claim that it was delivering better social conditions for the city's

workers *and* cheaper transport for the travelling public.

Glasgow was soon being held up as a model for the benefits of municipalising town transport services. The corporation had an imaginative and energetic first tramways manager, John Young, and was determined to use the trams as a means of driving forward visible improvements to the city. A very public fight with private operators had been won, but Glasgow's tramways in council control were still entirely horse drawn over some 40 miles of city streets, a system that was clearly outdated.

There was now prolonged uncertainty about the next steps in modernisation. Should it be cable traction or electric, and would overhead wires ruin the look of the city? Most engineers and technical experts were agreed on the best solution by the mid-1890s, particularly in the US, but elected councillors all over the UK were still undecided, and becoming particularly concerned about the aesthetics of the streetscape. Like the city residents they represented on the council, they had strong views, but most of them were not much better informed about the technicalities of transport than the general public. A subcommittee of Leeds councillors on a visit to Glasgow in 1895 found the elected members there in a similar dilemma to their own:

Their general conclusion appears to be that horse haulage should be discontinued as soon as possible… (but) that as between cable and electricity their town is well suited for cable, that overhead electricity would not suit them in the heart of the city on account of its unsightliness, though it might do in the outskirts.[22]

A year later Glasgow Corporation had still not taken a decision. As one of the members put it in yet another council debate in August 1896, they were 'on the

GLASGOW BRIDGE.

318

Electric trams and horse carts crossing the Clyde on Glasgow Bridge, c1904.

St George's Cross, Glasgow, c1903. Tram 618 is one of the new open top electric cars built at the Corporation's Coplawhill works in Pollokshields.

Argyle Street in Glasgow city centre, c1910. Tram 632 is another car built at Coplawhill as an open topper in 1902 and fitted with a top deck cover a few years later.

eve of great developments in electricity haulage. Perhaps within six months the conduit system might be demonstrated to be the best.[23]

Detailed reports on other electric systems, including conduit collection, were requested and provided by John

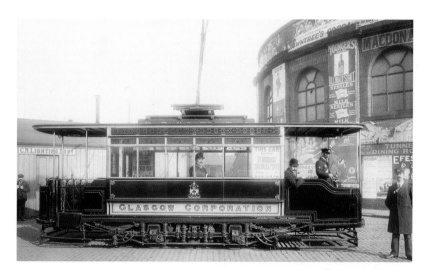

Car 92 was constructed as a double-deck horse tram in the 1890s then rebuilt in 1910 as an electric single decker for one-man operation on the short shuttle service from Finnieston Street to Stobcross Ferry in Anderston. It is seen here beside the north rotunda of the foot tunnel under the Clyde, which remained in use until 1986. Glasgow Museums

Young and his colleagues. Overseas inspection visits were made. Eventually, Glasgow set up its first electric line on a trial basis in 1898 between Mitchell Street and Springburn, using overhead wires supported in three different ways to show how this could be varied to suit a site: side poles, centre poles or brackets on buildings, all with tasteful decorative embellishments. The councillors were anxious to show that electric trams could even enhance a streetscape rather than ruin it, as their detractors claimed.

The Springburn tramline was generally well received by the Glasgow public and very well patronised. Young was able to press the council to finally commit to a programme of electrification with overhead wires throughout the city in January 1899. After the prolonged indecision, this was carried out with great speed. The last horse car was replaced in 1902, by which time Glasgow had the most extensive electric tram system in the country with the highest ridership, and both continued to grow.

Glasgow Corporation had also become adept at managing every aspect of its

Great Western Road at Botanic Gardens, Glasgow

Trams on the leafy Great Western Road in Hillhead beside Glasgow Botanic Gardens, c1904. The attractive local railway station on the right had only opened in 1896, but the arrival of electric trams and the cable-hauled Subway nearby virtually killed passenger traffic on this suburban steam line. The station closed temporarily during the First World War and permanently in 1939. It was later destroyed in a fire.

tramways in-house, from tracklaying and car building to system operation and maintenance, the complete opposite to the original private set-up at Bristol and Dublin. Glasgow used external contractors to manufacture much of its early electrical equipment, often built in the US, but soon developed its own capabilities in nearly every area, a less surprising step for a city of heavy manufacturing industry like ship and locomotive building. As one American historian has described it:

> *Glasgow drew heavily upon American technology, but it was not subservient to American enterprise…the municipal tramway system of Glasgow purchased advanced foreign technology to fit its specifications at competitive prices when that was expedient, and continued to rely on its own skill and initiative for operations.*[24]

In 1900, with electrification only half complete, Glasgow's cars were already carrying 20 per cent of the tramway passenger total for the entire country and transforming the way people lived in the

GLASGOW CORPORATION TRAMWAYS
OFFICIAL GUIDE
TO GLASGOW & NEIGHBOURHOOD 3D
JAMES DALRYMPLE, GENERAL MANAGER

Pride of the city. An *Official Guide to Glasgow and Neighbourhood*, history of the city and details of the sights and places of interest to be found on every tram route, c1910.

city. Five years later Frederic Clemson Howe, a leading American social reformer and administrator, spent some time in Glasgow investigating change and democracy in organising modern American and European cities. He described Glasgow as 'in many ways the most aggressively efficient city in Great Britain'.[25] The council-run tramways particularly impressed him as a key aspect of this and he found that every Glaswegian he spoke to was especially proud of their model system of 'caurs'.[26]

Liverpool

South of the border the English city that took the municipal route forward first with its tramways was Liverpool. The relationship between the city and the private horse tram operators was nothing like as confrontational as the stand-off in Glasgow. Even so, once the 1870 rule enabling local authorities to build and own but not run tramways was removed in 1896, Liverpool Corporation moved into the tramway business itself without delay. The private Liverpool United Tramway & Omnibus Company was acquired in 1897 when its lease expired, and with a less combative transition to council operation, plans for electrification were drawn up.[27]

As in Glasgow a new corporation committee took advice from external consultants, its own electrical engineer and went on extensive inspection tours of existing systems in Europe and America. There were the same debates over exactly what system to use, but Liverpool was more rapidly decisive than Glasgow in moving forward. Despite a later start to the project, the city quickly caught up with Glasgow and had its first electric line ready for opening from the city centre running east to Dingle in November 1898.

Although the process was rapid, the influence of continental tours and advice did lead to some idiosyncratic choices in Liverpool over their early electric trams. The expert engineers who advised the corporation believed that for safety reasons an electric car would have to remain static while passengers found their seats on the top deck. Experience proved this precaution unnecessary, but the idea led the councillors who went on the 'deputation to the Continent' to recommend strongly against using open double-deck cars. Their report was quite specific:

> *With regard to the cars, the deputation are of the opinion that to secure the full advantage of electric traction as regards speed and comfort, the cars used in Hamburg, without top seats, but with outside accommodation on the platforms, should be adopted in Liverpool, with the addition of open trailer cars for the summer service.*[28]

As a result the first batch of electric trams for Liverpool were ordered direct from its port city partner in Germany and supplied by W.C.F. Busch of Hamburg with motors and controllers from W.S. Schuckert of Nuremberg. Liverpool hedged its bets by also ordering a set of much larger single-deck American streetcars from the J.G. Brill Company of Philadelphia, to a design already used by the tramways of Cleveland, Ohio.

With so few precedents in England, the early months of electric tram

An open top Liverpool electric car built in 1899 at the Aigburth Vale terminus, c1900. The electric tram line was extended further east to the new city boundary at Garston in 1902, when the connecting corporation horse bus service shown here, the last in the city, was withdrawn.

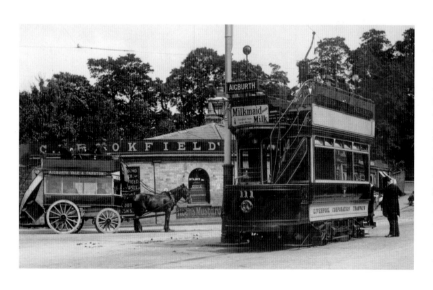

3403

View from Landing Stage, Liverpool

LIVERPOOL FROM THE LANDING STAGE

operation on Merseyside were effectively a series of full scale public service trials of equipment from Germany and the US. In the event neither of these overseas designs was adopted for general use. The tiny German tramcars and trailers proved unsuitable and were all withdrawn by 1901; the original American single-deck cars were in daily use for over twenty years, but were not to be the model

Aintree, Warbeck Terrace

This is the terminus of the Aintree Car.

The Wrench Series No. 4197

Warbeck Terrace in suburban Aintree, the western end of the electric tram line from the Pier Head. This card was posted on 8 August 1904 by Cissie to her sister Florrie in Ulverston letting her know that 'mother sailed on Saturday. Nellie and I went to see her off.'

The body shop of the ER&TCW at Preston, c1901. The wooden tram bodies under construction here will be given open-top decks and reverse stairs at either end then fixed to cast iron trucks, often imported from the JG Brill Company in the USA, and fitted with British-built Dick, Kerr control equipment.

Tramcars for Liverpool leaving the new Electric Railway & Tramway Carriage Works in Preston, c1900. The ER&TCW, established by Dick, Kerr and associates, supplied these Preston standard trams to more than fifty towns all over the country. In 1919 the manufacturing company was reconstituted as English Electric.

tram design for Liverpool or any other British city.

Liverpool Corporation decided to develop its own standard tramcar body design at the old horsecar works it had inherited, using bought-in American electrical equipment. First produced in 1899, variations of this open-top, single truck, double-deck design became the

popular choice of many council tramway committees all over the country. From 1900 the cars were built by the Dick, Kerr Company at its large new works in Preston, which first imported and then adapted or built under licence the American-pattern trucks and electrical equipment. The 'Preston Car' as it then became, first produced for Liverpool but

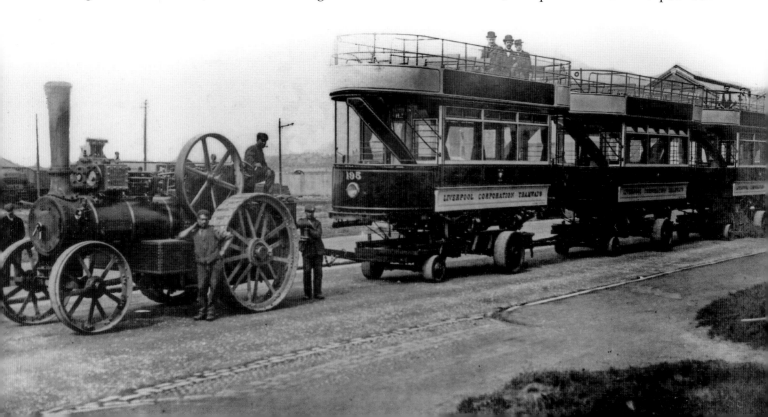

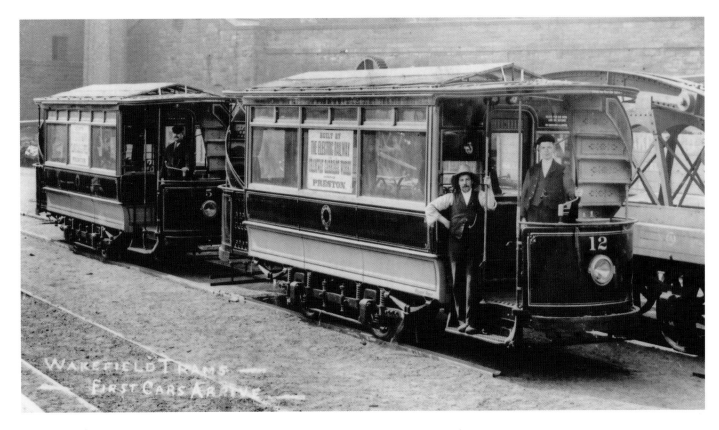

soon offered by Dick, Kerr as an almost 'off the shelf' product, appeared in different guises and colours on local authority tramways as far afield as Bolton, Colchester, Grimsby, Nottingham, Portsmouth and Reading among others.[29]

By 1902, when tramway electrification in Liverpool was virtually complete, the corporation's transport service mileage had doubled since 1897. It was committed to a low fares policy, and the attraction of this and the faster, more comfortable electric cars made the new trams very popular. Passenger journeys in the city trebled in the same period to nearly 110m in 1902.

As soon as electric trams were provided and fares were cut significantly, very large numbers of passengers starting using them without the need for significant advertising and promotion. It seemed to be a case of lay the tracks and wires and the passengers will come if the price is right. This was a capital investment choice that a local authority could afford to make in what it judged to be the public interest where a private company might be taking a considerable business and financial risk.

There was much debate at the time as to whether municipal trading gave local authorities an unfair advantage over private companies who now found themselves unable to compete with council-run electric tramways. The balance certainly shifted decisively in the late 1890s in favour of full council control in most of England, Scotland and Wales, though less so in Ireland. Liverpool Corporation's rapid tramway electrification was one of the first indications of what was to follow elsewhere. There the trams were also a significant contributor to, and reflection of, the city's civic and commercial confidence at the turn of the century. For a brief period its new electric tramways were ahead of the other great regional cities of England but Manchester, Leeds and Birmingham were all catching up fast.

Frederic Howe praised the way Liverpool, as well as Glasgow and the

Some Lancashire-built Preston trams were delivered to customers in two halves for convenience of transport. These vehicles for the Wakefield & District Light Railway will have their top decks fitted in Yorkshire.

Portsmouth was an example of a council operator that bought 'off the shelf' trams from Preston following the Liverpool pattern. It started electric operation with sixty standard cars in 1901. This postcard shows two of them at the Clarence Pier terminus, Southsea in 1904.

Southsea. The Common from Clarence Pier.

Almost ready to go. Doncaster Corporation also started with standard Preston products for its electric tramway system. Here is the first batch of electric cars being prepared for service in the brand new depot, 1902.

other big cities, ran their public transport under strong municipal control. He knew that his fellow Americans generally assumed that their own City Halls were incorrigibly corrupt and that the common British and German approach might look to them dangerously like socialism. His views were often dismissed in the US, but he continued to make the case that in key areas like urban transport it was clear that

European-style municipal management really did work:

'Citizens vie with officials in Liverpool in claiming that their tramways are the most up-to-date in Great Britain. Whatever merit there may be in the claim – a common one, by the way, heard all over Great Britain – the tramways are wonderfully efficient and comfortable, and are an ornament to the streets…The cars are cleaned every night, as are the trucks. The signs upon the cars give the routes and destinations in detail. Stopping places are marked by conspicuous signs. On the narrow streets the span-wires are carried from rosettes on the buildings, rather than from poles. Employees are picked after the most careful examination; they prize their jobs, and are courteous and considerate to passengers. There are no strap-hangers at any time, for the double-decker car offers more than twice as many seats as the average American single-deck car…

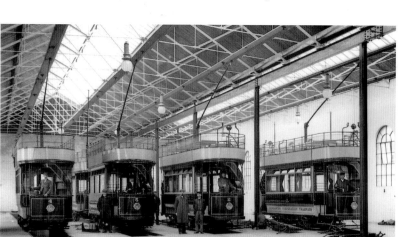

'Many other improvements have been
worked out in Liverpool which, so far
as the public is concerned, are far in
advance of the private lines in
America…a great workshop is
operated by the city where cars,
motors and machinery are both built
and repaired. There is a spirit of
enthusiastic rivalry to make the
service the best that can be offered.
Municipal ownership, far from
deadening initiative, seems to have
given it the fullest opportunity to
express itself. This is true all over
England, as it is in Germany.'[30]

The Town Hall (with tram).   Dover.

Across the country

At the end of 1894 there were only 65
miles of electric tramway in the whole of
Britain. By the turn of the century this had
increased slowly but steadily to 1,177
miles. There was nothing like the boom
that had taken place across the USA,
where by 1900 an estimated 40,000 electric
streetcars were covering more than 15,000
miles of town and country routes. All of
these were private company operations

and proving extremely lucrative to their
promoters if not always to the
communities they served. Throughout
Britain there was a change a decade after
this rapid development across the
Atlantic, but it came primarily from
public authorities that could learn from
experience overseas both in technical
development and management. With the
constraints on municipal tramway

Dover Corporation
opened the first
electric tramway in
southern England on 6
September 1897. This
card, posted in 1905,
shows car no. 9, one of
the ten original trams
supplied by Brush of
Loughborough, outside
the Town Hall.

The Bridge, Walsall

Walsall was the first
town in the West
Midlands to have an
electric tram route,
opened by the
South Staffordshire
Tramways Company
in 1893. This busy
town centre view was
taken about fifteen
years later and shows
open and covered top
cars after Walsall
Corporation had
taken over from
the private operators
and extended
local services.

Outside the Theatre Royal in George Street, Plymouth, where Corporation electric trams replaced horse cars in 1901.

At the close of the Victorian age council-run electric trams were introduced to towns as diverse and differing in size as Dover (1897), Bradford (1898), Southampton (1898), Sheffield (1899), Aberdeen (1899) and Hull (1899). Carlisle, Dundee, Norwich, Oldham, Southport, Sunderland and others followed in 1900 and were joined by another group in 1901 that ranged from Ayr on the west coast of Scotland to Southend in Essex. In the same year corporation tramways opened in the larger conurbations of Birmingham, Newcastle and Gateshead (on either side of the Tyne, but not yet bridged for trams) and Manchester and Salford (adjoining cities with no visible border but separately run council tram networks).

operation lifted and the end of company leases, local councils across the country, large and small, made plans to introduce their own electric trams.

Glasgow and Liverpool were the two big pioneers of corporation control, but were soon followed by other British cities.

These were all municipal systems electrified and extended after the acquisition of privately operated horse and, in a few cases, steam tramway companies. Only a handful of new company-run electric tramways were set up at this stage in urban districts but they were a diverse group with a wide

The terminus of the newly electrified line at Nether Edge, Sheffield, c1900. A delivery boy is collecting goods arriving by tram from town. One lady is stepping off the car while a family climb aboard. The conductor will swing the pole and the motorman will walk to the other end for the return journey to the city.

Top of Hilltown, Dundee, seen in a typically high quality 'real photo' postcard by local printer Valentine's, c1910. The steep tram route in this part of the city opened with steam traction in 1894 and was electrified when the Corporation took over in 1899. The Scottish-built single deck tram was supplied by Hurst Nelson of Motherwell in 1902.

geographical spread including Coventry (1895), Middlesborough (1898), Cork (1898), Potteries Electric Tramways (1899), Swansea (1900), Tynemouth & District (1901) and Merthyr Tydfil (1901). In most cases the local authority still owned, and sometimes built, the upgraded tram track, infrastructure and electrical plant. Most of the new companies were simply operators, just as they had been with horsecars, but now usually with shorter seven-year leasing agreements. The local authority's right of company purchase when these expired remained and a council takeover could still happen if circumstances changed.[31]

There were no real equivalents to the American inter-urban electric lines which connected towns across country in the US. The closest in the UK was probably the Blackpool & Fleetwood Tramroad (1898), a company project running mainly on reserved track and started as an independent operation to Blackpool Corporation's system, which later absorbed it in 1920. In Ireland the Great Northern Railway (Ireland) set up its own short but steep electric tourist line, the Hill of Howth Tramway near Dublin,

which from 1900 ran up to the summit of Slievemartin. It was similar in some ways to the Great Orme Tramway in Wales and the closest thing Ireland ever got to a mountain railway or tramway, patronised mainly by day trippers from Dublin in the summer season.

In August 1899 the leading American engineering journal *Cassier's Magazine* devoted an entire issue to the progress of electric traction in Europe and the USA at

In 1901 neighbouring Manchester and Salford opened separate electric tram systems, but ran through services across the borough boundary. In this view of Deansgate, Manchester, c1904, all five approaching cars are from the Salford Corporation fleet.

DEANSGATE, MANCHESTER.

Beverley Road, Hull, c1910. The tram is one of the original Milnes electric cars delivered in 1899 as open toppers and later fitted with short top covers in the council's workshops. They were soon known locally as 'kipper boxes'.

Clarence Bridge, Cardiff, soon after the introduction of electric trams by the corporation in 1902. The double tracks are interlaced over the narrow bridge meaning only one tram at a time could cross in either direction.

the turn of the century, featuring the opinions of expert professionals like Frank Sprague. In a detailed review of the latest UK tramway developments, Robert W. Blackwell makes a downbeat prediction on electrification prospects in the new century, noting that:

There is not the slightest evidence that any 'boom' is likely to occur. The progress will be quiet and steady compared with that made either on the continent or in America. The British public is by no means educated up to believe that a tramway of any kind whatever is necessary to its happiness and well-being, and it will acquire that education only by degrees…

His measured suggestion was that:

Both corporations and companies must, of necessity, move with deliberation. The tramway is still the 'poor man's carriage' in Great Britain, and it will take years before it will reach its proper estate and be recognised as an indispensable convenience by all classes.[32]

Blackwell's cautious assessment is understandable, but in fact electrification took off rather faster than he expected over the next few years. Although projects varied across the country in scale and speed of development, this was the start of a golden age for electric tramways which were to open in nearly

The tram stop and cab stand outside the Post Office and Town Hall, Ipswich. This early coloured postcard is an unusually accurate rendition of the green and cream livery of the electric cars introduced by the council in 1903.

every urban district of the British Isles in the Edwardian decade.

It is true that no overarching or co-ordinated national plan was ever put forward and co-operation across municipal boundaries was predictably wary. Local councils then, as now, were often doggedly independent and could be particularly competitive with their immediate neighbours. This sometimes led to nonsensical 'border breaks' where there was no through service or even a

A street scene in Prescot, just outside Liverpool, where an electric tram service was introduced by the St Helens & District Tramways in 1899.

Advertising card for the Blackpool & Fleetwood Tramroad, c1905. This was a company system opened in 1898, running north of Blackpool along the Fylde coast. It was purchased by Blackpool Corporation in 1920 and today forms the longest remaining stretch of the Blackpool operation.

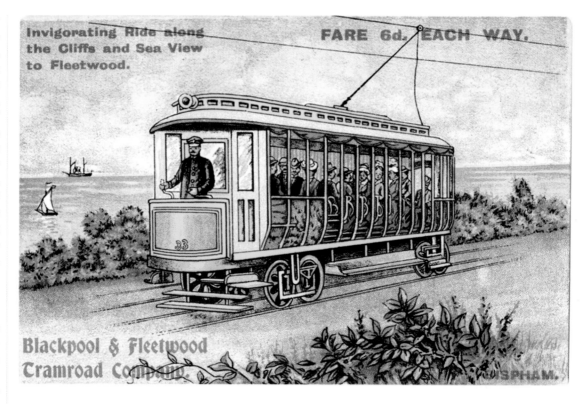

Car no.1 decorated for the opening of the short Hill of Howth Tramway near Dublin on 17 June 1901, a separate operation to the Clontarf Tramroad which had opened from Howth along the coast in 1900. This was destined to be the last electric tramway in Ireland, closed in 1959, though four of the ten trams used on the line survive in museums.

physical track connection between close running systems. The most ridiculous example of non co-operation was in West Yorkshire where the 11 miles between Bradford and Huddersfield was served by three electric undertakings working on different track gauges inside each local authority area. Six miles of tramline were in Bradford on 4ft gauge, one mile in Halifax on 3ft 6in gauge and five miles in Huddersfield on the odd 4ft 7in gauge, making through running impossible.[33]

A system break could also occur because legislation left the power of veto in the hands of the local authority. Private tramway companies felt strongly that councils exploited their position of control by in effect taxing them before giving consent to a proposal. A Mr Chaplin, President of the Local Government Board, stated in 1902 that 'What local authorities would describe as conditions are regarded by promoters – and very often no doubt with good reason – as neither more nor less than blackmail.'[34]

Giving evidence to the Royal Commission on London Traffic in 1904,

Opposite: Comic cards about the impact of electric trams traded heavily on popular myths and stereotypes. The main illustration here seems to be an exaggerated copy of the previous Chicago postcard. Belfast's new electric cars in 1906 were in fact all double deck and the idea of runaway pigs on urban streets is a hoary old caricature of the rural Irish in the modern city.

'A busy day on Dearborn and Randall Streets, Chicago'. Commercial postcard, c1905. Mixing fast electric streetcars with slow horse-drawn wagons could create traffic chaos in a big city. Similar jams to this were recorded in London and Manchester near the big railway goods warehouses.

A border break in south London, c1910. The Croydon Corporation tram in the foreground terminated at the borough's northern boundary in Norbury. Passengers for central London had to transfer to the LCC tram beyond. The two systems were not linked for through running until 1926.

A border break in the north at Wallsend, the eastern boundary of Newcastle, c1905. Passengers to and from the city had to transfer between the corporation car in the foreground, which is about to reverse, and the Tyneside Tramways company car beyond, which will return to North Shields. Through running and ticketing was agreed in 1910.

Clifton Robinson claimed that securing powers to construct 12 miles of tramway around Kingston-upon-Thames had cost the London United Tramways £154,000, or £12,800 per mile paid to the council. Other councils demanded even more as the 'price of permission' and their uncompromising attitude led his company to abandon 60 miles of proposed extensions and connections with other systems in Surrey as commercially unviable: 'Instead of giving such proposals sympathetic consideration, if not practical encouragement, the attitude assumed by the average local authority of today is one of hostility, inspired by a desire to extort the uttermost farthing from promoters.'

As an independent, commercial promoter of tramways, Robinson often found himself locking horns with local authorities, so his comments are not surprising. He was more concerned about securing a profitable deal for company shareholders than the wider social or community benefits that a tramway might

'A Trial of Patience'. A local postcard comment on the long delay in getting agreement for LUT trams to run through Malden to Tooting and Wimbledon in south-west London, 1906. One woman in the crowd is complaining 'My hat's going out of fashion.' LTM/TfL

The first London United tram over Kingston Bridge, finally extending the LUT system from Middlesex into Surrey, 1906. The Mayor of Kingston is at the controls; LUT Chairman James Clifton Robinson stands in front of the tram with his son. LTM/TfL

bring. It is a debate that still resonates today with developers, builders and local planning authorities.

A general enthusiasm for 'going electric' seemed to take over every sizeable town at the turn of the century, particularly as local authorities were released from some of their most restrictive legal obligations. Electric trams were now centre stage in more ambitious plans for municipal trading and a growing number of local councils realised that they were in a position to call the shots.

Late London
The area where a single co-ordinating authority could have brought the greatest benefit to city transport planning with electric trams was Greater London. The largest and wealthiest city in the country was, rather surprisingly, the slowest to introduce electric trams. Here the multiplicity of local authorities involved and sharp differences in attitude to the new mode of public transport caused many bureaucratic delays in the outer

suburbs, but the most lengthy transition was in the large central area covered by the London County Council (LCC).

The LCC was established in 1889 as the first elected local government body with powers across the metropolis including planning, housing and education. It was

Off the rails in the Old Kent Road, c1900. The LCC gradually took over the horse tram companies as their leases expired in the 1890s but dithered over how to modernise them. This horse car seems to have come off the tracks and been parked at the kerb while a problem is sorted out. LTM/TfL

the biggest, most significant and most ambitious English municipal authority of its day, but the sheer complexity of reforming the world's greatest city meant that progress in some areas was slow. There was also uncertainty and disagreement about whether its role should be largely advisory, regulatory and strategic or whether it should have direct operational responsibility for services.

Tramways became a particular bone of contention. At the time the LCC was created there were fifteen private horse tram companies working in the County of London, most of them on twenty-one year leases due to expire at various dates in the 1890s. Negotiating terms of acquisition under compulsory purchase was long and complicated, and it was not until 1896 that the LCC got the legal right to operate its own tramways. Surprisingly little thought

was given as to how these tramways might be modernised once they were in LCC hands. The Progressives, a coalition group of Liberals, Socialists and trade unionists who had political control of the new assembly, were keen to take over the old horse tramways but had no clear plans or ideas about how to improve them through an electrification programme.

A first stab at this came as late as 1898 in a report entitled *Tramway Traction* by J. Allen Baker, the Vice Chairman of the LCC's Highways Committee. Baker was a committed social reformer but had no experience or engineering knowledge of tramways and went on a study tour of US cities at his own expense before writing his report. He strongly advised the LCC to consider adopting a conduit electric system to avoid having overhead wires in the capital, a prospect that was already causing far more concern and debate in London than elsewhere in Britain. Baker had been particularly impressed with the heavy duty conduit construction then nearing completion in New York and Washington DC, both systems chosen to keep the broad streets of the showpiece downtown districts wire free. Clearly it would be considerably more expensive than a cheap overhead power line system for London, though Baker was vague about how much more it would cost to keep the capital's historic thoroughfares clear of power lines. Overhead wires might be acceptable, he concluded, for 'provincial cities with their wider and less busy streets and comparatively small populations', but 'the one in my judgement best suited to the requirements of London is the electric conduit.'[35]

Although no immediate decision was taken by the LCC, somehow the idea took hold that London had to have a wireless electric system no matter what the cost. Baker's report set the council on course towards adopting an electrification scheme which would turn out to be cumbersome, very expensive and take years to complete. The LCC started on this route by appointing as its electrical engineering consultant Dr Alexander Kennedy,[36] whose subsequent reports followed the same track in more detail but without much apparent expert knowledge.

It was a curious early example of almost unchallenged faith in a single consultant who was barely qualified for the job. By late 1900 the LCC had decided to commit to a conduit electric system but had still worked out very little of the detail. The Board of Trade authorised the initial scheme in April 1901 and construction work on the first line finally began with reconstruction of the old horse tracks in Tooting at the end of the year.[37]

No other local authority outside London could afford to install a complete conduit system, which was at least twice

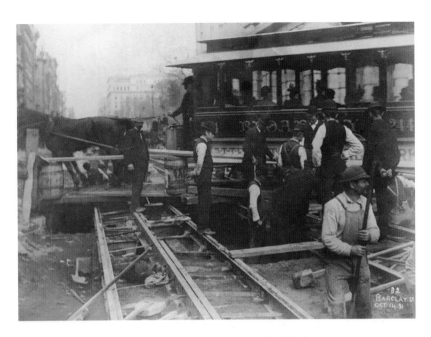

Installing the conduit electric system in New York while horse cars are still operating on a cross-track, 1891. This is a decade before the first electric tram appeared in London. New York Public Library

the cost of electrifying with overhead wires. Many local councils had the same tortuous debate about wires, but only a few decided to try other experimental supply systems. Bournemouth, Hastings,

Laying a major junction for Reading Corporation's new electric system in the town centre, 1903. This is standard trackwork without a conduit below it. A web of overhead wires will be erected over the intersection to power the trams. Reading Museum

A new ritual on the streets of most towns. The conductor swings the pole at Wibsey tram terminus on the outskirts of Bradford in readiness for the return trip to the city centre. Corporation electric trams arrived here in 1907.

Dick, Kerr Company labourers installing the LCC conduit system on the Thames Embankment in London, 1906. Putting in the heavy duty infrastructure for sub-surface power supply more than doubled the cost of electrification. LTM/TfL

Lincoln, Mexborough, Torquay and Wolverhampton were all persuaded to avoid unsightly wires by using partial or complete electrical pick-up through 'surface contact'. There were a number of slightly different commercial systems available but the principle was the same for all of them, as concisely explained by Charles Klapper:

The tram carried a long collector shoe or skate just out of contact with the road surface. Below the road at a similar depth to the conductor rails of the conduit system ran a continuous power cable, coupled at intervals with 'studs'. The skate was always above two or more studs and as each was passed over it was brought electro-magnetically into contact with the skate above and the power cable below.[38]

In theory the studs in the road only became 'live' when a tram was passing over them, going dead immediately afterwards, but the equipment was not very reliable. Klapper quotes from a hair-raising account in the *Yorkshire Telegraph and Star* of a night journey on the new Mexborough and Swinton Tramways in 1907:

We seemed at times to be travelling over sheets of fire, the electric flashes ever and anon blazing from beneath the wheels with almost startling vividness caused, I believe, by skidding over the studs and not finding contact evenly…To a passenger on a first run these flashes

Wolverhampton adopted the Lorain surface contact electric system in 1902. The corporation's trams picked up power through electro-magnetic skates as they passed over contact boxes laid between the rails. The surface studs can be clearly seen closely spaced along both tracks in this town centre view, with tall electric street lamps but no overhead wires for the trams.

Hastings & District Tramways used the alternative Dolter surface contact system for the section of route along St Leonard's Parade where the council felt that overhead wires would disfigure the elegant seafront. It opened in 1907 but was very troublesome. Wires were eventually put up here in 1921.

The Mexborough & Swinton Tramway trialled the Dolter system in 1907, but all its new trams were also equipped with trolley poles for overhead pick-up, as shown here. This was a wise precaution as the unreliable surface contact system was abandoned within a year.

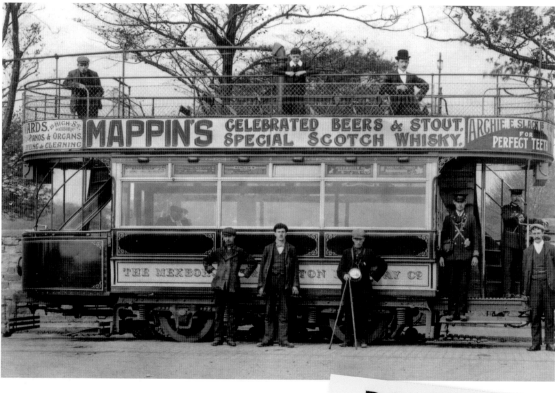

Torquay was also persuaded to adopt the Dolter system initially. Opened in 1907, it too was not a success and contrary to the company's optimistic advertising promotion at the time shown here, plans for its introduction in Oxford and Folkestone were soon abandoned.

are somewhat perturbing, but the element of danger is altogether absent, unless young horses are about and even they are fast getting used to it in these days of flying motors and quick travelling. With the flash comes a swishing sound similar to the send-off of a burning rocket. The lights in the car, too, dance in and out with frivolous frequency. Altogether the effects on a night journey lend a spice of variety to the run.[39]

Contrary to the safety claims of the Dolter and Lorain companies that installed these surface contact systems, there were many reports of horses getting electric shocks through their metal shoes from supposedly deactivated studs, and the reliability issue was never solved. None of these wire-free systems continued in operation for very long, the last to be abandoned being Wolverhampton's, which was converted to overhead wires in 1921.

By contrast the LCC's chosen conduit arrangement proved to be both robust and

reliable. Once installed it needed constant and labour-intensive cleaning and maintenance, but it remained in continuous daily operation for nearly fifty years until the end of London's trams in 1952.

Suburban progress

Before the slow-moving LCC had even started work, three separate electric tram systems had opened in outer west, south and east London beyond the county boundary in the course of 1901. These developments reflected the mixture of company and council initiatives that were in progress all around the LCC area in parts of Middlesex, Surrey, Hertfordshire and Metropolitan Essex.

The first and most impressive of these operations was the biggest new project of the Imperial Tramways Company, the private group led by George White and James Clifton Robinson. Following the same strategy they had used with the Dublin Southern Tramways in the early 1890s, Imperial had taken over a struggling horse tramway, in this case the West Metropolitan Tramways, and prepared a radical transformation scheme.

The WMT operated horse trams on the main roads west of Hammersmith and Shepherds Bush. They were short, isolated and unprofitable routes in suburban Middlesex, beyond the LCC's control, almost bankrupt and quite unable to fund their own modernisation and recovery.

After taking control of the WMT, Robinson proposed a new electric scheme to be developed over a much wider area of outer west London and renamed the London United Tramways. It required lengthy and patient negotiation both with Middlesex County Council as the principal local authority and the various individual boroughs, particularly those where attitudes to trams were sharply divided.

Ealing, which estate agents routinely described at this time as 'a very high class

George Wimpey's workmen reconstructing the former West Metropolitan horsecar lines in Hammersmith during preparation for overhead electrification as part of Clifton Robinson's London United Tramways, 1898. LTM/TfL

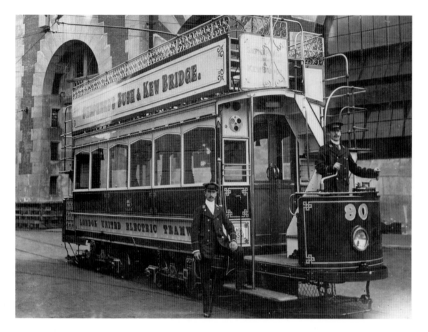

One of the first electric trams in London posed in front of the power station alongside the original Chiswick depot. Motorman Kellythorne, at the controls, drove the first LUT car in public service from Shepherd's Bush to Kew Bridge in April 1901. The former tram depot is now a London bus garage. LTM/TfL

residential suburb' was particularly difficult. Both the council and the wealthier residents were concerned that electric trams along the Uxbridge Road would lower the tone and reduce property values in the so-called 'Queen of Suburbs'. Robinson talked them round and this route became one of the first LUT lines to open. However, the company later faced prolonged haggling with Richmond, which would only accept expensive conduit electrification. The eventual outcome here was an end to the Kew Bridge and Richmond town's isolated horsecar service, but no electric upgrade or convenient tram connection to the rest of south-west London. There would be further tram battles ahead in Kingston and other boroughs.

Returning to 1901, another problem arose which threatened to derail the initial electrification scheme as it neared completion. Even after agreement with the local authorities had been secured, scientists at the prestigious Royal Kew Observatory in Richmond Park raised concerns that stray return electric currents from trams on the other side of the river would upset their delicate instruments. Robinson only resolved this on the day

before his new tram service was due to open with a last minute offer to meet the cost of removing the Observatory's equipment to a new site on the west coast of Scotland.[40]

London's first electric trams began running west from Shepherd's Bush and Hammersmith to Acton and Kew Bridge on 4 April 1901. Extensions through Ealing to Hanwell and Southall, and from Kew Bridge to Brentford and Hounslow, followed three months later on 6 July. Finally on 10 July, still beating the other London lines still under construction, there was a grand parade of nine decorated trams carrying guests to the formal opening ceremony for the whole network at Ealing Town Hall. Here Lord Rothschild declared the lines open and congratulated Ealing 'on having a scientific and comfortable system of locomotion brought to its doors'.

Everything about the opening reflected Clifton Robinson's exceptional skill in managing and promoting a tramway. This was his finest hour. The guest list rivalled Train's for the original Birkenhead tram launch forty years earlier, which Robinson had marvelled at as a boy. In the interim he had learned exactly who to target for maximum benefit, and unlike Train he was able to deliver an impressive project with tangible results.

All the appropriate people Robinson had been cultivating were there. Lord Rothschild, as one of the wealthiest men in London, and owner of Gunnersbury Park (just one of his extensive homes and properties), was an astute choice to perform the opening ceremony; American entrepreneurs Charles Tyson Yerkes and Pierpoint Morgan Jr, both busy planning investment in new London Tube projects were there; Granville Cunningham, manager of the Central London Tube Railway, whose trains met the LUT cars at Shepherds Bush; Arthur Balfour MP, leader of the House of Commons; W.J. (later Sir

William) Bull, MP for Hammersmith and a champion of Robinson's projects. The list goes on, an astute selection from the British political establishment and the new worlds of international finance and modern engineering. Most of the guests would probably never want or need to travel on Robinson's trams again, but as an influential launch party it was a huge success.

The decorated cars returned to Chiswick depot where the guests were shown the LUT power house, another ornate but tasteful structure by William Curtis Green, architect of the elaborate Bristol Tramways generating station. This too has been preserved externally and converted to house modern offices instead of turbines. Robinson's party sat down to a sumptuous luncheon in the newly constructed depot building alongside (now Chiswick bus garage). For the inauguration there were garlands decorating the plain interior and quality catering supplied by Messrs Ritz and Echenard of the luxury Carlton Hotel in Regent Street.

Balfour proposed a toast of success to the London United Tramways: 'I look to

this vast enterprise not merely to diminish the evils of metropolitan congestion, but greatly to add to the highest pleasures of life of the metropolitan inhabitants.'

Robinson had already primed the press, and the next day's issue of *Tramway & Railway World* predictably praised the LUT inauguration as one of the most important events in British electric traction history:

In transplanting the overcrowded masses to country or suburbs the

Electricity and Locomotion. This elaborate decorative cartouche is still in place on the London United Electric Tramways powerhouse in Chiswick, built in 1900. It is now a listed building housing offices and recording studios. OG

Hounslow, just west of London, was still a small market town when the LUT trams arrived in 1901. Improved public transport by electric tram and Underground train would soon suburbanise this part of rural Middlesex.

LUT appealed to philosophers and politicians and to all concerned in the housing question. The great men who attended the ceremony recognised a new factor in civilisation. The company's policy was to lay lines and await the traffic. On the inaugural trip to Southall it was noticeable that many houses were being erected along the route.[41]

The new trams attracted custom very rapidly, with more passengers in the first three months than the horse trams carried in a year. There was supposed to be a maximum three-minute service interval, with Clifton Robinson insistent about 'always allowing a passenger to see a car in sight one side or the other'. Speculative housing development continued all down the line, though not without further complaints from those existing residents

Electric cars at Ilford Broadway on one of the first council-run tramway systems to open in Metropolitan Essex, just east of London, in 1903.

and authorities trying to stem the tide of suburban spread across rural Middlesex.

A royal send off

While the London United planned (but did not always achieve) further growth in suburban west London, and south into Surrey, the county borough of East Ham opened the first municipally-run electric tramway on the other side of the metropolis in September 1901. To the south electric tram operation started in Croydon at the same time, initially run by the British Electric Traction company under contract but taken in-house by the corporation from 1906. By 1903 there were municipal electric services in Ilford, Barking and Bexley and more under construction by other outer London councils to the south and east of the LCC boundary. Across the rest of Middlesex east of the LUT districts the county

Broadway, Ilford

The first Electric Tram Car, leaving Stratford for Plaistow and Custom House on February 27, 1904

The grand opening of the West Ham Corporation Tramways in Stratford, east London, 1904. The sender of this postcard evidently appears in the photograph, presumably somewhere in the crowd.

council decided to build electric tram lines on its main roads running north out of London for operation under contract by the Metropolitan Electric Tramways, another BET subsidiary. Electric trams were arriving in nearly every London suburb through a complicated range of municipal and public/private agreements.

Most Londoners knew nothing of the detailed arrangements and probably cared less whether their new transport services were run by a public or private authority. But the procedural wrangles were important because in the end they delayed both electrification and the creation of a single transport authority which could have planned and developed an integrated system across the whole vast urban area more effectively. The London County Council, unlike corporations elsewhere in the country and even in the suburbs just outside its boundaries, was not its own street authority. It was subject to the veto powers of the metropolitan boroughs and the City of London still in force under the 1870 Tramways Act. Even as its first

electric tram line, built under the costly conduit system, neared completion in 1903, it was clear that expansion plans, through running and co-ordination with other authorities would only be agreed and enacted slowly.

In contrast to its initial 'uninformed amateur' approach to tramway engineering, the LCC was admirably progressive and organised in its social housing policy, which was closely linked to cheap transport. Improving inner London's appalling housing conditions was a priority. In 1900, before any decisions had been made on tramway electrification, the council had bought a large site in south London at Totterdown Fields, Lower Tooting, to build its first inner suburban cottage housing estate. Over 1,000 arts and crafts style homes with gardens designed and built by the LCC would house more than 8,000 people. Living conditions would be vastly improved for anyone moving out of overcrowded central London, but cheap and easy travelling facilities to work were also essential. Electric trams were the

THE ARCHWAY TAVERN, HIGHGATE.

Transition in north London. Cable (left), horse and a new MET overhead electric tram meet at the Archway Tavern, c1906, just before the LCC electrified both the horse and cable car lines on its conduit system.
LTM/TfL

obvious way to provide this, and hence the LCC's first choice for electrification of the Tooting–Westminster Bridge horse line that it had recently acquired.

This made the opening of its first electric tram service by the Prince of Wales on 15 May 1903 a double publicity coup for the LCC. It may have been two years behind Robinson's pioneer electrification in west London, but a royal opening trumped a Rothschild. There was also the opportunity to show off the LCC's new social housing provision at the end of the tram line with a royal visit to a family that had just moved into one of the new council cottages. The future King George V was accompanied by the Princess of Wales and their two boys, the future Edward VIII and George VI, who were dressed in sailor suits. John Williams Benn, chairman of the LCC's Highways Committee, in top hat and morning dress,

collected halfpenny fares from the royal party before their special white tram moved off at the head of a procession of fifty cars. Cheering schoolchildren and 'hundreds of thousands' of other Londoners lined the route all the way to Tooting. That evening a public service was available to all.

Here it does seem to have been working people and not property speculators who benefited most from the LCC's enlightened approach, which saw electric trams as agents of social progress rather than private profit. The number of cheap early morning workmen's tickets sold on the tramway to Tooting was 582,000 in the last year of the horsecars (1902/3). Four years later, for the year 1906/7, it had grown to 3,342,000.[42] As the LCC electric network developed, it had a similar dramatic impact on tram riding throughout the metropolis. By 1910 thousands of smart

A souvenir of the royal opening of the first LCC electric tram route from Westminster to Tooting, 15 May 1903.
LTM/TfL

Transition in south London. Early LCC electric trams surround a horse bus at New Cross Gate, c1905. These small open-top cars could not cope with the surge in passenger numbers which followed electrification in London and were soon replaced by large enclosed bogie cars from 1907.

chocolate and cream coloured trams, a livery known officially as 'deep purple lake and primrose', were running all over the city and carrying Londoners on more than 500 *million* rides each year.

Social Impact

The statistics alone are astonishing, but more significant still is the minor social revolution that electric trams helped to bring about, particularly in London. Charles Masterman, a reforming Liberal politician, described these from his own observations and experience in the Edwardian period. Writing in 1906, when the electric system was growing rapidly and he had recently become an MP, Masterman vividly recalled what it had been like eight years earlier when he first went to live in Camberwell, then still a working-class area of south London:

'Our sole communication with London over-the-river - where our people worked – was a few erratic horse omnibuses, and lines of slow-moving two-horse trams, which diverged fan-like to the bases of the various bridges. Here at evening a tired, indignant crowd fought silently for entrance into each successive conveyance; the young and the old were squeezed out and occasionally trampled under. The crowded tram jogged off quietly into the night. By the dim light of two odorous oil lamps we contemplated dismally the dismal countenances of our neighbours. Half an hour afterwards, or perhaps three-quarters, we were deposited amongst the crowded warrens we called our home...
'What is the condition today? We have fast lines of electric trams, brilliantly lighted, in which reading is a pleasure, hurrying us down from over the bridges at half the time expended under the old conditions. Each workman today in this district has had an hour added to his life – half an hour actually saved from the transit, and half an hour given back to him in the transit. And you may see the young of both sexes – especially the young working girls – eagerly using that half hour.'

Masterman enthused about the lifestyle change that electric tram travel had brought to London's working classes:

'What are the results in human wellbeing? The ring which cramped in the overcrowded millions of the Abyss is actually at the point of breakage. Family after family are evacuating the blocks and crowded tenements (of inner London) for little four roomed cottages, with little gardens, at Hither Green or Tooting...
'The two greatest boons which have come to our working people are the gas stove and the fast electric tram. The combined energies of statesmen and philanthropists in half a century have created no such desirable change as has been wrought by these absurd mechanical inventions.'[43]

The LCC's photographer recorded this moment very precisely: it is 7.12am on 18 April 1912 at Brownhill Road tram terminus, Catford, in south-east London. Cheap workmen's tickets were only available before 7.30am. LTM/TfL

Even the facilities the public never saw were proudly presented on official postcards. This is the interior of the LCC Tramways' largest depot at New Cross with its state-of-the-art electric traverser for moving cars between tracks. LTM/TfL

Masterman was a committed social reformer but even making allowances for some hyperbole, there is no reason to think that he is exaggerating the changes he observed. Tram ticket sales figures make a sharp upward curve at this time across the country as electrification spread, though different conclusions can be drawn about the social impact of greater tram travel across Britain.

In Manchester, for example, tram traffic grew impressively from 23.6 million passengers in 1902, when the city's first electric trams started running, to 206 million in 1913/14, nearly a tenfold increase. The corporation tramways committee there, like the LCC, adopted a policy of reducing ordinary fares as much as possible and making everyone pay

As the LCC's electric system expanded passengers needed help to negotiate its massive and complex network. Routes were numbered, and free folding maps and guides became available with regular updates. This is the cover of the last map to be issued before the outbreak of war in August 1914, featuring the Horniman Museum in Forest Hill, south London, opened in 1901.

New Birmingham Corporation electric cars ready for service at Witton depot, close to the Aston Villa football ground, c1913. Witton was to be one of the last working tram depots in the city when the system closed in 1953. It survives today as a listed building with the tram tracks still in situ.

good deal which must have encouraged all social classes to use the trams.[44]

The unexpected volume of traffic on the electric cars seemed to take some council tramway departments by surprise, but the principle of cheap fares was maintained nearly everywhere. Electrified routes were longer than horsecar services and the trams were twice as fast, but the really significant factor was the fare reduction. In every town the distance a passenger could travel for one penny (1d) by electric tram was several times its horse equivalent. For example, in 1912 Birmingham's penny (1d) workman's tickets gave early morning passengers a 4 mile electric tram ride. No wonder this facility was being used by over 15million people a year.[45]

alike. In 1910 it was calculated that over 60 per cent of the city's tram passengers paid a fare of just 1d (one old penny) and that there were on average 187 journeys made in a year per head of population. The undertaking not only paid for itself but was soon contributing more than £75,000 per year in support of the corporation rates and a further £70,000 to their own renewals fund. Even with cheap fares across the board, both the council and the passengers were getting an extremely

There were various attempts to deal with the serious overcrowding that arose on some electric tram services, but this never involved pricing people out by increasing basic ticket prices. The loudest complaints from passengers were very likely to be that minority of middle-class travellers who did not really want to mix with the hoi-polloi at all. Trams are, by their nature, democratic equalisers with no class divisions and

Trams outside the Council House in Handsworth, Birmingham, c1912. Corporation electric trams had just replaced cable cars to this point on the Soho Road and there was now through running well beyond the city boundary towards the Black Country.

597 Soho Rd. & Council House, Handsworth, Birmingham

Trams outside Lime Street station and the North Western Hotel, Liverpool, c1914. The cream-coloured car is one of the luxury first-class trams introduced on routes running out to middle-class suburbs.

everybody paid the same fare. Railway travel was different, where a first-class ticket bought the wealthier passenger comfort and seclusion even on a short-distance suburban service. This distinction was not possible within an open-saloon tram, but one British city did try using first-class trams on selected services.

This was Liverpool again, where in 1908 a proposal to introduce some first-class luxury trams came from Sir Charles Petrie, chairman of the corporation's tramways committee. Apparently 'the idea met with scorn in many places', but it went ahead for a trial period on the Garston-Pierhead route. The cars were easily distinguished from standard Liverpool trams (then painted crimson lake and cream) by a special livery in two shades of cream with elaborate gold, red and blue lining. Inside, the lower saloons were upholstered in blue plush, with coir carpets, cut glass lamp bowls and curtained windows.

There was soon a demand for these glamorous trams on other routes, particularly those with a high proportion of middle-class female passengers. By 1914 there were sixty-eight first-class cars in service, normally running out to middle-class suburbs like West Derby, Knotty Ash and Aintree. Liverpool's large scale experiment in premium travel under city

Little and large. The crew of a first-class Liverpool Corporation tram, c1914.

London County Council trams on the Embankment below Waterloo Bridge, 1908. On the left is the southern portal of the newly opened Kingsway Subway, which linked the LCC's northern and southern networks. This could only be used by single-deck cars until it was enlarged in 1931. The Embankment was the closest that trams got to London's West End. LTM/TfL

conditions was not repeated anywhere else in Britain, and its impact on passenger numbers is unknown. The luxury cream cars were probably loss leaders, but although the service continued for fifteen years, it seems that no attempt was ever made to measure or estimate the additional traffic they attracted.[46]

In Edwardian London the electric trams were certainly used by nearly everyone, although the social make-up of different parts of the city would have meant higher middle-class patronage in the LUT's suburban heartlands like Ealing or Twickenham than the inner LCC districts of Tooting or Clapham. Kensington, Chelsea and the City of London continued to keep trams off their streets and a large tram-free void remained at the heart of London. The LCC could only eventually get close to the centre along the

Stuck on the dead, c1920. The crew of an LCC car stranded on the gap at the Vauxhall crossover try to shift their ten ton tram back on to the power line, an almost impossible task. The policeman will have to direct traffic around the junction until the next tram comes up behind to give this one a gentle push. LTM/TfL

Embankment once it was allowed to cross the Thames on a loop via the bridges at Westminster and Blackfriars. It was then possible to link its north and south London systems through the Kingsway Tram Subway, an American-style one-off feature which was not adopted elsewhere in London nor in any other British city.[47]

The main characteristic of the LCC system that did not apply anywhere else was the conduit pick-up arrangement. Apart from the laborious cleaning and maintenance procedures, the conduit required particular driving skills in the LCC's motormen. At every junction and crossover on the system, of which there were many, there were gaps in the sub-surface conduit rail which had to be negotiated without stopping. Braking on a cross-over could leave a tram 'stuck on the dead' without power, unable to move and blocking the road junction. The tram was effectively stranded until the next car came up behind and pushed it forward on to the power line. A motorman who caused service disruption like this, whether he was to blame or not, would inevitably get it in the neck from the timekeeper or 'regulator' and be disciplined. The LCCT was run with military-style efficiency and rigorous standards had to be maintained by all staff.

Where the conduit sections met the overhead lines of the outer boroughs at the LCC boundary, an ingenious changeover system was devised to allow through running. If a tram was heading out of central London the pick-up plough was shot out to a central island between the tracks and the conductor raised the trolley pole to pick up power from the overhead wire. The operation would only require stopping for a few seconds at the 'change pit'. This procedure was reversed for trams in the opposite direction: pole lowered and tied down with a rope at the back of the tram by the conductor, plough pushed under the tram by a 'ploughman' with a large fork stationed on the centre island,

electrical switch thrown by the motorman before moving off on to the conduit section. Described in words it sounds arcane and primitive, but the process was fast and efficient, and is best understood when seen on film, which fortunately was recorded just before the system ended in 1952.[48]

A unique London feature introduced from 1908: the change pit where trams swapped from overhead wire to conduit and vice versa at the LCC border. This is the Mile End Road in east London with a tram leaving the wires and having a plough forked underneath as it heads for Aldgate on the conduit, 1934. LTM/TfL

Inserting a pick-up plough at the Clapton change pit under a tram running off the overhead. This changeover ritual continued daily until the end of London's trams in 1952. LTM/TfL

THE RIDING HABIT
IN EDWARDIAN BRITAIN

Between 1900 and 1913 tramway traffic throughout Britain trebled as electrification spread through all the big cities and most large towns. This was a rise from about 1m to 3.3m passengers per year. In 1904 there were 6,783 electric trams operating around the country, and by 1910 this figure had nearly doubled to 11,123.

Perhaps the most telling statistical change was the increase in per capita use of trams between the horsecar peak in the late 1880s and twenty-five years later when electric cars had taken over almost everywhere. In 1887 three of the leading regional cities in Britain averaged only fifty annual tram rides per head: Glasgow 61, Liverpool 51 and Birmingham 37. By 1913 the average for these three was 202 or four times as many journeys: Glasgow's trams were carrying each member of its population 271 times per year, Liverpool's 187 and Birmingham's 179. Other major regional cities were within this range so that when Manchester, Leeds, Sheffield, Nottingham and Bradford are included we reach an average of 189 tram rides a year per head of population, four times the horse tram use.[49]

Crowded seafront at Scarborough.

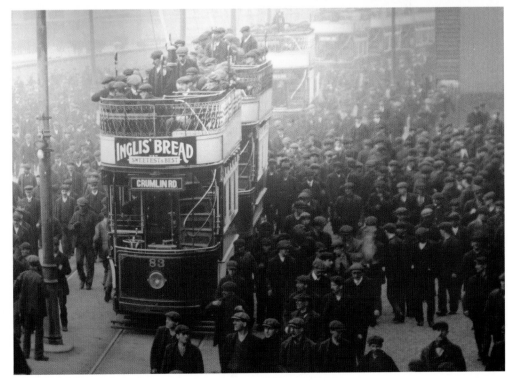

TOP LEFT:
At the Crystal Palace,
Sydenham, south London.

TOP RIGHT:
Dinner time at Platt's
Mill, Oldham.

CENTRE LEFT:
Through the city walls, York.

CENTRE RIGHT:
Moor Street, Sheffield.

LOWER:
Going home time at the
giant Harland & Wolff
shipyard, Belfast. These men
were probably building
the *Titanic*.

TOP LEFT:
Workmen's cars outside the Carron Iron Works in Falkirk, Scotland.

TOP RIGHT:
Halifax car at Brighouse, West Yorkshire

CENTRE LEFT:
People and parcels for Ferndale in the Rhondda, South Wales.

CENTRE RIGHT:
An outing on the Burton & Ashby Light Railway.

LOWER:
Bank holiday queues in Forster Square, Bradford.

The entire staff, including managers and their wives, of Colchester Corporation Tramways, probably photographed on a Sunday morning at the depot, with three of the system's sixteen cars behind them, soon after the official opening in 1904.

Most smaller cities and towns also had electric trams by this time, all well used by the broad mass of the urban population. Everywhere seemed to reflect a significant increase in what contemporary writers began referring to as 'the riding habit' as soon as electric trams appeared. A comment by the local newspaper in Keighley, Yorkshire, when the town's own electric service had just opened in 1904 is typical: 'Trams have ceased to be a luxury and are now a necessity of town life.'[50]

Trams gave everybody the opportunity to have an affordable ride to work, an evening out in town, a cheap excursion to the countryside on Sundays and holidays or even, in some areas, parcel and postal services by tram. They were also starting to shape the outward spread of the town. In some of the larger cities, Liverpool and Manchester being prime examples, new corporation electric tramways were 'not simply following suburban development, but leading that development by extending their services in advance of existing demand'.[51] In these cases trams really were 'growing the town' American style, but under the control of local authorities rather than developers. Early in 1914 Liverpool city engineer John Brodie gave a conference paper on 'Town Planning in relation to Tramways' at which he showed the city's plans for developing new tree lined highways in the suburbs and rural areas beyond the built-up town, with wide dual carriageways and segregated grass tram tracks in a central reservation. An early example of this was a new extension to a proposed garden suburb and the first municipal golf course in England at Bowring Park, Huyton, 7 miles east of Liverpool. The road and tramway opened in September 1914, a month after the declaration of war. Implementing this concept more widely had to wait until the post-war 1920s, but it was then taken up by several other cities including Glasgow, Birmingham and Leeds.

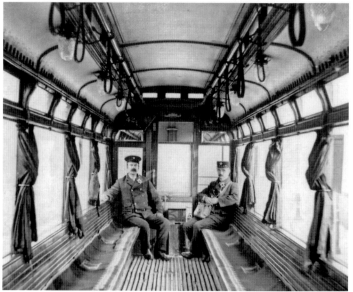

SMART SERVICE

LEFT:
Manager and staff at
Cottingham Road
depot, Hull.

TOP RIGHT:
Tram guards
(conductors) at
Queen's Road depot,
Manchester.

CENTRE RIGHT:
Motorman and
conductor in a
Burnley car that even
has curtains.

Electric tramways offered new
employment opportunities all over
the country in the 1900s and the
smart military-style crew uniforms
gave the staff a status and self-respect
that had never been evident on the
horse trams. Pay and conditions were
much improved, although strikes
were not unknown. These men are all
obviously proud of their jobs and the
public service they provide. The LCC
tram conductor here even featured in
a commercial postcard series called
'London characters'.

ABOVE: Birmingham Corporation Tramways crew on
car 247 in Lodge Road, Hockley.

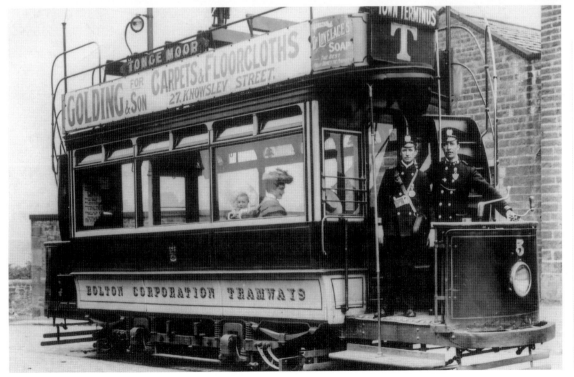

TOP LEFT:
Studio portrait of a
Torquay conductor.

TOP RIGHT:
London County
Council Tramways
conductor on duty.

LOWER:
A smart crew ready
to depart from Tonge
Moor to Bolton town
centre.

ABOVE: Collecting sand from the beach at Blackpool. The motorman had to release sand from boxes on each tram to reduce wheel slip on greasy rails.

RIGHT: A Maidstone Corporation crew on the route to Loose, on the edge of town, 1907.

ABOVE:: Ready for service at the Aberhill depot of the privately owned Wemyss & District Tramway, built by the local laird to serve the pits and villages on his estates in Fife by the Wemyss Coal Co. Ltd.

LEFT: LCC Regulator (Inspector) George Cooke, one of the team who maintained strict military-style timing and discipline on London's tramways. A local photographer has captured his sergeant major's demeanour perfectly. LTM/TfL

CITY OF LIVERPOOL
PROGRAMME OF INSPECTION
OF
STREET IMPROVEMENTS · & · TRAMWAY EXTENSIONS
AND
OFFICIAL · OPENING · OF · MENLOVE · AVENUE
ROADWAY · & · TRAMWAYS
MONDAY. 21ST MARCH
·1910·
CITY ENGINEER'S OFFICE
LIVERPOOL.

C. Tinling & Co., Ltd., Typ.

Trams and town planning. A council invitation to the opening of a tramway extension and street improvements in a newly developed area of suburban Liverpool, 1910.

Vickerstown, a company-built housing estate for shipyard managers and workers at Walney Island, on the edge of Barrow-in-Furness, was started in the early 1900s. The tram line linking the estate with the town centre and the Vickers shipyard over a new bridge opened in 1911.

« L'Entente Cordiale », Illuminated Car Portsmouth, August 1905.

PICTURING TRAMS
AND SPECIAL OCCASIONS

L'Entente Cordiale with France, Portsmouth 1908.

Electric trams feature extensively in two popular new media that took off in Britain at almost exactly the same time in the 1900s. Picture postcards and cinematography both cover trams as a theme, though in rather different ways. It was a fortuitous coincidence that has left us a wide ranging visual record of everyday life at the dawn of the twentieth century.

As the latest evidence of modernity, each town's new electric trams appeared in photographic postcards of the locality, whether to mark a line inauguration by the mayor, day trippers riding on the promenade or the convenient modal interchange at the railway station. Trams appear alongside local landmarks, terminating at the market place, squeezing through historic town walls, posing outside the town hall or serving the suburbs.

Some feature comic observations about the new practice of tram travelling, with the inevitable music hall style jokes about drunks catching the last car, the problems of overweight passengers and little old ladies nearly getting run over or an electric shock. These were often generic cards overprinted with a local name so that a cartoon scene showing Wakes Week in Oldham

THE ILLUMINATED TRAMCAR, BLACKBURN SHOW WEEK, NOV 1909

Blackburn show
week, 1909.

Roker Gala,
Sunderland, c1910.

Coronation Day of King George V, Doncaster, 1911.

Lifeboat day, Croydon, 1908.

could easily become the last car from the Franco-British Exhibition in London.

There are colour tinted photographic cards showing trams elaborately decorated for special occasions like the 1911 Coronation or a royal visit. A few are even turned into rather inappropriate Christmas and Valentine cards. Finally, there are the postcards recording the aftermath of tram accidents, not particularly common but invariably spectacular and often fatal when a runaway car crashed or overturned. Local photographers and printers could always find a market for this grim sensationalism, often accompanied by full details of the death and destruction caused. Convenient as they were, electric trams were the largest and fastest vehicles on the road, and could do a lot of damage if something went wrong or the brakes failed on a steep hill.

Early film-makers worked with large, heavy movie cameras and could not shoot outdoors with steady mobile dollies or long adjustable lenses. Mounting a camera on the platform of a moving tram was the ideal way to achieve a smooth tracking shot on the street. It was also the easiest method of breaking away from static film-making with a fixed tripod. Moving pictures of everyday life were as popular as studio-bound dramas, particularly for local audiences who might see themselves or their neighbours on screen in a local church hall or cinema. Many of these films were shot from trams or included trams in street footage.

The great majority of these early silent movies have now been lost, but some amazing material has survived. A remarkable re-discovery in a house clearance in the 1990s was a long forgotten cache of film made by Mitchell & Kenyon, a company based in Blackburn, Lancashire, who prided themselves on making 'local films for local people' from 1897. The surviving reels have been restored and copied by the British Film Institute (BFI)

and include many valuable glimpses of newly opened electric tramways in operation on busy city streets in the early 1900s including Belfast, Bradford, Glasgow, Halifax and Wigan.[52]

Not surprisingly, the greatest tramway showman of them all, Clifton Robinson, arranged for the ceremonial inauguration of his London United system in 1901 to be recorded on film. William Kennedy-Laurie Dickson, cameraman for the British Mutoscope and Biograph Company, set up his state-of-the-art electric movie camera on the front platform of a tram in the grand opening procession. His film, entitled *Panorama of Ealing from a Moving Tram*, was later shown at the Empire Theatre both to LUT staff and the general public.[53]

King Edward VII's visit to Leeds, 1908.

COMIC CARDS

Where shall I get the tram?
In your back if you don't move.
Ma'am !

THE POLICEMAN SAID "FOLLOW THE TRAM-LINES."

The Last Car
from Goswell Road

Comic cards featuring trams appeared all over the country in the 1900s, often with the same basic joke and the locations overprinted to give it local relevance.

OPENINGS

ABOVE:
Halifax, 1898.

RIGHT:
Ayr, 1901.

THE OPENING OF THE ELECTRIC TRAMWAY LINCOLN

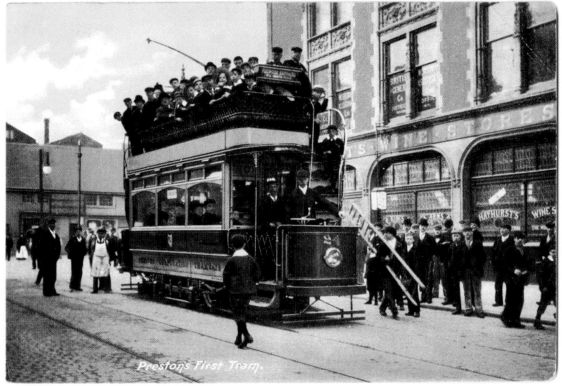

Preston's First Tram.

ABOVE:
Lincoln, 1905.

LEFT:
Preston, 1904.

ABOVE:
Exeter, 1906.

RIGHT:
Pudsey, 1908.

RIPLEY'S FIRST TRAM

LEFT:
Ripley, 1914.

BELOW LEFT:
Keighley, 1904.

BELOW RIGHT:
Morley, 1911.

KEIGHLEY ELECTRIC CARS
OCTOBER 12TH 1904.

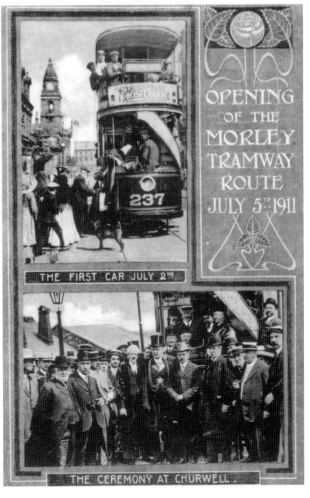

OPENING OF THE MORLEY TRAMWAY ROUTE JULY 5TH 1911

THE FIRST CAR JULY 2ND

THE CEREMONY AT CHURWELL.

GREETINGS

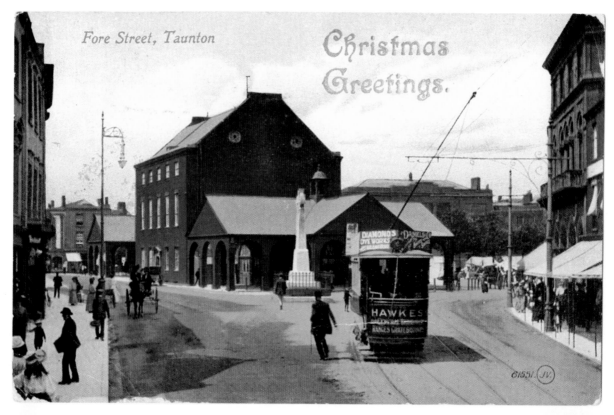

Tettenhall Road, Wolverhampton.

Christmas greetings
from Taunton,
Coventry and
Wolverhampton, and
a Tram Valentine (?)
from Newcastle.

ACCIDENTS

Tram accidents were major news stories in the 1900s, with the scene always recorded by local photographers and the results often turned into postcards.

The steep descent to the harbour on Madeira Road, Ramsgate, was an accident blackspot for the Isle of Thanet Tramways. On 3 August 1905 a tram crashed through the wall on the curve to the left and plunged down to the lower level. Amazingly, the driver was the only person to be badly injured.

The Bournemouth tram disaster on 1 May 1908 involved even more fatalities, with seven passengers killed and twenty-six seriously injured. This was a brakes failure following poor maintenance and safety checks. The tram crashed on Poole Hill, as sensationally described and illustrated in this local card (right).

An incident in Swindon on 1 June 1906 was much more serious. The brakes failed on a crowded, brand new tram which was descending a hill. The speeding car derailed on a curve and overturned, killing five passengers and injuring more than thirty.

A GOLDEN AGE

'Just arrived at Blackpool'. A circular tour of the resort in a toastrack tram was a well publicised attraction, with the unspoken implication that this was a town where you might encounter attractive young women on or off the trams.

The grand parade of nine decorated cars leaving Shepherd's Bush for the ceremonial inauguration of the London United Tramways on 10 July 1901. The day's events were professionally filmed and later presented as a picture show at local cinemas in west London with the gripping title *Panorama of Ealing from a Moving Tram*.
London Transport Museum/TfL

Illuminated Gondola, Blackpool by Night.

Gondola or tram? Blackpool's elaborately disguised and decorated showcars first appeared in 1912 and have been a feature of the town's famous illuminations ever since. Inevitably they quickly found their way on to Blackpool postcards.

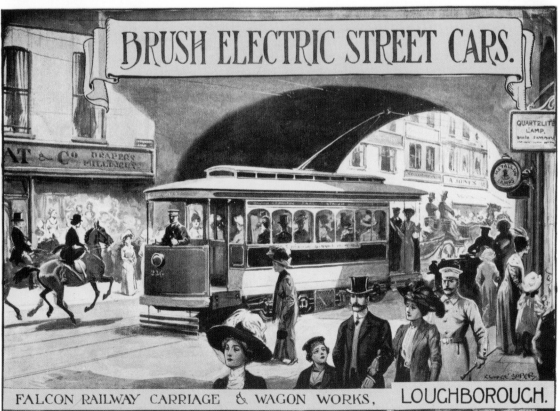

BRUSH ELECTRIC STREET CARS.

FALCON RAILWAY CARRIAGE & WAGON WORKS, LOUGHBOROUGH.

The Brush Electrical Engineering Company at Loughborough was the second largest builder of electric tramcars in Britain after Preston. This illustration is from the company's 1912 catalogue, which features trams built for a wide range of operators both in the UK and overseas. Exports were mainly to the British Empire, but Brush also supplied trams for St Petersburg in Imperial Russia.

LEFT:
'Riding on top of the car'. A popular Edwardian music hall song memorably used fifty years later in the documentary film recording the end of London's trams, *The Elephant Will Never Forget*.
London Transport Museum/TfL

RIGHT:
This postcard could be overprinted with the name of any town. As this one is numbered 176 there were presumably at least 175 others which were just as lovely as Salford!

"*Riding on the Top of the Car.*"

" Then we go, go, go for a ride on the car, car, car,
For you know how cosy the tops of the tramcars are,
The seats are so small, and there's not much to pay,
You sit close together, and spoon all the way ;
There's many a Miss will be Missis some day,
Thro' riding on top of the car."

176

A RIDE ON THE TRAM FROM SALFORD IS JUST LOVELY

Whitsun Bank holiday trippers to Kew at Shepherd's Bush, 1903. LTM/TfL

Chapter 4

THROUGH WAR AND PEACE

A Gathering Storm

The age of development and expansion for electric tramways in Britain turned out to be quite short and concentrated in the Edwardian decade at the start of the twentieth century (1901-11). By early 1914 the electric mileage figure for the whole country had reached 2530, roughly the same position the USA had got to after the boom in the 1890s (2540 track miles on city streets by 1896), but there was already a slowdown in the UK. Most towns had opened a basic electric network and it was extensions rather than new start-up projects that were postponed by the outbreak of war in August 1914.

Although passenger numbers continued to rise, the financial position of tramway operators, whether company or municipal, was insecure. Neither private operators nor councils put aside any of their short-term revenue 'profit' into renewals and there was very little strategic thinking about the future. Having opened the Pandora's Box of the cheap travel habit, local authorities found it was proving difficult to manage, especially in London. The passenger numbers kept going up because of the LCC's progressive social policy of subsidising cheap workmen's tickets, but its revenue income started to decline. The numbers carried on workmen's cars nearly doubled between 1910/11 (42m) and 1913/14 (77m), straining capacity even with the latest big seventy-eight-seater trams in service. In 1913 the LCC got permission to use double-deck trailers on the busiest routes, but these were difficult for conductors to manage. It was almost a problem of success. The LCCT had grown into the largest electric

A heavily loaded LCC tram and trailer on a busy evening service somewhere in London, December 1913. There are about 120 passengers on the two vehicles, which seems to require the combined efforts of three conductors to issue tickets. LTM/TfL

Gardiners Corner, Whitechapel, east London, 1912. Eight LCC and West Ham Corporation electric trams and just two LGOC B type motor buses are in the frame. By this time, London's trams were carrying nearly 800 million passengers a year. LTM/TfL

Competitors on the streets in 1910 on static display in the London Transport Museum a century later: a B type bus and a West Ham tram. Buses appeared cheaper to run, but they were far less hardy and reliable than trams, which were often in service for over thirty years, more than twice the usual life of early motor buses. OG

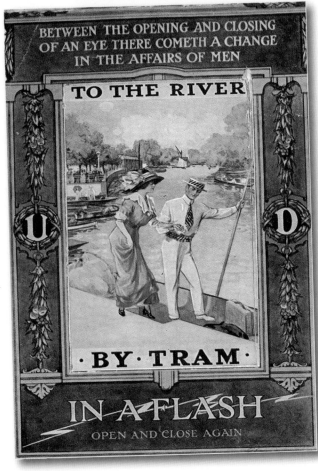

tramway operation in the world, with a massive fleet of reliable, well maintained cars, but the council had dug itself into a hole with its fares policy. The trams were hugely popular but were already running at a loss and the LCC had no strategy to correct this.

London was a particular problem area because trams were not the only mode of public transport in the city. There was growing competition from new motor bus and electric Underground services, neither of which were controlled by the dominant tram operator, the London County Council. When the LCC's electric tram services began in 1903 the old Metropolitan and District Railways were still steam operated, only two electric

By 1913 the Underground Group had absorbed the three private tram companies running in London's suburbs, the LUT, MET and SMET. They were soon benefitting from Frank Pick's stylish poster and publicity campaigns. LTM/TfL

Tubes were running and the few primitive motor buses were hopelessly unreliable. A decade on, these latecomers were becoming more of a threat. The whole of the Underground had been electrified, with three new deep Tube lines opening under central London in 1906/7. The main London bus company, the LGOC, developed the first reliable, mass produced motor bus, the famous B type, and replaced its entire horse bus fleet with them in 1910/11. Finally, the privately run Underground Group had taken over both the LGOC and the three company tramways in outer London, the LUT, MET and SMET, creating the so-called London Traffic Combine.

Despite these company mergers and some co-operation between the various council tramways, there was still no move towards creating a single transport authority for London. The municipal/private enterprise divide and related mutual antagonism was particularly strong in the capital and the idea of collaboration for the sake of economy and efficiency made absolutely no progress here.

The LGOC's motor buses, which already ran throughout the tram-free City and West End, now began to invade the LCC's tram routes. Buses were no longer middle-class vehicles charging middle-class fares and starting in the morning when most of the labouring classes were already at work. They were now carrying passengers of all classes at profitable rates and were not constrained by the LCC's policy of issuing cheap workmen's tickets. Individually, buses could not compete with trams and had less than half their carrying capacity (usually 34), but they were more flexible and much cheaper to run because they did not need the fixed infrastructure of tracks and power supply.

A cartoon called 'Beaten on Points' appeared in *Punch* magazine in 1914, neatly summing up the problem facing

the LCC. A bus and a tram are shown competing in a boxing match, with the nimble bus getting the best of the lumbering tram and a brief exchange between them:

LCC Tram: 'Hard lines on me.'
Motor bus: 'Yes, it's always hard lines with you, my boy. That's what's the matter, you can't side step.'

By 1914 London's various tramways were carrying just over 800m passengers, 90m more than the total for the buses, but the gap was narrowing. The LCC had no

'Beaten on Points'. Artwork for a *Punch* cartoon by Leonard Raven-Hill underlining the flexibility of the motor bus over the electric tram, 1914. LTM/TfL

Liverpool Corporation first ran motor buses in 1912, introducing two Tilling-Stevens petrol electrics that provided an extension service beyond the Calderstones Park tram terminus to Woolton, just outside the city boundary.

loss-making tram and Underground services. Merging the whole lot together made perfect sense, but nobody was keen to do this.

Outside London bus competition was not yet a problem for tramways. Some of the larger local authority systems, including Liverpool and Sheffield, ran motor buses themselves on feeder services to complement their busier tram routes but that was all. At this stage motor buses in the provinces were more likely to be run by small independent operators in semi-rural areas where there was not enough traffic for trams to be viable.

There were also some early experiments with 'rail-less' electric vehicles, soon known as trolleybuses, which picked up power from overhead wires but could be steered like a motor bus and were not confined to rails in the road. As a hybrid mode, they were marketed as cheaper to set up and run than a tram network but more reliable than early petrol-driven buses.

The first public services, provided by the Railless Electric Traction Company

powers to run buses even if it wanted to, but also had no flexibility to adapt its tram services to more efficient operation. Meanwhile the private London Traffic Combine could use its buses to augment its LUT and MET tram routes as well as its Underground services, and offered popular excursions into London's countryside at weekends. The expanding and profitable LGOC buses could cross-subsidise the Combine's own essential but

The UK's first two public trolleybus routes were officially opened at 12 noon on the same day, 20 June 1911, by long term city rivals Bradford and Leeds. Here the first Leeds rail-less car stands waiting for the Lord Mayor, who will drive it the 4 miles from the city centre to Farnley Moor Top and back.

(RET), began simultaneously in Bradford and Leeds, both already tram operators, on 20 June 1911. By 1914 there were six more fledgling operations set up in the UK in Aberdare, Keighley, Ramsbottom, Rotherham and Stockport, but the first trolleybus service in Scotland, opened in Dundee in 1912, had already closed down. Another system in the Rhondda, South Wales, opened in December 1914 but failed in only three months because the poor road surface collapsed.

A railless vehicle had been demonstrated in the capital at the Metropolitan Electric Tramways depot in Hendon, north London, in 1909 but never entered passenger service. In 1913 the RET showed off its first double-deck trolleybus in Brighton, but the trial runs were an embarrassing failure, graphically described by the *Brighton Herald*:

> *To go along a road at nigh on twenty miles an hour, after the fashion of an inebriated person going home and visiting each side of the road with strict impartiality , is more like a ride on a switchback than a trolley 'bus.*

Trolleybuses would have their day, but not yet.[1]

As early as 1912 Edwin Pratt, the author of the first comprehensive history of inland transport in Britain, was suggesting rather negative future prospects for the electric tram:

> *Today we have the further question whether electric tramways, which have always constituted a more or less speculative business, have not attained the height of their possible development, and whether they are not already on their decline in face of other systems more efficient or, at least, less costly and less cumbersome.*

Pratt's analysis of the likely problems facing tramways, and the potential of motor buses and electric trolleybuses to

supersede them, was remarkably astute and far-sighted. As he wisely concludes:

> *The whole history of transport shows constant change and progress, the achievements of one generation or the 'records' of one pioneer being only the starting-point of fresh advance or of still greater triumphs later on. Electric tramways themselves were, undoubtedly, as great an improvement on horse tramways as the drawing of vehicles by horses along a pair of rails had already been an advance on locomotion over the rough and rugged surfaces of badly made streets or roads. But electric tramways did not necessarily constitute finality and local authorities who built them as though for eternity are now faced by the rivalry of the motor-omnibus.*[2]

He had a point, of course, but he must have known that no local politician, councillor or tramways manager wanted to hear Jonah-like home truths when they were still getting praise for providing their town with

Leeds Corporation opened two more trolleybus routes in 1915, both feeders to its tram services. This is the terminus at Burley in Wharfedale of the short trolleybus route to Guiseley, where it met the trams from Leeds city centre.

Northumberland Street, Newcastle, c1914. Trams and horse-drawn goods vehicles are the traffic policeman's main concern, but a single motor car and a motor cycle are also evident on the right hand side of the photograph. Today this central shopping street is entirely pedestrianised and traffic free.

Two B type buses demonstrate their trackless flexibility around an LCC tram at the terminus outside Aldgate East Underground station in 1914. The District Railway also offered much-improved electric services by this time. London now had three competing modes of public transport. LTM/TfL

the best and cheapest form of transport anyone had ever seen or experienced. In 1912 electric tramways were still widely considered a modern marvel.

The First World War

When war broke out in the summer of 1914 nobody in Great Britain or any of the other European combatants could have foreseen the consequences. The sheer scale of the war, the level of death and destruction, and its immense social and economic implications were beyond anybody's experience or imagination. The tramways were affected by the war from the start, first as an aid to recruitment in the initial euphoria of creating a military fighting force, but before long faced with the challenge of running a critical part of the Home Front with diminishing staff and resources. Britain had been involved in various colonial conflicts within the previous thirty years, most recently in South Africa (the Boer Wars), but these were remote battles in far flung parts of the British Empire. From the autumn of 1914 the artillery of the Western Front was within earshot of the south coast of England, and at Easter 1916 the Republican uprising in Dublin brought fighting on to the streets of what was then considered a British city. War was no longer distant.

It was clear from the outset that Britain would need a much larger army to fight in Continental Europe, a task that had not been faced for nearly a century since the Napoleonic Wars. Initially Lord Kitchener, the Secretary of State for War, was able to avoid introducing conscription by asking for locally-recruited volunteer groups of friends, families and colleagues to create what became known as Pals Battalions.

Glasgow was the first and fastest city to respond to this appeal with three volunteer divisions created in September 1914 for the Highland Light Infantry (HLI). James Dalrymple, the dynamic manager of Glasgow Corporation Tramways, showed a remarkable combination of patriotic persuasion skills and administrative ability in getting more than one thousand men enlisted from his department in a sixteen-hour period, forming the First Battalion of the HLI.

In *An Epic of Glasgow,* the story of the 15th Battalion of the HLI published in 1934, historian Tom Chalmers describes Dalrymple as:

Probably the greatest recruiting agent that Scotland produced in the war. For resource, energy, enthusiasm and organising ability, in the self-imposed task of raising recruits he had no peer. In the first fourteen months of the war…his methods induced ten thousand men to accept military service. He was more or less the direct means of raising a brigade of artillery, two infantry battalions and five companies of engineers. He was a clever propagandist and used the tramway resources exhaustively. Illuminated cars with concealed bands stirred the suburbs; advertisements for the first time appeared on tramcar windows and streamers on the sides; the Tramways pipe band paraded the streets…he astonished the citizens with an open air cinema and even overawed Nature by arranging physical exercise classes for men whose chest measurement was below the Army requirement.

Soon after the outbreak of war, most towns turned the decorated cars they used for celebration into mobile recruiting aids, all with a similar message: 'A Call to Arms', 'Enlist Today', 'Your King and Country Need You'. These examples (clockwise from top left) are from Huddersfield, Leicester, Cardiff and Oldham and were echoed all over the country.

Off to war by tram? A family snapshot beside the elaborate tram shelter in Marton, Blackpool, c1915

Dalrymple's success as a military recruiter soon gave him problems in staffing his tramways, which in turn led to another initiative first promoted in Glasgow but soon copied by other tramway operators across the country. This was the employment of women in a range of jobs

for which they had never been considered before the war, but which now became essential as men joined the colours. Women had worked for tramway companies before, but mainly in office jobs as clerks and typists, or in light factory bench tasks such as armature winding in the works. They were certainly never seen in a public-facing job like tram conducting, and in uniform, but this was exactly what Dalrymple now proposed.

In March 1915 Glasgow became the first city in the country to employ female tram conductors, and by the following year thirty-three women had been trained as drivers on the same terms as the men: 29 shillings a week. This was a step change in employment practice which was widely opposed by management and staff alike before becoming reluctantly accepted as inevitable in wartime conditions. One year into the war almost half the male staff on the Glasgow trams had enlisted: 2,178 out of 4,672. Female recruitment began as an experiment, but by October 1915 over 800 women had been taken on as conductors.

Mary Campbell, one of the first five young women to be trained as 'lady drivers' in Glasgow was interviewed by the *People's Journal* in December 1915 about the demands of her new role. 'Speaking candidly' she said 'I don't consider the task beyond women folks. I prefer driving to conducting; there may be occasions when dilatory carters make me wish that my command of the King's English could be more forceful and still be lady-like, but taking it all over it is a grand life. Out in the open air, with no one to bother you as long as the work is going on and the wheels revolving to time.'[3]

Most male staff came to regard it as a temporary necessity in order to keep the service running, but there was a widespread assumption that women would not prove up to the job. Dalrymple admitted that he and his colleagues had

TRAMWAYS DEPARTMENT.

Good Work

AND

Good Wages

FOR

Good Women

Call at 46 BATH ST.
10 A.M. OR 4 P.M.

'Good Work and Good Wages for Good Women'. A Glasgow Tramways Department recruiting poster, 1916.

Imperial War Museum

been 'at the end of our tether' but relieved at how 'altogether satisfactory' the women were. Glasgow's new conductors were 'strong physically and knew what it was to do a day's work'.[4]

There was also a general agreement by the men that women would have to go when the war ended and former male employees needed their jobs back. Having women as drivers was a step too far for some tramway authorities however short-staffed they became in wartime conditions. The London County Council Tramways, for example, took on hundreds of women as conductors but never trained any of them as 'motorwomen'. At the other end of the scale, the little company tramway in the coastal resort of Weston-super-Mare, struggling to keep its 3-mile system operational at all in wartime, was more progressive. It was the first in the south west of England to employ a female driver, Beatrice Page, in January 1916. By 1917 women were showing their aptitude for a wide range of supposedly 'male' jobs and on some tramways were outnumbering men on the payroll. Dalrymple commented at the time that 'they were rapidly coming to the point when a majority of the tramway staff would be of the gentler sex and that he would not hesitate to have the whole service run by women.'[5]

The issue of female employment on the trams remained controversial throughout the war and in 1918 J.M. McElroy, General Manager of Manchester Tramways, was asked to compile a full report on the matter for the War Cabinet. McElroy surveyed all ninety municipal tramway departments in the UK and received comprehensive data on employment statistics together with a great deal of rather unscientific opinion and comment, all of it from male managers but none from the female employees!

The figures showed that by 1918, the last year of the war, there were just over

Glasgow Corporation provided their newly recruited female tram drivers and conductors with specially designed uniforms of a short military jacket with a long, tartan skirt. Black straw hats with an enamel corporation badge were worn in summer. This rare survivor is on display in the Imperial War Museum's First World War galleries.

Imperial War Museum

THE BIG PUSH!

LEFT:
'There's room for you!' One of a set of 'Women in Wartime' postcards issued by Raphael Tuck, c1916.

RIGHT:
The output of comic postcards continued in wartime. This example by Dudley Buxton references the popular name given to the Somme offensive in 1916 which cost thousands of lives but did not break the stalemate on the Western Front.

New tramway recruits often had their picture taken in uniform at a local photographer's studio and printed as a postcard to send to relatives and friends. This card was produced for a woman conductor in Shirley, Southampton.

13,500 drivers and 14,500 conductors working on municipal tramways in the UK. Only 724 of those drivers were women, but there were 11,671 female tram conductors (about 80 per cent) and nearly 10 per cent of inspectors were women. There were 1,664 women car cleaners, but all 6,688 maintenance staff (grouped together as 'shedmen') appeared to be men. In addition the tramways employed 1,685 boys and 400 girls aged under eighteen, who covered a range of tasks like operating point levers at junctions and helping adult conductors manage crowded cars (the 'trolley boys' and 'trolley girls' as they were called in Manchester, where conductors were known as 'guards').

The replies McElroy received tend to reflect conventional social attitudes of the time about a woman's role in the male workplace, but they are not as hostile or negative as might be expected. It is

A group of female MET conductors with two inspectors at a photographer's studio in north London, c1916. LTM/TfL

interesting to note that only twelve of the ninety authorities paid women less than the basic rate of wages for doing the same job as a man and in most cases the managers acknowledged that the female staff had made an important contribution. At the same time, women were said to be less reliable under pressure and more likely to give up the job because they found the shifts too arduous. Their customer care, as we would call it today, was also said to be less dependable than the men.

In answer to the question 'are they as courteous to passengers?' McElroy comments:

There is no question that we have far more complaints of rudeness by female than by male conductors. They are, naturally, more argumentative. When women were first employed on the cars, the public were exceedingly tolerant and I am satisfied that many cases of discourtesy were passed over, simply because the travelling public did not like the idea of reporting a woman.[6]

A few tramway managers, Dalrymple included, were in favour of keeping women on the cars after the war but in practice this rarely happened, especially where there was a formal agreement that it was a time-limited wartime expediency 'for the duration'. In Bristol, where there were still a lot of ex-servicemen out of work in 1920, there were some violent attacks on trams and conductresses who had refused to give up their jobs. The

Women at work as wartime tram conductors in Southport (top left), York (top right) and, Leeds (above), 1916-18.

incidents led the tram company to cave in and quickly dismiss all its remaining female staff with little thanks for their contribution to the war effort.

There were clearly different circumstances in towns across the country. A Chesterfield woman driver, recalling her wartime employment on the trams, said: 'I loved the work. It was tiring at times, and often cold, but I didn't mind that. There was a wonderful fellowship on the trams,

and I kept in touch with nearly all the girls for many years afterwards.'

She recalled that one of her fellow women drivers received an award for averting an accident by knocking aside a learner and applying the brakes on a tram that was about to crash into another. The tramway committee commended the woman for 'her conduct, presence of mind and nerve'.[7]

The temporary role reversal, or at least adjustment to a very different balance of the sexes in wartime Britain, with some women in a position of uniformed authority like a tram conductor or inspector, was clearly quite unsettling for both sexes. One of the oddest semi-fictional accounts of women on the trams appears in a short story called *Fares Please* written by the novelist D.H. Lawrence in 1919. It is set on the 'Ripley Rattler', the long cross-country tramway serving the towns and coalfields between Nottingham and Ripley,

Training a female tram crew at Walthamstow Tramways' depot in north-east London, c1917. The motorwoman looks particularly confident. She and her conductor are both wearing their summer dustcoats.
Vestry House Museum/Waltham Forest

A Black Cat cigarette card of a tram conductress, c1917. The caption suggests that women might stay on the trams after the war, but this female employment did not continue for long after the peace.

the area where Lawrence grew up and which he knew well.

This, the most dangerous tram service in England, as the authorities themselves declare with pride, is entirely conducted by girls, and driven by rash young men unfit for active service…the girls are fearless young hussies. In their ugly blue uniform, skirts up to their knees, shapeless old peaked caps on their heads, they have all the sang-froid of an old non-commissioned officer. With a tram packed with howling colliers, roaring hymns downstairs and a sort of antiphony of obscenities upstairs, the lasses are perfectly at their ease. They pounce on the youths who try to evade their ticket-machine. They push off the men at the end of their distance. They are not going to be done in the eye – not they. They fear nobody and everybody fears them.[8]

BLACK CAT
CIGARETTES

TRAM CONDUCTOR

WOMEN ON WAR WORK

No. 28. TRAM CONDUCTOR.

THE lady tram conductor is now quite a familiar sight in all the big towns. There seems no reason why they need give up this work after the war, although it is quite likely they may do so.

Issued by
CARRERAS LIMITED
ESTAB. 1788
LONDON & MONTREAL
ENG.   QUE.

Cleaning and maintenance staff of the Yorkshire (Woollen District) Tramways at Dewsbury depot, c1917. Women and boys are present but no young men of military age.

Wartime operation in Bentley New Village, Doncaster, with a female inspector and driver, and a very young boy conductor, c1917. The tram has been fitted with a headlamp mask as a blackout measure following Zeppelin raids.

'Remember Scarborough!' A tram in Scarborough dressed as a naval gun raising funds for the war effort during the shell shortage of 1915. The slogan refers to the shock bombardment of east-coast towns by the German fleet in December 1914 when the Royal Navy had been unable to retaliate.

Lawrence's tale becomes a female revenge drama when a group of women tram conductors assault and tear the tunic off the male inspector who has flirted with all of them but never committed himself to any one of them. ('Come on…you've got to choose!' they shout as they gang up on him in the messroom). The story may be more revealing of Lawrence's own curiosity and fantasy about the limits of masculine and feminine behaviour than about real life on the Ripley trams, but it highlights a major social change that women in the workplace brought about during the war, if only temporarily.[9]

If the working environment on the tramways changed during the war, with large numbers of female and almost under-age male operating staff, so too did the general experience of management

East Street, Bedminster Bristol

Bedminster was the hub and depot for Bristol's south-eastern tram routes. This wartime photograph shows tram crews waiting for their next turn of duty on East Street, with three male drivers in a noticeably separate group from their female conductors, c1917.

Cover of *Bristol & The War* magazine, January 1917. The photograph shows the first twenty-five 'lady conductors' recruited by the Bristol Tramways Company, which then had one hundred female staff in training.

Bristol Record Office

and all workers. Where competition with buses had developed immediately before the war, this disappeared when motor vehicles were commandeered for military use. At the beginning of the conflict the army had very little motorised transport and more than a thousand London buses were taken off the streets to provide troop transport both at home and on the Western Front. This put more pressure on the trams, particularly as war industries like munitions developed and workers flocked to those areas for this well-paid employment. Outer London districts like Woolwich (for the Arsenal), Enfield Lock (the small arms factory), Waltham Abbey (gunpowder factory), and the new aircraft assembly works set up in Kingston and Hendon all required more intensive tram services to transport their wartime workers.

Trams played a military recruitment role all over the country, with decorated cars acting as mobile billboards for the army. In Scarborough there was even a recruitment tram dressed as a naval gun with the slogan 'Remember Scarborough!' following the public outrage at the bombardment of three east coast towns by the German

LONDON COUNTY COUNCIL TRAMWAYS

General Order No. 683—Amended

MOTORMEN and CONDUCTORS

HOSTILE AIRCRAFT

The following is a copy of an Order made by the Field-Marshal Commanding-in-Chief, Home Forces, in connection with anticipated attacks by hostile aircraft:—

1. "The Order to take air-raid precautions will be communicated in a manner approved by the "Commissioner of Police of the Metropolis to the car drivers throughout the area.

2. "The normal service of cars throughout the area must be maintained, and the cars shall not "be brought to a standstill in the road, except for the purpose of picking up or setting down "passengers, nor return to the depot except at the conclusion of their normal journeys.

3. "The speed of all cars must be instantly reduced (by running on series only) so as not to "exceed six miles an hour until the warning is withdrawn.

4. "Only one lighting circuit may be used, and no additional circuit may be put on until the "warning is withdrawn.

5. "Trolleys must be connected with and disconnected from the overhead wires in such a manner "that flashing is avoided.

6. "Drivers must throw-off at all section insulators and when passing frogs, ears, &c., where "flashing may occur.

7. "Special precautions must be taken that no defective trolley wheels are used."

The warning will be conveyed to the motormen by the traffic or sub-station officials.

It is of the utmost importance that these precautions should be rigorously carried out, and employees must make themselves familiar with the above, as any person found offending by the Military or Police Authorities, may be liable to severe punishment.

62 Finsbury Pavement, E.C.
10th November, 1916

A. L. C. FELL,
Chief Officer

fleet on 10 December 1914, the first enemy attacks on British civilian targets.

When London was bombed by Zeppelin airships, and later aircraft in 1915-17, trams played a significant role in the capital's rather limited civil defence. Several open top cars were commandeered by the War Office and converted into mobile searchlight carriers, manned by soldiers of the Royal Engineers who had been drivers in peacetime on the Tynemouth and South Shields tramway systems. The searchlight trams were stationed in outer London at locations including Barnet, Enfield, Bexley, Croydon and Hounslow. They proved useful in tracking slow-moving airships and contributed to the first successful counter-attack on a Zeppelin raider just north of London on the night of 3 September 1916. Held by searchlights and attacked by anti-aircraft guns on the ground, the giant airship was famously finished off in the air by 2nd Lieutenant William Leefe Robinson in his tiny BE2c fighter. The stricken Zeppelin fell to the ground at Cuffley in Hertfordshire, killing every member of its crew, with the falling fireball clearly visible to thousands of spectators up to 30 miles away across north London. Robinson was awarded the Victoria Cross by King George V in a ceremony at Windsor Castle five days later.[10]

Both civilian casualties and damage were modest in the First World War compared to the Luftwaffe's onslaught in the Second World War, but the tramways did take direct hits in air raids. On the night of 23/24 September 1916, Zeppelin L31 dropped a series of incendiary and explosive bombs across Streatham and Brixton in south London, hitting an all-night LCC tram and killing the driver, conductor and four passengers. A year later another LCC car was hit in the first night raid on London by Gotha bombers on 4 September 1917. A high explosive

bomb landed on the Embankment beside Cleopatra's Needle just as a single-deck subway car was passing. The tram took the full impact of the blast, killing the driver and the only two passengers. The conductor was blown from one end of the tram to the other but survived.[11]

There were a number of Zeppelin raids on urban centres in England well away from London during 1916, and in at least two of these attacks tramways were hit. On the night of 31 January two airships bombed Tipton, Bradley, Wednesbury and Walsall in the West Midlands, leaving thirty-five local people dead. One bomb exploded in the centre

Wartime LCC Tramways staff at Camberwell depot, south London, c1916.
LTM/TfL

OPPOSITE:
'Hostile Aircraft'. LCC Tramways poster warning motormen and conductors about the dangers of air raids and what to do in them, 1916.
LTM/TfL

IT IS FAR BETTER
TO FACE THE BULLETS
THAN TO BE KILLED
AT HOME BY A BOMB

JOIN THE ARMY AT ONCE
& HELP TO STOP AN AIR RAID

GOD SAVE THE KING

Christmas card from Barnet Searchlight Station, north London, featuring the Zeppelin shot down with their help at Cuffley, Hertfordshire, on 3 September 1916.

Questionable logic in a recruiting poster produced after several German Zeppelin raids had been experienced in 1915. IWM

of Walsall close to a tram in which Mary Julia Slater, the town's lady mayoress, and her sister were travelling. Both women were severely injured in the blast, the mayoress dying in hospital from her wounds several weeks later.

A Zeppelin raid on Sunderland on 1 April killed 22 people and injured 128. One of the bombs fell on the Wheatsheaf tram depot, destroying a tram and killing an inspector who was sheltering inside. Incidents like this were isolated but particularly shocking in a country that had never experienced aerial attack on

the civilian population. They were also somewhat random as the Zeppelin crews were often confused by poor visibility and bad weather. The commanders of the two airships that bombed the West Midlands, for example, were hopelessly off course and thought they were hitting Liverpool, their intended target, which they never reached.[12]

The common experience of travelling by tram during the war was not fear, disruption or injury in an air raid but a general exasperation at the increasingly unpleasant journey conditions. A growing

The Crescent, Sheerness

The Sheerness & District Tramway closed in 1917, unable to source spare parts for its German electrical equipment during the war. The rather cumbersome Siemens & Halske bow collector fitted to all the company cars can be seen on top of both trams.

shortage of serviceable tramcars meant frequent cancellations and serious overcrowding. On one occasion 500 passengers were reported to have crammed on to three Belfast cars, though it is not clear how anyone counted them.[13] It was generally worse in London than anywhere else because of the sheer numbers of people wanting a ride. One account of the early months of 1917 recalled some years later that:

> Getting home during rush hours was a daily terror, especially on dark winter evenings in London. The crowds of office workers were vastly increased and the scramble to get into some of the longer distance trams and omnibuses constituted a bear fight out of which those of both sexes, who were worsted or driven off the overladen vehicles by the conductors, retreated to the pavements with hats bashed in, umbrellas broken, shins and ankles kicked and bruised, in a dazed and shaken condition.[14]

It sounds unpleasant, though as a 'daily terror' hardly a match for life in the trenches of the Western Front. When the Armistice was declared in November 1918 there was no rapid return to 1914 conditions. The Versailles peace treaty was not hammered out until six months later and most men in the armed forces who had survived the fighting did not return to civilian life until well into 1919. This also meant that the thousands of women working on the trams did not lose their relatively well-paid wartime jobs immediately, but most were sacked at

Celebrating the Versailles peace settlement on a Rotherham tram, 1919.

Memorial to the Manchester Corporation Tramways staff killed in the First World War. This brass wall plaque was originally commissioned for the main depot and works on Hyde Road in the early 1920s and is now on display in the Greater Manchester Museum of Transport. OG

fairly short notice in the course of 1919. After nearly five years of austerity many trams were still running in drab wartime grey rather than their usual colourful liveries. With minimal maintenance and repair despite growing passenger numbers, the nation's tramways were in poor shape to face the 1920s.

Renew or replace?
Sheerness, on the Isle of Sheppey in Kent, has the dubious distinction of being the first town in the UK to lose its electric tramway, in 1917. The Sheerness & District operation was a small company-run system opened with three short routes over nearly three miles of track in 1903. It was part of the BET group, with trams purchased from Brush of Loughborough and electrical equipment supplied by Siemens & Halske of Berlin. This combination of modest size, geographical isolation and German suppliers brought about its demise in less than fifteen years. Of the twelve original Brush tramcars, four were sold on immediately to the City of Birmingham Tramways as being excess to requirements, not an auspicious start. Poor patronage soon led the company to offer the system for sale to Sheerness Urban District Council but this was declined. Bus competition arose in 1913 and the final nail in the coffin came when the company was unable to source spare parts for its Siemens electrical equipment

Deansgate, Manchester.

from Germany during the First World War. Final closure in 1917 seemed inevitable.[15]

The fate of the Sheerness system might be taken as the start of a period of decline for British tramways after the Edwardian golden years but this would be misleading. Circumstances on Sheppey were unusual, if not unique, and this particular decline was neither typical nor the first sign of a trend. In fact, although the great days of tramway expansion were over by the First World War, tramways were still in the ascendant. It was not until the late 1920s that tram numbers began to decline from their maximum figure of over 14,000 cars, and total passenger numbers dropped for the first time. However, the overall financial position of most tramways was already starting to look quite serious. The increase in passenger numbers during the war was

sustained, giving twice the revenue income in 1920 over 1914, but wholesale prices had trebled in the same period so trams were running at a loss.

The cheap fares that had attracted such large numbers to the electric trams in the 1900s remained a characteristic of the post-war period nearly everywhere. A.L.C. Fell, the renowned and long serving manager of the LCC Tramways, had an oft-quoted dictum 'I'll make it too dear for you to walk.'

His poetic name Aubrey Llewellyn Coventry Fell was spelt out in full publican-style on the side of every LCC car, but Fell was like a mythical pub landlord whose prices keep going down. In 1920 cheap midday fares from 10am to 4pm were introduced, with a maximum fare of 2d all the way. Five years later the LCC launched the one shilling 'all day

Tram jam in Manchester, c1920. There are eight trams in this view of Deansgate, blocking the street in both directions.

Blackfriars Bridge. London

Blackfriars Bridge, London, looking across the Thames towards Southwark, c1927. This was the closest that trams from south London got to the City before running along the Embankment (in the foreground) and looping back over Westminster Bridge. Trams finally reached the City on an extension over Southwark Bridge after it was rebuilt in 1925 (see poster opposite).

ticket' which offered unlimited rides in the County of London for twenty-four hours. Some routes even had 'all night' cars. Fell had retired in 1924, but the council's cheap fares policy remained, keeping the trams well loaded but not contributing enough to the LCC's revenue account.

Outside London the big city local authority tramways continued to expand into the suburbs. Birmingham Corporation opened its new extension from Selly Oak to the Lickey Hills near Bromsgrove for the Whitsun holiday in 1924. The line was constructed on segregated 'reserved' track on the centre strip of the Bristol Road dual carriageway. The fare was 5d single for the 8 mile ride from the centre of Birmingham to the country terminus, or 9d return. An even longer country excursion service was available from Birmingham Council

House to Kinver (advertised on the cars as the 'Switzerland of the Midlands'), 36 miles return for 1s 6d. In the industrial areas of the Black Country, works outings and Sunday school excursions usually ended up at one of these two destinations, often with a fleet of tramcars hired for the day.[16]

Although the new tramway extensions in Birmingham were well used for leisure trips, their main purpose was to serve the new housing estates built after the First World War. Providing 'a land fit for heroes to live in' was a winning promise in Lloyd George's election victory in 1918, and both local authorities and private builders were encouraged to create new homes on the suburban periphery of all the big cities. Creating tramway extensions in the centre of new arterial roads seemed the obvious way to provide public transport

LONDON'S TRAMWAYS

TRAMWAY SERVICES
3 & 5 TO HAMPSTEAD
7 TO PARLIAMENT
HILL FIELDS.

LONDON'S TRAMWAYS

UNKNOWN KING

DULL DAYS MADE
BRIGHT IN THE
MUSEUMS

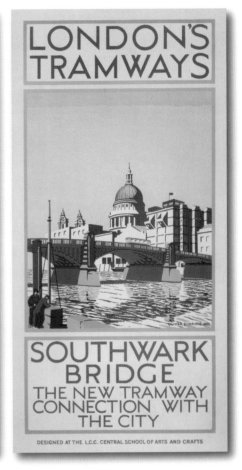

LONDON'S
TRAMWAYS

SOUTHWARK
BRIDGE
THE NEW TRAMWAY
CONNECTION WITH
THE CITY

DESIGNED AT THE L.C.C. CENTRAL SCHOOL OF ARTS AND CRAFTS

to these suburbs when few of the new residents owned a car, though the inability of the tram to serve estates off the main roads would later make the bus a more flexible alternative.

There was no realistic possibility of trams being supplanted by buses in the larger towns and cities in the 1920s. Despite rapid strides in motor bus development in this decade, including the drop-frame chassis, covered top decks and pneumatic tyres, all of which improved passenger comfort, buses could not compete with trams in mass urban transit. Besides, some big city systems like Glasgow had been able to pay off their entire capital debt by the end of the First World War and were able to plan for renewals, extensions and investment in their ageing infrastructure. Birmingham was the first to replace trams with trolleybuses on a single route

LONDON'S TRAMWAYS

TRAVEL BY TRAM FOR
COVER AND COMFORT.

DESIGNED AT THE LCC CENTRAL SCHOOL OF ARTS AND CRAFTS.

In the 1920s London County Council trams and shelters carried advertising posters designed by students at the LCC's Central School of Arts & Crafts. These four striking examples are by Muriel Jackson, Margaret Curtis Haythorne, Oliver Burridge (top left to right) and F.H. Spear (lower). LTM/TfL

Manchester tram staff formed their own B.M.G. (Banjo, Mandolin and Guitar) Orchestra, who gave regular performances on stage in the entertainment hall at the new Birchfields Road depot opened in 1928. Trams were at their peak in the city, but two years later the first double-deck bus replacements arrived, signalling a decade of decline for the trams.

Birmingham Corporation tram on the Bristol Road route near Selly Oak where the tracks were laid in a central reservation in the 1920s, running south through the city's growing suburbs to the Lickey Hills at Rednall.

(to Nechells) as early as 1922, but elsewhere in the city tramway expansion and the purchase of new cars continued throughout the twenties.

On the other hand, smaller tram networks began to look uneconomic by the twenties. Most electric systems were now 20-25 years old and local authorities had to consider whether to modernise their existing trams and equipment, or abandon trams completely in favour of cheaper motor buses or trolleybuses. Keighley, in Yorkshire, was the first local authority to close its entire electric tramway system in 1924 and also the first to replace its trams completely with trolleybuses, which it had originally trialled just before the war.

Most of the smaller systems chose the motor bus instead of the tram from the late 1920s. Early local authority shutdowns included Colchester (1929), Lincoln (1929), Chester (1930), Exeter (1931), Lowestoft (1931), and Wigan (1931) which all introduced bus services. The City of York Corporation introduced trolleybuses on feeder routes to its tramways in 1920, but found both systems were losing money by the end of the decade. In 1934 they set up a Joint Committee with the West Yorkshire Road Car Company and by 1935 had

TOP: From 1901 the popular beauty spot of Kinver could be reached by tram from all over the West Midlands. This is one of the open-sided summer cars at the Kinver terminus. Traffic declined in the 1920s with bus competition and the line closed in 1930.

CENTRE: A tram heading down North Hill, Colchester, c1910. This was one of the first local authority systems to close when buses took over in 1929.

LOWER: A newly introduced trolleybus in York getting dangerously close to pedestrians in the narrow city streets, 1920. The corporation was soon losing money on its trams and trolleybuses, and replaced both networks with motor buses outsourced to the West Yorkshire Road Car Company in the early 1930s. LTM/TfL

TRAMMING TIN STONE, EAST POOL MINE, NEAR REDRUTH

The only electric tramway in Cornwall, the Camborne & Redruth, closed its passenger and postal services in 1927. Its freight operations, using small electric locomotives to haul tin stone from a local mine, continued until 1934.

replaced both their trams and trolleybuses with motor buses.

The smaller company systems found it particularly difficult to sustain operations. The Taunton Electric Tramway, an isolated system with less than 2 miles of track, closed in 1921. The Burton & Ashby Light Railway (B&ALR), originally opened as the sole tramway subsidiary of the Midland Railway in 1906, was inherited by the LMS Railway at the Grouping in 1923. Bus competition and falling passenger numbers, especially after the General Strike of 1926, meant the B&ALR could no longer cover its operating costs from declining fares revenue. The LMS was not prepared to cross-subsidise the tramway from its more profitable lines, and shut it down in 1927.[17] In the same year the only electric tramway in Cornwall, the Camborne & Redruth, closed its passenger operations. The little Barnsley & District Electric Tramway in Yorkshire, a BET subsidiary, succumbed in 1930.

Sometimes a local authority stepped in to purchase a struggling company system only to close it down and introduce motor buses, as happened in Worcester (1928)

The little Barnsley & District Electric Tramway, seen here in the town's market place in 1914, was another private operation hit by bus competition in the 1920s and closed in 1930.

The small, company-run Mexborough & Swinton Tramway also decided to modernise its operations in the late 1920s, buying a fleet of new single-deck trolleybuses to replace its trams and appointing a team of female conductors. This occasion is probably a press launch for both at the company's Denaby depot in 1928.

and Carlisle (1931). Other local councils , for example Ayr in Scotland, sold their tramway operation to a bus company which then carried out the closure and brought in replacement bus services, in this case the Scottish Motor Traction Company (SMT) of Edinburgh (1931).[18]

Ambitious bus companies like SMT were often equally predatory with smaller private tram operators. The Falkirk & District Tramways in central Scotland, first opened in 1904, were rationalised and modernised under new owners in the 1920s, with trackwork replaced and a fleet of new single-deck trams acquired from 1929 onwards. These improvements did not secure the tramways' future for very long. In 1935 the SMT bought enough company shares to give it a controlling interest. A year later Falkirk's tram system was closed down and replaced by SMT bus services.

Early conversions from tram to trolleybus included towns where local vehicle manufacturers developed their

A woman conductor in her summer uniform poses beside a newly delivered Brush single-deck tram on the Falkirk & District Tramways, c1930. Modernising this run down company-owned system did not save it from takeover, closure and bus replacement by the Scottish Motor Traction Co. in 1935/6.

The huge disruption caused when a major tramway crossover had to be replaced is well illustrated by this view of new conduit trackwork being installed in Aldgate High Street, east London, in 1929. LTM/TfL

Wolverhampton Corporation replaced its entire tram network with trolleybuses between 1923 and 1928. By the time these four locally built Sunbeam trolleys were delivered in 1933, the town had briefly become the largest trolleybus operator in the world, with ten routes and more than seventy-five vehicles.

Collecting fares on the upper deck of an LUT Feltham, 1931. The upstairs seating on the fast new trams was still reversible but was now fully upholstered and much more comfortable than on the old cars. LTM/TfL

own brand of rail-less transport. The two which stand out are Ipswich, where the engineering company Ransomes built trolleybuses as well as agricultural machinery, and Wolverhampton, home of Guy Motors and Sunbeam, who both diversified into trolleybus building. Ipswich Corporation replaced its last trams with locally built trolleybuses as early as 1926. Wolverhampton followed in 1928, joined by nearby Walsall from 1931. Hastings also converted to trolleybus operation in 1928; Nottingham introduced trolleybuses gradually between 1927 and 1932. Trolleybus design was still quite crude in the 1920s, but the vehicles became much more sophisticated and reliable in the following decade.

The typical British tramcar of the mid-1920s was very similar to its pre-1914 predecessor. New and refurbished trams were more comfortable but basically hand built with traditional construction methods in much the same way as before, and largely without any novel features. Mass production on assembly lines, which Henry Ford had pioneered for the American car industry, was never

considered for trams, and a British tramcar manufacturing industry as such never really developed. Very little effort had been made to bring the tramcar up to date and practically no research was being done in Britain to improve it technically. This was in complete contrast to the rapid evolution in the design of buses and trolleybuses, which boosted the adoption of both alternatives to the tram.[19]

The main exception to this traditional approach was in the Underground Group of companies in London, which was already in the vanguard of bus and tube train development, often adopting innovative practices from the American motor industry. Its experiments with new prototype trams in the late 1920s led to the creation of a radically modern all-steel body design in 1930. One hundred 'Feltham' cars, named after the west London suburb where they were mass-produced in a new factory by the Union Construction Company (UCC), entered service on the London United and Metropolitan Electric systems in 1930/31. The luxurious Felthams were the fastest

and most advanced trams in the country at the time, but appeared just as the whole future of tramways in Britain was being called into question. Were they too late?

The Royal Commission Verdict

Developments in the 1920s were not all in one direction, and at the start of the 1930s it was uncertain whether the future of urban public transport in Britain lay with trams, trolleybuses, motor buses or a combination of these different modes. A Royal Commission Report in 1931 acknowledged 'the great part played by tramways in the past' but came down strongly in favour of the motor bus as the transport of the future:

We believe tramways to be superior to any other form of road passenger vehicle at the present moment in London, Glasgow, Liverpool, Manchester and other large towns where the volume of passenger traffic at certain hours is very great, but we cannot believe that even in these populous centres the present state of things is likely to be permanent… improvements in motor omnibuses in recent years as regards comfort, capacity, design, reliability and economical running has been so remarkable that we feel certain that the time will soon arrive when the motor omnibus, supplemented, perhaps, by new tube railways, etc, will be able to carry the public, even in London and other big cities, as expeditiously and cheaply as the tramcar.[20]

The Commissioners itemised a number of specific disadvantages of tramways, including:

- The location of tramlines in the middle of the road, resulting in obstruction to other traffic and danger to passengers
- 'Intolerable' congestion when trams and buses operate on the same streets

Boarding and alighting from trams in the middle of the road was becoming hazardous as other road traffic increased. This is the stop outside Finsbury Park station in north London in the evening rush hour, 1930. LTM/TfL

- The inability to steer a tramcar makes it more liable to collision and especially dangerous if it leaves the rails and has no braking control
- Danger to cars and cycles of skidding on tramlines in wet weather
- Heavy interest payments on capital costs and expensive track and road maintenance.

Their considered view was that tramways 'if not an obsolete form of transport are at all events in a state of obsolescence, and cause much unnecessary congestion and considerable danger to the public'. They therefore recommended:

- That no additional tramways should be constructed and
- That, though no definite time limit can be laid down, they should gradually disappear and give place to other forms of transport.

The members of the Royal Commission did not explore alternative solutions which might have led to a more favourable consideration of tramways. Whilst it might have been acceptable for trams to run down the middle of narrow streets when there was less other traffic, it was not, in their opinion, in 1931. The right of buses and cars to unobstructed passage was not challenged, with trams seen as a cause of congestion rather than as a means of carrying heavy passenger loads more economically and using less road space than other vehicles to do so. There was no perception at the time that cars would become the primary cause of congestion, or that buses, despite becoming bigger and more efficient, would not be able to cope with such heavy passenger flows as trams. The freedom of the bus and trolleybus from fixed tracks was also accepted uncritically as beneficial to all concerned.[21]

Nevertheless, the attitude of the Royal Commission on Transport towards trams

probably reflected public perceptions at the time. By 1931 trams were widely considered to be old fashioned, a threat to road safety, and the major cause of traffic congestion in towns. None of this was strictly accurate, but the Commission Report appeared to give the popular view its official seal of approval. This did not translate into national policy, but the disparagement of trams and recommendations for replacement set the tone for a decade of decline across the country.

In the early 1930s trams also became indelibly associated with the problems of the industrial North and Midlands. Old trams seemed to be in their natural habitat against a background of grim, dirty and traditional heavy industry. This was ironic as trams themselves provided a clean, efficient and non-polluting transport service to districts where the air and urban environment had been blackened for decades by coal fires,

A safety alert for motorists following a tram to be aware of alighting passengers. This poster appeared on LCC trams in 1933. LTM/TfL

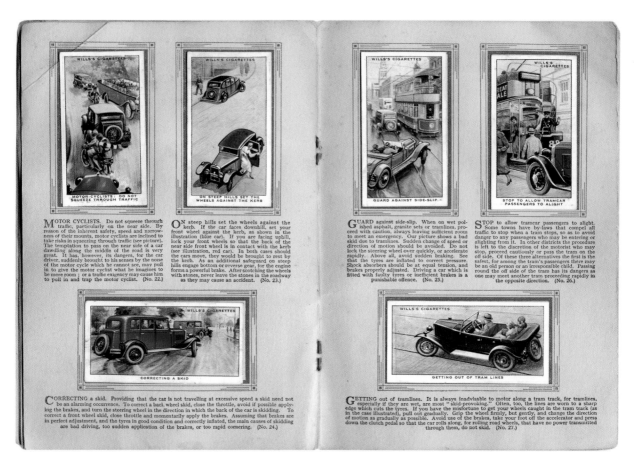

Pages from *Safety First*, a cigarette card album 'of national importance' issued by W.D. & H.O. Wills, part of the Imperial Tobacco Company, c1935. Popular opinion was that trams had become outdated, obstructive and even dangerous by this time. LTM/TfL

factory chimneys and steam trains. Yet trams had become perceived as part of that Victorian and Edwardian urban setting that in the Depression years was even more unattractive to contemporary critics. Sheffield deliberately adopted an all-over cream livery for its trams in the 1930s in a bid to counter the city's smoky industrial image.

The slump of 1929/30, which saw unemployment soar in key northern industries like steel and textiles, also had a direct effect on tramway finances because people out of work are less likely to travel. Ian Yearsley, the historian of the Manchester tramways, suggests that the effect of mass unemployment in the nearby cotton town of Rochdale, for example, was to precipitate the complete shut-down of the local tramway system in favour of buses in 1930-2.[22]

In his celebrated travelogue *English Journey*, published in 1934, the novelist and playwright J.B. Priestley, a self–styled northerner and man of the people, is typically unimpressed by trams. Travelling cross-country in the south he is enthusiastic about the comfort and luxury of the new long-distance motor coach but finds his trip on a Manchester tram grim and depressing. Or was this just a bad day for a Yorkshireman in Lancashire? Priestley would no doubt have been heartened to know that R. Stuart Pilcher, General Manager of the Manchester Tramways, was already announcing a programme of tram to bus conversion as track renewals became due on each route in the city.[23]

Seaside contrasts

The north/south divide is particularly apparent in the contrasting fate of the tramways in two of England's leading seaside resorts, Bournemouth and

Blackpool, which both wanted to update their image in the 1930s.

Bournemouth Corporation, along with almost every seaside town in the south, was looking for alternatives to its trams from the late 1920s. It sold its lines running west of the town to Hants & Dorset Motor Services and these routes to Parkstone and Poole were replaced by buses. Within the borough boundaries and east to Christchurch, the corporation introduced its own new electric trolleybuses to replace all remaining tram routes between 1933 and 1936.

Bournemouth's modern primrose-coloured trolleybuses soon became part of the town's image as the premier middle-class holiday resort. The local trams, some of them only ten years old, but still of traditional Edwardian open top appearance, were sold for further seaside use on the Llandudno & Colwyn Bay system in north Wales. Back in Bournemouth the council's compact trolleybus network operated for over thirty years, with a complete fleet renewal in the 1950s, making it the most up-to-

date system in the UK and the last on the south coast to close in 1969.

Blackpool was a bigger, brasher resort than Bournemouth with a northern working-class mass holiday and day tripper market. The trams had always been a much more significant part of the Blackpool seaside experience than on the south coast. There was a service all along the seafront linking the main Blackpool attractions from the Pleasure Beach to the

Blackpool's new streamlined trams built by English Electric promoted on a picture postcard, c1935.

The newly completed modernist Casino and Pleasure Beach building at Blackpool, designed by Joseph Emberton in 1939, with one of Walter Luff's stylish open boat cars in the foreground.

A beautifully renovated Blackpool boat car in operation at the National Tramway Museum, Crich, in 2013. OG

An English Electric 'Balloon' car still in regular service aged seventy-five outside Blackpool Pleasure Beach in 2010. OG

Tower, with branches into the town and a lengthy run northwards up the Fylde coast to Fleetwood. Over the years Blackpool Corporation's tramways department had become as much a part of the town's entertainment industry as a public transport authority, and ran circular tours and elaborately decorated cars linked to the famous illuminations.

A new General Manager, Walter Luff, arrived in Blackpool in 1933, just as Bournemouth started replacing its tramways. There were many local councillors who favoured getting rid of the town's trams and replacing them with buses, but Luff had other ideas. He realised that modern, eye-catching trams could give his system a tremendous boost and quickly presented the members with a comprehensive five-year plan for his department to do just that. Blackpool was the first authority to introduce a fleet of new streamlined trams in 1934/5, developed and built in partnership with nearby English Electric at Preston, and soon followed up with modern cars from other suppliers.[24]

Luff's trams looked nothing like the traditional Edwardian cars that most Blackpool visitors were familiar with in their home towns. They had a smart new cream and green livery, stylish lightweight bodywork, wide staircases, air operated centre doors, curved roof lights for a better view out and comfortable cushion seating, all features that more than matched the appeal of the latest buses, trolleybuses or even the new motor coaches Priestley so admired. The streamlined tram fleet also came in different weather variants, including single-deck, double-deck and the particularly swish 'open boat' cars.

The best in modern industrial design styling had at last reached the British tram. Gliding up the seafront to the matching modernism of the Pleasure Beach Casino, opened in May 1939, Luff's sleek 'railcars' gave Blackpool a touch of American-influenced glamour that staid and conservative Bournemouth would never quite match. The latest Blackpool cars were also extremely well built, and with attentive care and maintenance at Blackpool's Rigby Road depot some of them are still operational more than eighty years later as a heritage fleet alongside the new Flexity trams and running past the equally chic Casino building, fully refurbished in 1930's style for the twenty-first century.[25]

The end of modernity
Most new tramcars built in Britain from the mid-1930s incorporated the modern features first seen in Blackpool, but they only appeared in some of the larger towns and cities which remained committed to the tram as their principal mode of transport. Birmingham never saw a modern tram, bought no new cars after 1930 and progressively replaced tram routes with motor buses or trolleybuses throughout the decade. Belfast, Manchester and Newcastle all began converting to trolleybus or bus operation in the 1930s. Only a few city systems such as Aberdeen, Leeds and Sunderland continued to invest in modern trams while trimming back their networks.

The only British cities that continued to plan the expansion of their tramway systems in the 1930s *and* build modern tramcars to run on them were the two municipal pioneers of the 1890s, Liverpool and Glasgow. Both Corporations had the skills, facilities and experience to design and build their own new trams with the latest technical and design features and began to do so after 1935.

Liverpool built a fleet of 175 large streamlined bogie cars (known as 'Liners') at its Edge Lane works in 1936/7, followed by 100 similar but smaller single truck cars ('Baby Grands') in 1937-42. These modern lightweight trams were extremely fast and would often overtake private cars when running on the extended reserved track sections in the city's suburbs, which accounted for a third of Liverpool's tram route mileage by the 1940s.

Glasgow's Coplawhill works built 152 modern trams, known as the 'Coronation' type from their year of introduction, between 1937 and 1941 when there was a switch to war production. They were claimed to be 'the finest short stage vehicles in Europe' and were proudly shown off to visitors attending the great Empire Exhibition held in Glasgow in 1938 as war clouds loomed on the Continent. A further 100 'Mark Two'

A Liverpool streamliner, built at the corporation's Edge Lane workshops in 1936, after restoration to immaculate working condition at Crich in 2006. This tram had been passed on to Glasgow when the Liverpool system was cut back in the 1950s and finally withdrawn from service in 1962.
Neil Cossons

Seeing Glasgow By Tram and Bus. The city guidebook produced for the Empire Exhibition in 1938 featured one of Glasgow Corporation's sleek new Coronation cars on the cover. The final batch of post-war Coronations, built in 1950, were the last new double-deck trams built in the UK.

Coronation cars were built in Glasgow after the war in 1948-52, the final full-sized double-deck trams to be built in Britain, for what was to be the last big city system to close.

London Transport

Developments in London in the 1930s were, as usual, rather different to every other city in the country but helped to reinforce opinion against the tram. At the start of the decade forward planning for public transport in the rapidly growing metropolis was still hampered by the lack of a single overarching authority. This had long been recommended but never enacted, leaving operational responsibility for local transport across the city hopelessly divided between various company and council undertakings of different sizes which cut across road and rail services.

The big players were the LCC Trams and the Underground Group, which between them ran most, but not all, of the buses, trams and underground railway services. On the trams alone there was a fundamentally different approach by the giant LCC and the three company tramways of the Underground Group, the LUT, MET and SMET. The LCC, once progressive and innovative when it first introduced electric trams, had become conservative and traditional in the 1920s, and was not inclined to cooperate on research and development or anything new. The Underground Group, by contrast, was progressive and forward-thinking under the dynamic leadership of Lord Ashfield and Frank Pick. There was a restless quest for improvement in every area, which included the tramways.

Ashfield and Pick were well aware that London's transport could only work with a combination of modes including buses, railways and tramways, but they also encouraged change and innovation in all areas. Hence it was their tramways division that experimented both with the new Feltham cars and the alternative option of trolleybuses in 1931. The much larger LCC built new trams to traditional designs, refurbished its old fleet and infrastructure, but did not plan effectively for the future. By the time the LCC engineers had finally come up with their own modern tram prototype in 1932, working with the English Electric Company, the London County Council was about to lose its responsibility for transport altogether.[26]

A solution to London's intractable transport problems had been found by Herbert Morrison, Minister of Transport in the 1929 Labour government. He had rejected a proposal for a joint authority by the LCC and Underground Group, recommending instead the creation of a new public corporation, the London Passenger Transport Board (LPTB) to run all bus, tram and underground railway services in the capital. Morrison was out of office before his Bill came before Parliament, but on 1 July 1933 the LPTB, soon to be known simply as London Transport, came into being. London's trams were no longer under council control, but were one division of the largest public transport organisation in the world. Ashfield became the LPTB's first chairman and Pick its chief executive.

The Board was independent of political control but had the daunting task of providing suitably integrated public transport over a vast urban, suburban and country area. London Transport had to meet its operating expenses through fares, but was able to fund the capital costs of

new development by borrowing against Treasury guarantees through a separate finance corporation, an option not available to local authorities. By 1934 the LPTB had announced an ambitious £40m New Works Programme that included both new Underground line extensions and the

The LCC at last began to refurbish its ageing tram fleet in the late 1920s to compete with buses, calling the upgraded interior decor 'Pullmanisation'. All trams were given a new exterior livery of red and cream which was similar to the LGOC's bus colours. LTM/TfL

The last major infrastructure development by the LCC Tramways was the enlargement of the Kingsway Subway to take double-deck cars in 1930/31. This underground tram station at Holborn still exists below the road, disused since 1952 when the Subway closed. LTM/TfL

The LCC was too late with its research and development of a new advanced tram design for London. No.1, known as *Bluebird* because of its distinctive dark blue colour scheme, was built in 1932. but remained a unique prototype. A year later London Transport took over and announced that the trams would go. *Bluebird*, repainted in LT red, ran in London until 1950, when it was sold to Leeds. It is now in the National Tramway Museum collection at Crich. LTM/TfL

complete conversion of London's massive tram network to trolleybus operation.

London's electric tramways were unlike any other urban operation in the UK. There was no consistency in their planning, administration or technical operation because of their fragmented development over more than thirty years. The decision to replace the tramways, announced so quickly after the LPTB came into being, has often been seen by tram enthusiasts as a flawed, retrograde step by Ashfield and Pick. It is proof, they claim, that the Underground duo had always favoured buses and Tubes as the appropriate transport modes for London, and that they seized this opportunity to get rid of the trams with undue haste.

In fact Ashfield's background was in streetcar management in the USA before he joined the Underground, and Pick had studied the transport needs of different metropolitan areas very carefully for many years. Neither of them made impulsive decisions. In his presidential address to the Institute of Transport in 1931, Pick had commented 'That tramways worked to their reasonable capacity are almost the cheapest form of urban transport is not to be denied. For a regional city with a population rarely reaching 2 million people, tramways constitute the most convenient and economical system.'

The problem with tramways, he believed, was the inadequacy of many city streets to accommodate them coupled with an operational inefficiency 'when they stretch out to cover too vast a territory'. London, to his mind, had not got its transport right because its development had never been co-ordinated with the growth of the city. Both had been haphazard, and when new opportunities had arisen, like the LCC's creation of a huge out of town housing estate at Becontree in the 1920s, there had been no provision of rapid transit facilities. Some 115,000 people were added to outer East London, but the promised trams never got there. As a planning authority for transport and housing, the LCC had failed to deliver an integrated outcome.

The creation of the LPTB as the sole transport authority for London, with a new means of capital funding, gave Ashfield and Pick a unique opportunity to do things differently. They were not constrained by local authority financial rules nor the political policies of councillors. The LCC conduit system they inherited in 1933 was cumbersome, costly and could not be modernised. Trolleybus operation on part of the LUT system had been successfully trialled since 1931 and could now be applied right across London using the existing electrical distribution system for the trams. Larger trolleybuses could replace trams on a one-for-one basis, which their latest diesel buses could not. The Underground's unrivalled experience in managing big infrastructure projects gave them confidence that tramway replacement could be achieved very quickly.

Looked at in the round, London Transport's plans to ditch its tramways still look pragmatic, operationally sensible and financially sound. The first

London Transport's standard 70-seat trolleybuses were large enough to replace trams on a one-for-one basis while its motor buses, with 56 seats, were too small. This illustration is from a Leyland brochure of 1936. LTM/TfL

conversions took place in 1935 and by the time work was halted by the war in 1940, well over half the huge tram network had gone. London's approach to tramway replacement under the LPTB was unique

The LT tram to trolleybus conversion scheme began with the former LUT routes in west London. This is the final night of the trams in Hounslow, with a line of cars returning to the depot on Saturday, 26 October 1935. Next day the new trolleys took over. LTM/TfL

A busy scene at Burnley Centre, c1930. Burnley Corporation's tram fleet was completely replaced with motor buses soon afterwards between 1932 and 1935.

One of the last trams in Stockton-on-Tees surrounded by motor vehicles: cars, motor-cycles, a lorry and at least four single-deck motor buses, which replaced the local tram service in 1932.

BROADGATE, COVENTRY. (4)   220297.J.V.

and could not have been emulated anywhere else in the UK. None of the big regional cities ran their urban transport in a comparable way, but the London Transport conversions added weight to the Royal Commission's recommendation that tramways should eventually be phased out everywhere.

By the late 1930s it was not only the smaller tramway systems that were being replaced. The company-run Bristol network, the urban tramway pioneer, was purchased by the council in 1937 and the first bus replacements followed in 1938. Nearby Bath closed its tramways in the same year. There were selective route closures in Leicester, Plymouth, Cardiff and most other medium sized cities. Some major tram operators introduced trolleybuses as well as motor bus replacements, including Newcastle,

Belfast and Manchester. None of these larger cities had phased trams out completely when the Second World War brought a temporary halt to replacement schemes in 1939/40, but the number of trams in Britain had fallen to about 7000, roughly half the peak figure of 1927.

The Blitz spirit

The outbreak of war in September 1939 led to the scaling down or postponement of a number of tram replacement programmes that were under way, but not completed. Some conversion work continued into 1940, but when heavy air raids began later that year it inevitably became more important to sustain existing transport services than to create new ones. Huddersfield completed a ten-year conversion programme in the blackout conditions of 1940 before any bombing

Coventry's trams were phased out from 1932 as new motor buses were introduced. This view of Broadgate in the mid-1930s shows one of each. The German Blitz attacks of November 1940 devastated the city centre and led to the premature suspension of the last tram route, which was formally closed down in 1941.

restarted when Blitz attacks devastated the city in November 1940. Services were suspended again, and the remaining tram system was formally closed down and replaced with buses in February 1941.

Bristol's remaining tram services, down to just two routes by the start of the war, were brought to a premature end in April 1941 when a German bomb cut the main power supply. The damage was considered beyond economic repair and the system was abandoned prematurely. Southend quietly withdrew its last trams in 1942, and Belfast continued to close individual routes throughout the war years.

Hull, which had replaced the northern half of its tramway system with trolleybuses by 1937, also continued its tram replacement during the war. One route was converted in February 1940 before the city was bombed, but the last tram route did not close until June 1945, just as the war in Europe ended. Unlike Bristol, whose antiquated trams had all

Tram replacement continued in Hull during the war despite the severe Blitz attacks of 1941. This is one of twelve redundant cars sold to Leeds in 1942. It has been painted in drab wartime grey and its windows have been taped to reduce splintering in a bomb incident. A woman conductor is in charge.

began, but Coventry was less fortunate. Much of the Corporation's tramway system had closed between 1932 and 1937; the remainder was suspended on the outbreak of war in 1939 and had just been

A bomb crater with twisted tracks and a wrecked tram nearby in Kennington, south London, October 1940. LTM/TfL

gone for scrap, Hull was able to sell many of its redundant cars to Leeds.

Plymouth was another unlikely war survivor. The trams had been gradually cut back in the 1930s and replaced with buses, though the remaining services were sustained with second-hand cars bought from Exeter and Torquay when their systems closed. One route survived the city's virtual destruction in air raids and was still running through the rubble strewn centre in 1945, the last tram service in the south west.

Liverpool, still bucking the trend elsewhere, actually enlarged its tram network during the war. The last of its lengthy reserved track extensions, serving the huge Royal Ordnance Factory at Kirkby, which employed some 20,000 war workers, opened as late as 1942-4 and was operated by the corporation's latest 'Baby Grand' streamliners.[27]

Tram staff and systems were remarkably resilient in the face of aerial attack by the Luftwaffe and it became a matter of pride to repair bomb damage wherever possible and keep the trams running as an important morale booster for the civilian population. This was not always possible, particularly where high explosives had torn through the track and overhead wires. The London conduit system was particularly difficult to deal with when conduit track was hit, but

Clapham tram depot after an air raid, April 1941.
LTM/TfL

Sheffield city centre, December 1940, with a tram and a department store engulfed in a firestorm created by incendiary bombs.

Glasgow car no.6 took a direct hit from a parachute mine on the first night of the Clydebank Blitz in March 1941. The tram was virtually destroyed and eleven people on board were killed though twenty more were rescued. When another no.6 emerged pristine from Coplawhill works in 1942, the myth of a miraculous reconstruction from this wreck was born. It was, in fact, a completely new tram given the missing fleet number.

Glasgow Herald

astonishing repairs were achieved while the Blitz attacks continued on a nightly basis for months in 1940/41.

A direct hit on a depot, as happened at Clapham, south London in April 1981, could knock out a number of trams or a group could be destroyed in the street, like the attacks on Sheffield in December 1940 when a row of abandoned trams and most of the city centre buildings around them were engulfed in a firestorm started by incendiaries. In two devastating raids, thirty-one Sheffield trams were initially thought to be damaged beyond repair but eventually only fourteen of these were written off completely. These were replaced in due course by redundant trams acquired from London, Newcastle and Bradford which all needed reconditioning; the remainder were rebuilt at the Corporation's Queens Road depot.[28]

In the spring of 1941 the Glasgow area became the target of several German 'blitzes', with Clydebank heavily hit in March and Greenock in May. On the first night of the Clydebank raids, 13 March 1941, tram no.6 took a direct hit with heavy casualties as it travelled down Nelson Street. Pictures taken a few days later by a *Glasgow Herald* photographer show the car completely wrecked and clearly fit only for the scrapyard. When a pristine no.6 emerged from Coplawhill works in 1942, a mythical tale of remarkable reconstruction and repair developed. In fact the 'reborn' number 6 was a completely new tram but the story persists as one of the myths of the Blitz.[29]

Yet working on the trams in cities experiencing aerial bombing was as dangerous as any Home Front occupation, and again it was war work shared by men and women. In April 1940 the first 200 conductresses were engaged in Glasgow; in February 1941 the first group of 26 women started work as tram drivers. Thousands of women were again recruited as conductors all over the country, though as in the First World War very few became drivers, either on trams or trolleybuses, with notable exceptions like Glasgow and Manchester. This time, however, women were able to stay in the job after the war nearly everywhere and the firm female tram conductors of Glasgow in particular, who had learned how to control wartime shipyard workers and American GIs alike, became the stuff of legend. A well-known post-war cartoon by Bill Tait in the Glasgow *Evening Citizen* showed a conductress barring a meek male passenger's entry to her tram with the words 'come on, get aff!', also transcribed as the single Glaswegian admonition 'cumoangerraff!'

Tramway Twilight

When the war ended in 1945 there were still about 6,000 trams operating in Britain. Most of these were running on borrowed time where the war had held up conversion programmes. As new buses and trolleybuses became available the trams were scrapped, but deliveries of new vehicles were slow in the austerity years of the immediate post-war period, and until they arrived the trams had to be kept going.

This section takes its title from one of the best accounts of the final years of

The top deck of a rundown Bolton tram photographed soon after the war just before the system was replaced in 1947.

British trams, published in 1962. Its author vividly evokes the run-down feel of Manchester's remaining trams in the mid-1940s, the remnants of one of the great city systems:

The last night in Southampton, New Year's Eve, 1949. Buses took over on 1 January 1950.

A visit shortly after the war showed the trams in a sorry state. They juddered over the rail joints, the windows vibrated, the seats rattled and the noise reverberated through the cars as they ground their way along the corrugated track. The wooden seats were hard and the coloured glass in the top lights cast strange spectral hues over the passengers. For those passing through Manchester, the trams were a familiar part of the journey for the change of station between London Road and Exchange, a slow grinding ride across Piccadilly and down Market Street. For exhilaration, though, there was the ride to Belle Vue on a 'Pilcher', which sped tail-wagging along Hyde Road, flinging you violently against the side of the car and determined that if it could not throw you off it would beat you into submission.[30]

QUEEN STREET, CARDIFF.

The rundown of the remaining system began in 1946 and ended with the closure of route 35 to Hazel Grove three years later. Manchester's last car ran without much ceremony from Piccadilly to Birchfields Road on 10 January 1949. Its most up to date trams, the thirty-eight 'Pilcher' cars built in 1930-32, were offered for sale and all found new homes on four remaining systems in Aberdeen, Edinburgh, Leeds and Sunderland.

In the five years after the war most of the towns and cities that had begun tram replacement in the late 1930s finished the job. Trams disappeared from Bolton (1947), Salford (1947), Bury (1949), Dublin (1949), Blackburn (1949), Leicester (1949), Southampton (1949), Cardiff (1950), Newcastle (1950) and Bradford (1950).

These closures brought the number of trams operating around the country down to about 4,700.

In London 'Operation Tramaway' did not even see its first post-war tram replacements until September 1950. This was because priority was given to completing the Central line Tube extensions postponed in 1939, which were opened in 1947-49. All other outstanding parts of London Transport's ambitious 1935-40 New Works Programme were cut back or cancelled as a post-war economy measure. London Transport was nationalised in 1948 along with the 'Big Four' main line railway companies, and reported to the government's new British Transport Commission (BTC), with no direct control over its own planning and

Queen Street, Cardiff, in the late 1940s. The final tram ran here in 1950.

Last tram on London route 31 to Wandsworth about to enter the Kingsway Subway at Southampton Row, Holborn, 1950. LTM/TfL

Regular London tram passengers on the final day, 5 July 1952. Next week they will be on the bus. LTM/TfL

finances. It was decided not to extend the trolleybus system, already the largest in the world, and to use diesel buses instead to replace the remaining tram network in a phased two-year programme.

Even at reduced cost, this was a massive £9m scheme that involved London Transport replacing about 830 trams which by 1950 were carrying nearly 300m passengers a year. Around 100 route miles of tram track would be torn up and a huge fleet of new standard RT and RTL type buses introduced in stages. A special 'tramatorium' was set up in Woolwich to which London's trams made their final journey to be broken up and burned. The last week of operation in July 1952 was announced on the side of every car, and all passengers were issued with special 'Last Tram Week' souvenir tickets.[31]

The last night, 5/6 July, became a big public event with crowds lining the streets and the last car unable to reach New Cross depot until the early hours of the morning. It was a curious occasion in some respects because Londoners had never before expressed any particular attachment to their public transport. The trams were given an emotional send-off that was almost reminiscent of VE night in May 1945, but there were now no all-night cars to take south Londoners home past the Elephant & Castle and down the Old Kent Road. A sentimental, but beautifully filmed short documentary, *The Elephant Will Never Forget*, was made by British Transport Films to capture the final days of London's trams, and shown after the closure in cinemas.[32]

Last Tram Week in Greenwich, south London, July 1952. Thousands of these special tickets were issued. LTM/TfL

Culturally informed graffiti at the London 'tramatorium' in Woolwich, 1952. The film of Tennessee Williams' play *A Streetcar Named Desire*, starring Marlon Brando and Vivien Leigh, was released a year earlier. By then the suddenly famous Desire route in New Orleans had just been replaced with a bus service but other historic streetcar lines in the city survive today. LTM/TfL

It took six months to break up and burn the 740 London trams sent to the Penhall Road scrapyard. This is the last car to be set alight, on 29 January 1953.
LTM/TfL

Chapter 5

RELICS AND RENAISSANCE

While the tramway systems that had already begun replacement in the 1930s acted as quickly as possible to buy in bus substitutes for their remaining trams after the war, there were a few apparent moves in the opposite direction. As Joyce points out in *Tramway Twilight*:

> Some cities, far from intending to scrap their tramways, were building new trams and planning extensions. New trams were put into service in Leeds, Sheffield, Glasgow, Edinburgh, Aberdeen and Blackpool, while new tramway extensions were built in Glasgow, Leeds and Sunderland. It appeared that, on these systems at least, the tram was likely to remain into the foreseeable future.[1]

In fact, what Joyce describes as a 'minor tramway renaissance' was a very short-lived phenomenon in the post-war years, though looking back seventy years later it represents a fascinating 'what if' scenario. The seven local authorities mentioned all remained committed to improving their tramways rather than getting rid of them and did so with new trams and/or network extensions. The new developments were all promising, but they were strictly individual initiatives which were never likely to take trams forward. A tramway renaissance in the UK, if that is the right word, was fifty years in the future.

The Light Railway Transport League (LRTL), formed in 1937, advocated the retention of urban tramways, not by preserving them as they were but by modernisation. There were divisions in the LRTL from the start and disagreement about whether it should take an active, propagandist approach as a pressure group or be primarily concerned with the specialist interest of studying tramways. Its membership and magazine, *The Modern Tramway*, both flourished in the post-war years, but unfortunately its influence on transport policy in Britain was marginal.

Nearly everyone and everything was firmly against trams in 1950's Britain.

'The Fruits of Tram Scrapping'. An early poster produced by the Light Railway Transport League, who campaigned in vain against tramway closures in the 1940s and 50s.

Town planners preparing schemes for post-war reconstruction of bomb battered city centres and the development of New Towns never included tramways in their proposals. Priority was always given to the bus and, increasingly, the private car, with a blinkered assumption that trams could not be accommodated in new street layouts that had gyratory systems and underpasses. The result was more destruction of city centres by the planners than the Luftwaffe and a general failure to use the opportunity to create improved and better laid out urban environments. Towns and cities became dominated rather than liberated by new urban highways and inner ring roads. Bristol and Birmingham, once well served by trams, fell to post-war planning blight and extensive rebuilding to accommodate the private car, later followed by Leeds, Glasgow, Liverpool and other cities. While competition with the car before the war had been for road space, after 1950 it was for passengers, and substituting buses for trams did not bring them back. Public transport of every kind went into

decline as car ownership began to grow dramatically from the mid-1950s and brought serious congestion problems to busy urban areas.

There were occasional grand ideas, such as the 1940s plan to put trams underground through the centre of Leeds, with a sub-surface transport interchange at the main railway station. Birmingham could have done something similar. However, expensive reconstruction schemes like these were pie in the sky in austerity Britain. No local authority could afford them and it was clear that none would get government assistance for such a project however much it might appeal to local councillors and municipal pride. Tram subways later materialised in some European cities, notably in Brussels, where they are still in use, but they never caught on in the UK.

Rising costs hit the tramways hard and were an almost insuperable problem after the war. By the late 1940s, the price of rails was about 60 per cent higher than before the war, and electricity costs were up by about 50 per cent. Electricity was also

The future that never arrived. Newly built prototype tram 602, with its special royal purple livery, is shown off in City Square, Leeds, in May 1953, just before the Coronation. The proposed subway interchange, with modern single-deck trams running under the city centre, would have been built directly below this spot. Only a month later the newly elected Labour Council decided to phase out trams altogether. No.602 survives in the National Tramway Museum.

R.B. Parr/Tramway Museum Society

PIER HEAD AND RIVER MERSEY, LIVERPOOL.

The transport hub at Liverpool's Pierhead, seen from the tower of the Liver Building in about 1949, when the first tram route closures were taking place on Merseyside.

Streamliner 293 was painted white to become Liverpool's official last car in 1957. It was then sold to an American buyer and still resides, unrestored, at the Seashore Trolley Museum in Maine. Identical 'Baby Grand' number 245, owned by National Museums Liverpool, has recently been fully restored by Merseyside Transport Preservation Society with the help of a Heritage Lottery grant to run on the Wirral Tramway in Birkenhead. TMS

beyond local authority control, part of a newly nationalised industry that could no longer offer reduced prices to a local transport supplier. Operating and maintenance costs were rising all round, with even the larger remaining operators reporting heavy losses. In 1950/51 Liverpool and Glasgow showed deficits of around £500k and £200k respectively on their tramway accounts.

Even ordering new trams was a problem, both in terms of cost and supply. There were few suitable tram builders and because there was no likelihood of mass production orders, commercially produced trams were very expensive. A new tram might cost up to £10,000 while a new bus would be less than half the price at about £4,000. When Leeds Corporation invited tenders for fifty new trams in 1948 they had no offers.

Only a local authority the size of Glasgow still had the capacity and facilities to build their own tramcars, but they were not empowered to supply them to anyone else. When in 1945 the General

Manager of Aberdeen Corporation Transport enquired whether he could order twenty new tramcar bodies from Coplawhill Works he was told there was no provision in Glasgow Corporation's Tramways Acts of Parliament that would allow such a proposal to be undertaken![2]

The extent of co-operation between operators at this time was a flourishing

Leeds was still committed to its tramways in 1950 and acquired London's redundant Feltham cars. Car 2099 (on the right), still carrying its LT number, was the first to arrive, seen alongside one of the Leeds high-speed Middleton bogie cars built in 1935. This particular Feltham was saved by enthusiasts when the system closed in 1959 and is now in the London Transport Museum's collection. TMS

In 1951 Leeds had its own Festival of Britain events and displays, using this decorated tram to celebrate and promote the city's commerce and industry. Trams did not remain part of this for much longer.

trade in second-hand cars as more systems closed and offered their trams to the survivors. London's superior Felthams and eleven Southampton cars went to Leeds, Liverpool sold many of its streamliners to Glasgow and the Gateshead & District, last of the BET company systems to close in 1951, sold nineteen cars to the Grimsby & Immingham line, the only electric tramway inherited by the newly

nationalised British Railways. The sales gave all these trams an extended life of about ten years and are indicative of the rather hand-to-mouth management of the final years of decline. In the end the remaining tramways were closed down as the quickest way to save money on public services that would never pay.

The cost of new tramway extensions was by now almost prohibitively high. In the early 1950s it was £50-60,000 per mile for double track, a substantial addition to the cost of building new council housing estates on the edge of town which required public transport. Not surprisingly, most councils chose the cheaper bus in these situations. Only three local authorities invested in extensions at this time. Glasgow and Leeds were just about big enough to afford it but Sunderland, which opened its only reserved track extension in 1949 to serve new housing on the Durham Road, decided to abandon the line only five years later, one of the shortest lived tram routes in Britain.[3]

With persuasive arguments about cost, flexibility and street congestion all stacked

Passenger numbers on Sheffield trams dropped in the 1950s as private car ownership rose. This scene shows the hilly western route to Walkley in 1954 with two new Morris saloons, a Minor and an Oxford, passing a pre-war tram. The tram replacement programme was accelerated, but Sheffield was still the last of the big English cities to lose its trams in October 1960. TMS

The Grimsby & Immingham Tramway, the only electric tram system inherited by British Railways in 1948, was run entirely with long single-deck cars. The line was replaced by a bus service in 1961 which was much slower than the cross-country trams because the road route was not direct. TMS

against them, even the big tramway stalwarts had to throw in the towel. Liverpool started conversions and closures in 1949, Aberdeen in 1951, Sunderland and Edinburgh in 1952, Dundee in 1955. By 1958 there were only just over 1,000 trams still running in Britain and Ireland. The last electric tramway in Ireland, the Hill of Howth near Dublin, succumbed in 1959. In January 1960 the historic Swansea & Mumbles Railway, successor to the original Oystermouth Railway and Tramroad Company, and now the last in South Wales, was closed down. The final three big city operations were already preparing for closure. The last Leeds tram ran in 1959, the final Sheffield car in 1960 and two years later, in 1962, Glasgow gave up its last trams.

In the ten years since the end of London's trams, system closures had become increasingly large and emotional public events. Glasgow, which had identified with its trams more than any other British city, had only taken the reluctant and unpopular decision to

abandon its whole system in 1955. The final send-off was almost a week-long drawn out affair that seemed to involve a majority of the city's residents. The date, 1 September 1962, was the last day of 'normal' service on the final route, the number 9 from Dalmuir West to the wonderfully named Auchenshuggle.[4] By popular demand, a special service of

Sunderland Corporation opened this reserved track extension in 1949 to serve new housing along the Durham Road. It was closed only five years later, one of the shortest lived tram routes in Britain.

Alan A Jackson

sixpenny rides from Anderston Cross to Auchenshuggle was run for the next three days. Then on 4 September there was a ceremonial parade of twenty trams which moved slowly through the city like a funeral procession, watched by an estimated crowd of 250,000 people who braved the rain to pay their final respects.[5]

Preservation and survival

When the Glasgow system closed in 1962 it left Blackpool as the only extensive urban, street-running electric tramway in Britain. That too was about to be cut back to the seafront promenade and the inter-urban line to Fleetwood. On the Isle of Man the Douglas horse trams, the Manx Electric Railway and the Snaefell Mountain Railway continued seasonal operations, as did the cable-worked Great Orme Tramway in North Wales, Volk's Electric Railway in Brighton and a miniature tramway for holidaymakers opened at Eastbourne in 1953.[6] None of them, apart from Blackpool, offered a regular public transport service. In due course they would become part of the heritage leisure industry with its mixture of popular entertainment and nostalgia for lost times, but in the early sixties their future looked precarious.

As one writer observed at the time 'The tram as it now survives in Britain is

Trams in Dundee High Street, c1952. The council began tramway abandonment soon afterwards and the last tram ran here in October 1956.

largely a holiday attraction and a seaside amusement. Its other role is as a museum piece, where it stands as a reminder of its past glory.'[7]

It was an over-used expression in the 1950s and early 60s to describe trams as being 'consigned to museums' when in fact very little active preservation of this kind had taken place. Glasgow was the only municipal operator to commit to the creation of a publicly accessible museum in which to preserve and display, amongst other transport items, a selection of the council's trams covering a period of more than sixty years' service. The first Glasgow Transport Museum was duly opened in 1964 by the Queen Mother in the appropriate location of the former Coplawhill Works in Pollokshields. It has since moved twice, eventually to the dramatic purpose-built Riverside Museum opened in 2010, designed by award winning architect Zaha Hadid on the site of a former Glasgow shipyard. The new museum is extremely popular and a great success, though ironically it is not well served by the city's diminished public transport system.[8]

Elsewhere very few of the former municipal tram operators took steps to preserve even a fraction of their tramway heritage when systems were closed down, although most of the same local authorities ran a public museum whose role covered the collection and display of their town or city's history. A tram is a particularly large object for any museum to collect, but a combination of lack of storage and display space with disinterested councils and curators probably accounts for the tram's general absence from even the larger regional museum collections.

It seemed the electric tram was not old enough to be considered historically significant yet too commonplace to be thought worthy of museum preservation. One or two were

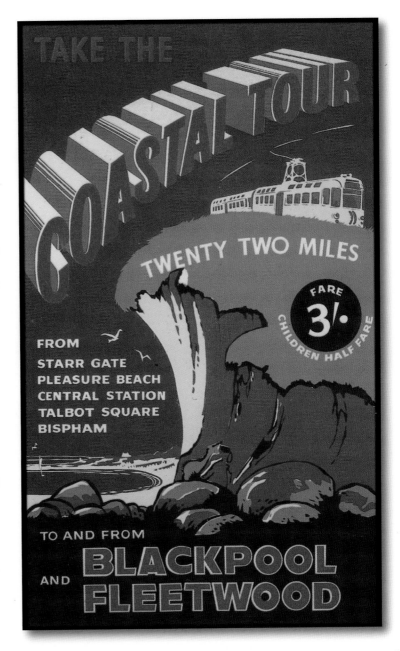

squirrelled away by council transport departments in their own works, as happened in Bradford and Edinburgh, but others like Bristol and Nottingham scrapped, burned or otherwise disposed of every withdrawn car as quickly as possible when their tramways closed. Very few local authorities resolved to save a tram for their own museum, as Birmingham did, for example. London Transport, nationalised in 1948, also still had a sense of history and preserved two 40-year-old municipal tramcars when its

Blackpool was still promoting its coastal tours by tram in the early 1960s. After 1962, when the Glasgow system closed down, it became the only regular street tramway operation in mainland Britain for the next thirty years.

Blackpool Transport

The first exhibit that greets the visitor entering Glasgow's Riverside Museum is this 'Room and Kitchen' tram, one of the original electric cars of 1898. A short black and white video presentation on the last Cunarder car displayed here evokes a Saturday night in 1950s Glasgow with two girls going out to a dance hall by tram. OG

remaining system was replaced in 1950-52, though it did not yet have a museum to put them in.[9]

In the late 1940s there was, understandably, little nostalgia for the recent past and a general impatience to move on quickly with post-war reconstruction and modernisation. Preservation and conservation of heritage assets was not a priority in any field either at national or local level, and a great deal of historic material was lost or actively destroyed as a result. Two Manchester trams were scrapped in 1948 ten years after they had been earmarked for preservation just before the war. Leicester Corporation set aside one of its own trams for transfer to its museum service when the city's system was closed down in 1949. This too was summarily broken up by the council's transport department only a year later when no suitable home had been found for it.[10] Incidents like this were not unusual in the bleak austerity years. In addition, local authorities tended to favour their gallery collections of art and archaeology over social and industrial history at that time. Trams and other transport items were not considered culturally significant and would often fall outside local museums' principal collecting remit.

The only exception for many years was the transport museum in Hull, established by the City Corporation as early as 1925. Here the notoriously acquisitive curator Thomas Sheppard built up an extensive collection of vehicles and transport-related material including two early trams with no local connection to the city. One was a horsecar from the Ryde (Isle of Wight) Pier Company, built in 1867 and used until 1935. The other was a steam tram built in 1882 by Kitson's of Leeds for the Portstewart Tramway in Northern Ireland, which closed in 1926. Both found a distant long-term home in Hull some time after withdrawal from their operational context as representative of vehicle types rather than any local relevance.[11] Sheppard also secured a fine large-scale model of an experimental tramcar designed and built in Hull Corporation's own workshops for exhibition at the British Empire Exhibition at Wembley in 1924. A full size electric tram was not added in the pre-war period while the city's trams were still running, but a Hull car of 1910 is now part of the transport collection displayed in the city's Streetlife Museum.[12]

Very little tram preservation came from official sources either at national or local level but a remarkable movement was to grow out of the efforts of individual groups of enthusiasts. In the post-war years the Light Railway Transport League (LRTL) continued its campaign for the modernisation of existing tramways, but as closures continued the thoughts of some members turned to what might be salvaged before they all disappeared. The first unplanned step was taken after an LRTL tour of the remaining tram system

Only one tram survives from Birmingham's once huge fleet of nearly 850 double-deck cars. Tram 395, built in 1913, was set aside by the council when the last routes were closed forty years later and is now on display in Thinktank, the city's science museum.

Thinktank

in Southampton in August 1948, shortly before buses were due to take over. Denis Dunstone describes what happened:

The tour was made on a fine day and, when the group passed a row of open-top trams stored out of service, a request was made to transfer to one of those. The accommodating management readily agreed and the tour continued in the condemned car, no.44. At the end of the day it was revealed that no.44's next journey would be to the scrapyard. This was too much for the visitors, and a decision was made to offer to buy it. The management agreed, and for £10 offered no.45, which was in better condition than no.44. Furthermore, they overhauled and painted it. The main problem was where to put it, but it was also necessary to raise £45 for its transportation. Eventually a home was found for it in a depot in Blackpool.[13]

Ian Yearsley, who remembers giving half-a-crown (2/6) to the appeal for no.45's

Breaking up cars at the Southampton tram dump in 1949. The enthusiasts who saved car 45 from this fate by buying it for £10 started a preservation movement that led eventually to the creation of the National Tramway Museum at Crich.

removal costs at his local LRTL branch meeting in Manchester, takes up the story of what was to inspire preservation progress in Britain once the Southampton car had been secured:

All this may have seemed like a foolhardy venture on the part of the LRTL members. But from the United States they already had several examples of what amateurs could do, not merely to preserve, but to operate trams. Branford Electric Railway Association, launched in 1945, had taken over an operating line in 1947and continued to run it, and a brief but telling description of this was published in the LRTL's journal Modern Tramway in November 1948. Two other American trolley museums, Seashore Electric Railway at Kennebunkport and the Connecticut Electric Railway museum at Warehouse Point, had also been formed....just as in the early days of electric tramways much of the technology came from across the Atlantic, so much of the inspiration for a concerted programme of tramway preservation in this country came in 1948 from America.[14]

In 1949 the LRTL set up a Museum Committee with the vision of creating a working tramway museum run by an enthusiast body. Various potential sites were considered but none seemed suitable or within the LRTL's financial resources. A number of individual tram preservation bids around the country failed when unsecured cars fell victim to vandalism or weather damage, and as more systems closed the division within the society about its essential purpose (preservation of the past or modernisation for the future) only grew. With these conflicting aims unresolved, it was decided in 1955 to

A former Bournemouth car on the Llandudno & Colwyn Bay Tramway in north Wales, 1953. This last remaining private tramway in the UK might have become the first working line in preservation but it was closed and dismantled two years later. TMS

establish a separate Transport Museum Society (TMS).

A scheme to take over and run the last remaining privately-run tramway in the country, the Llandudno & Colwyn Bay line in north Wales, looked briefly like a viable preservation opportunity in 1955. Plans for closure had been announced, but the asking price for the sale of the system nearly quadrupled during negotiations, and the project failed. This might have taken active tramway preservation in a different direction with a volunteer-run street railway in a seaside resort, but it was not to be.[15]

Breakthrough came in 1959 when a potential site was found for a working museum in a derelict limestone quarry at Crich, near Matlock in Derbyshire. It did not look particularly promising, but the site offered the prospect of both accommodation and a running track. The TMS agreed a lease, soon converted to a freehold, and volunteers got to work. Southampton 45, the tram that had started it all, arrived on site in October 1960. Trams stored in various locations were brought to Crich for restoration, new

buildings erected and track laid. From the start the museum followed a strategic, disciplined approach, becoming a limited company and an educational charity.

The first tram operation, using a preserved Sheffield horsecar, began in

When the Bradford system closed in 1950 the body of the last tram, number 104, was given to the city's Odsal sports stadium to serve as a scoreboard. A few years later the Council took it back and began a restoration project in its own transport workshops, which was completed in 1958. Since 1974 no.104 has been on static display in Bradford Industrial Museum alongside one of the trolleybuses that replaced it. OG

impressive start to a project which grew to attract over 100,000 visitors a year, and became far more than either an enthusiasts' plaything or a simple visitor attraction offering rides on old trams.

At Crich the TMS was soon to break new ground and set new standards in the operation of a volunteer run, but highly professional independent working museum. The title National Tramway Museum was adopted in 1980, and 'registered' status, the recognised quality standard for museums in the UK, was awarded by the government's Museums & Galleries Commission in 1990. In 1995, when the TMS celebrated its golden Jubilee year, the museum was also 'designated' for the quality and significance of its collections, which had grown to over sixty trams and a wide range of associated material through which to record, interpret and explain the history of tramways. For marketing purposes, and to attract a wider general audience beyond the enthusiasts and specialists, it was rebranded as 'Crich

1963. A year later electric cars were run 'under the wire' for the first time, public services beginning on 5 July 1964. As word spread around of what was happening at Crich, the public came and kept on coming. The electric cars carried 30,687 adults and 15,503 children in the first operating season in 1964. It was an

The main exhibition hall at Crich which covers the first century of tramways in Britain from the 1860s to the closure of the Glasgow system in 1962, with about 20 trams from the museum's large collection on display. OG

Tramway Village, home of the National Tramway Museum'.

Around the country other museums followed Crich's example by creating heritage tramways where visitors could see and ride on preserved and restored historic vehicles. Short working tramways were established at the East Anglian Transport Museum at Carlton Colville (opened in 1972), Beamish, the North of England Open Air Museum (1973) the Black Country Museum near Dudley, (1980), Heaton Park Tramway in Manchester (1980), The Museum of Scottish Industrial Life at Coatbridge, near Glasgow (1988) and the Wirral Heritage Tramway at Birkenhead (1995). Numerous other preservation projects have taken place involving the restoration of individual trams for static display in museums from the London Transport Museum in Covent Garden (opened in 1980) to the rail and road galleries of the Ulster Folk and Transport Museum at Cultra, near Belfast (opened in 1993).

Most of the working tramway projects took off in the first great heritage boom

of the 1970s and 80s, when open air museums developed on historic sites with rescued and reconstructed buildings became popular visitor attractions. Trams operating in authentically recreated street scenes with stone setts and traditional shops give successive generations who do not remember trams

A post-war Sheffield tram (left) and a Belfast trolleybus, both operating a long way from their original homes at the East Anglian Transport Museum, Carlton Colville, near Lowestoft, 2015. OG

Gateshead 10, built in 1925, was the first tram to arrive at Beamish Museum in County Durham, where it has been operating since 1973. The car has recently been repainted in the green British Railways livery it wore on the Grimsby & Immingham Tramway in the 1950s after the closure of the Gateshead system. OG

Newcastle 114, one of the original open-top electric cars supplied to the city in 1901 by Hurst Nelson of Motherwell. It was restored to operational condition at Beamish in the 1980s and is seen here at the museum after a full overhaul and repaint in 2015.
Paul Jarman/Beamish Museum

operating in Britain a convincing historical context. Beamish, Crich and the Black Country Museum all transcend any notion of being simply heritage theme parks, although other temporary tram operations like the popular Glasgow Garden Festival in 1988 have been equally enjoyable as pure entertainment.

There has also been a growing interest in re-purposing the considerable amount of tramway infrastructure which remains on our city streets, largely unnoticed, more than half a century after the trams have gone. Understandably, there was initially far more concern to save complete trams when they were disappearing, and the buildings associated with them were mostly far too large to be transferred to a museum site.[16] Many of them continued to function as bus garages or found new commercial uses, but with no sense of deliberately protecting them as heritage facilities.[17] In most cases those that are still in everyday use are better described as survivors than preserved structures.

Only a handful of historic tramway structures have been given the statutory protection of 'listing' by English Heritage (now the responsibility of Historic England) and the majority go unrecognised. They are, with a few exceptions, strictly functional sheds and maintenance buildings, and were never for public use. Hence they were rarely embellished with architectural flourishes or given the same care and attention in

The tramway at the Black Country Living Museum has been operating since 1980. This is Dudley and Stourbridge single-deck tram no.34, built locally at Tividale in 1920. The Albion Depot behind it here is a reconstruction based on Handsworth Tram Depot, built in the 1880s. OG

Riding on the Seaton Tramway in Devon, 2015. This is a modern, narrow gauge leisure tramway running on the trackbed of an attractive country branch line closed in 1966. The trams are miniature versions of full-size heritage trams, such as this passing London Feltham. OG

Restored Liverpool and Birkenhead electric cars running on the Wirral Heritage Tramway in Birkenhead, 2010. This is close to the site of Train's original horse-drawn street railway opened in 1860. OG

The Tramshed bar/restaurant now occupies the former depot in Bath, last used by trams in 1939. The adjacent power station building has been converted into offices and studios. OG

A computer generated impression of another tramshed, a new arts centre, performance space and creative industries hub opened in Cardiff in 2015. This is a conversion and re-use of the former Grangetown depot of Cardiff Corporation Tramways, built in 1902, which had become a council store after the trams' demise. TShed Developments/Ellis Williams Architects tramshed

The craftsmen of Coplawhill. Carpenters and painters in the body shop at Glasgow Corporation's famous tram building and overhaul works, 1926. Compare this to the same location as a modern art venue ninety years later (below).

After closure in 1962, part of Coplawhill was adapted to house Glasgow's first transport museum. When the museum moved out it became the Tramway arts centre. Here it is hosting the annual Turner Prize art show, held in Scotland for the first time in 2015. The original latticed roof and embedded tracks of the tram works remain above and below. OG

their design detail as Victorian railway stations. However, a number of them have been successfully converted in recent years to become bars, restaurants, offices, design workshops, theatres, and arts centres, with or without reference to their original purpose.

The latest ambitious project is a major scheme to redevelop a disused former tram depot in South Wales. It was built by Cardiff Corporation in 1902 at Grangetown, near the city centre, to house part of its new electric tram fleet. Transformation of this Grade 2 listed building into Tramshed, a substantial new arts centre and 'business incubator' for the creative industries, began in 2015. Its facilities will include two dance studios, an art gallery, live music venue, community space and studio/office units. A unique feature of this will be an exhibition gallery and café built into the surviving tram inspection and repair pits, last used for their original purpose seventy years ago in 1946.[18]

Apart from the depots, tramway power stations and offices have also survived for

adaptation to become, amongst other new uses, an industrial museum in Sheffield, a hotel in Leeds and apartments in Bristol.[19] The long disused northern access ramp to the Kingsway Subway in central London, with its conduit track still in place, is a well-known survivor. Less obvious is the original function of the prominent windowless brick building in the centre of

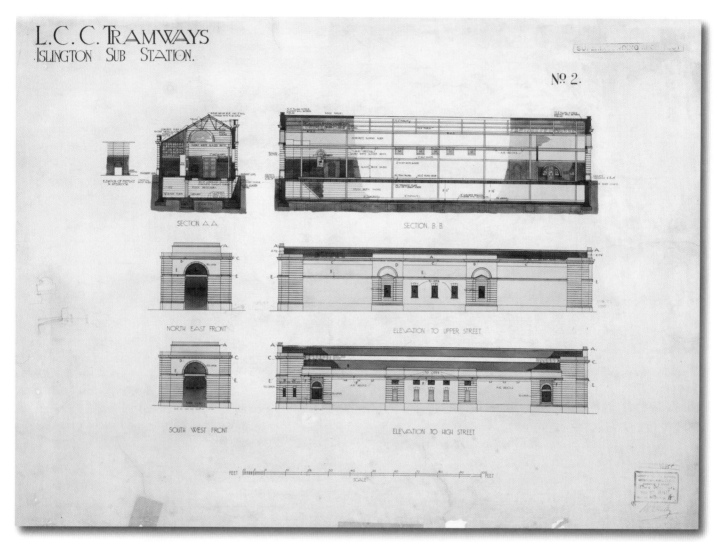

LCC architect's drawings of the tramway sub-station in Islington High Street, 1905. The design was a tribute to the style of Newgate prison, which had then just been demolished. Redundant and disused for over fifty years, the listed structure has been turned into a retail unit, seen here in 2010. LTM/TfL and OG

Islington High Street. It is now a large retail unit, but was built in 1905/6 as a London County Council Tramways (LCCT) sub-station.[20] The former LCCT power station which looms over the waterfront at Greenwich no longer supplies tramways but still houses an emergency back-up generator for the London Underground should the electricity supply from the national grid fail.

Light Rail

There was an almost universal belief in 1960s Britain that trams or any related form of electric street transport were features of the past, to be nostalgically remembered but only seen in a museum context. This was also true of their hybrid successor the electric trolleybus, which had been adopted by quite a number of towns in the 1930s but was now also on

The northern access ramp to the Kingsway Subway in Southampton Row, last used by London's trams in 1952, survives almost intact, with granite setts, tiled walls and conduit track all in place. Much of the Subway itself, including the underground tram station at Holborn, remains unchanged.
OG

First and last. Preserved 'Diddler' trolleybus no.1 at Fulwell, west London, on the final day of London's trolleybuses, 8 May 1962. This site was originally the LUT's largest tram depot, opened in 1902. It became London's first trolleybus depot in 1931 and has been part-used as a bus garage since 1962.
LTM/TfL

the way out. London Transport (LT), which by 1950 had the largest trolleybus system in the world, decided to standardise on diesel buses. A conversion programme began in 1958 and LT ended its last electric services in May 1962, four months before the last tram was withdrawn in Glasgow. Trolleybuses only lasted another ten years in Britain, the final system closure being Bradford, one of the original trolleybus pioneers in 1911. There was no financial advantage to running electric trolleybuses against the cost of modern diesels, and the oil crisis of 1973/4 came too late to have any impact on transport policy. The obvious environmental benefits of clean electric power on the streets were also given little thought at the time. The invisible but deadly air pollution of petrol and diesel emissions simply got worse as road congestion increased, particularly in urban areas.

Charles Oakley's final words in his epitaph for the last trams in Glasgow was typical of the general feeling at the time:

> *What the future holds for local public transport no one could possibly say. But it would almost certainly be a delusion to suppose that, after the last car has run on route no.9, tramcars will ever run in the streets of Glasgow again. They have reached the terminus.*[21]

Trams have not yet run again in Glasgow, but thirty years later they did appear again on the streets of Manchester at the start of the light rail renaissance in Britain. It was a long absence and the tram revival as a public transport mode rather than a heritage attraction in the 1990s needs some explanation.

While trams disappeared completely from Britain's local government and town planning agenda in the 1960s, many cities in Continental Europe continued to rely on trams as their main form of public transport. This was particularly true of the Communist Eastern Bloc countries aligned with the Soviet Union, where there was no private car market and public transport was the only available option for almost the entire population. In the USSR itself, government policy was to develop full metro systems for cities with a population of over one million, and many urban centres had large tram and trolleybus networks as well. Moscow and Leningrad (now St Petersburg) had two of the biggest tram systems in the world in the late twentieth century. East Germany retained nearly all of its tram systems after the war whilst Prague in Czechoslovakia and Budapest in Hungary continued to operate extensive city networks.

In Western Europe some cities such as Lisbon and Turin continued to run antiquated traditional trams, which have since become tourist attractions themselves. In Austria, Belgium, the Netherlands, Switzerland and West Germany in particular there was considerable new investment in tramway modernisation and rolling stock development from the 1970s. Only the smaller and hopelessly uneconomic systems disappeared in the post-war

The revival of light rail in Europe. Barcelona closed its last regular tram routes in 1971, apart from one short heritage line for tourists. New light rail routes were opened in the suburbs in 2003 using Alstom Citadis trams built in France. OG

period and by the fall of the Berlin Wall in 1989 there were still more than 150 tram systems across the whole of Europe. Cities in France, Italy and Spain, where public transport had declined in the 1950s and 60s, began investing in new tramways from the 1980s.[22]

In the US and Canada, where the majority of traditional streetcar lines had closed by the early 1960s, only seven major North American cities continued to operate street railways. Others planned new networks from the 1980s, looking at European precedents and turning to Germany in particular for technology and rolling stock. The long held American belief, particularly on the affluent west coast in California, that it was possible to satisfy everyone's desire for personal transport with ever more automobiles and continuous highway building in both rural and urban areas was becoming unsustainable. Even Los Angeles, the largest metropolitan area in the world, where nearly 30 per cent of land was given over to highways and almost 40 per cent more to vehicle parking, was running out of space. The first light rail metro line opened in that ultimate city of the automobile in 1990 and LA's rail-based rapid transit has continued to grow ever since.[23]

In 1972 the US Urban Mass Transportation Administration (UMTA, the precursor to the Federal Transit Administration) coined the term *light rail* to collectively describe new tram and streetcar transformations that were taking place in Europe and the United States. It became a new generic name which encompassed quite a wide range of new urban public transport systems from street line systems to operations on exclusive rights of way above or alongside roads and conventional railway lines. Edmonton in Alberta, Canada, was the first city in North America to introduce a complete new light rail

The steep grades and tight curves of the old city in Lisbon have led to the retention of tiny traditional trams in the Portuguese capital, a regular public service that has become a significant tourist attraction. These trams were last 'remodelled' in the 1980s from much older vehicles dating back to the 1930s and earlier. The operator, Carris, was originally a British owned company. OG

The Swedish capital Stockholm closed its original tram network in the 1960s. A short heritage line was opened in 1991 using historic streetcars in summer only. This has developed to become an extended year-round service called Sparvag City, with modern light rail vehicles. These are Bombardier Flexity Classic units introduced in 2012. OG

As the sole remaining tramway operator in mainland Britain after 1962, Blackpool continued its quirky mix of innovation and entertainment. *Tramnik One*, launched in 1963, was next in a long line of disguised and decorated trams designed to complement the town's annual illuminations.

The Tyne & Wear Metro, opened from 1980, is a cross between a light and heavy rail system, running entirely off road and mainly using former suburban rail lines. This 2003 view shows a Metro train crossing the River Wear in Sunderland, heading for Newcastle. Until 1954 Sunderland Corporation trams linked the two sides of the city over the Wearmouth road bridge on the left. OG

system in 1978, soon followed by San Diego in the USA. Since that time more than twenty North American cities have joined the light rail revival in addition to the handful of cities that never completely abandoned the trolley.[24]

Having closed all but one of their traditional street tramways, Britain and Ireland were not initially involved in any serious planning or commitment to new developments in urban light rail. The first

toe in the water of innovative public transport planning came in the mid-1970s when a proposal from the new Tyne and Wear Passenger Transport Authority was agreed for the metropolitan area around Newcastle and Wearside. The plans involved converting the existing, but run down network of local rail services into an electrified rapid transit system with new tunnels, viaducts and bridges linking them up and running directly below Newcastle and Gateshead city centres. Street running was not proposed, but it was intended to create an integrated local transport network with buses acting as feeders to purpose-built interchanges. The Tyne & Wear Metro, which opened in 1980, was the first modern light rail system in the UK, although strictly speaking it is a hybrid combining elements of light rail, heavy underground metro and longer distance suburban railway systems. Thirty-five years later nearly 40 million passenger journeys are being made annually and patronage is still growing.[25]

Despite its undoubted success and subsequent extension, the Tyne & Wear

Metro was not adopted as a model for urban transport planning in any other UK city. Government assistance for regional areas and especially expenditure on public transport was contrary to the privatising free market philosophy of the eighties. The Conservative government elected in 1979 did not support 'big state' spending on infrastructure projects and was keen to encourage the private sector, although the prime minister herself did cut the ribbon on the final section of the M25, London's new orbital motorway, in 1985.

Docklands Light Railway

The next light rail network in the UK was designed to meet a rather different agenda. When plans were formulated to redevelop the decayed and derelict former docklands of east London, it was realised that a new public transport system was essential to enable both commercial and residential regeneration. The original intention, in the 1970s, had been to extend London Underground's new Jubilee line eastwards, but by the early 1980s there was strong pressure from government to explore cheaper alternatives. Light rail – as opposed to express bus, guided bus or conventional Underground – was chosen as the most cost-effective transport solution.

In 1982 construction of the Docklands Light Railway (DLR) was authorised, designed as a stand-alone rapid transit system that provided a low-cost link between the isolated Isle of Dogs, where a new business hub was planned at Canary Wharf, and the existing financial centre in the city, together with wider areas of east London. Through re-using the trackbed of some derelict freight lines linked by new elevated sections featuring tight curves and steep gradients, the DLR would be the updated equivalent of a conventional tramway, though without any street running. It would employ articulated passenger cars based on the modern trams used in German cities, but with no drivers. The latest computer technology would allow remote, fully automated train control, and as the DLR would be off-street it could use third rail power pick-up instead of overhead wires. A complete

An early poster for the newly opened Docklands Light Railway (DLR) in east London, 1989. None of the office development in the derelict former West India Docks had yet taken off, but the towers of a massive new business and financial centre, Canary Wharf, would rise here in the 1990s. LTM/TfL

Most of the London DLR is elevated above ground level, with tight curves and steep gradients that are more like a tramway than a metro system. This view towards the City shows the complex central intersection of the main DLR branches near the Poplar hub in 2011. OG

great success, but a confident prediction in 1987 when it was about to launch, was rather wide of the mark:

The Docklands Light Railway has already acted as a catalyst in improving land use and employment opportunities in Docklands. It seems likely that it could provide a pattern for urban transport planning both in other parts of London and provincial cities in the 1990s.[27]

The benefits were genuine, but as ever, it proved unwise to predict even the short-term future. The boom and bust course of the British economy in the nineties, financial deregulation in the City and changes in government policy soon highlighted this.

A now almost forgotten private light rail scheme for the Bristol area was unveiled to the public and press in November 1987, only months after the opening of the DLR. This was the Avon Metro, promoted by a company called Advanced Transport for Avon (ATA), the brainchild of architect Brian Tucker and Richard Cottrell, the Conservative MEP for Bristol. Capitalising on the idea that the DLR had inflated the value and development potential along its route in east London, the Avon Metro was to be financed by land development along its lines. A start would be made by converting the old rail line through the Avon gorge out to Portishead, 'a route which passes sites fat with development potential' according to an enthusiastic endorsement in *The Times*.

Cottrell, who was the principal front-man for the scheme, claimed that it would not cost ratepayers or tax payers any money, but be 'a free gift to the people of Avon'. It was an unfortunate phrase, which seemed to echo the heady heyday of James Clifton Robinson when he advocated electric trams for Bristol in the 1890s. As ATA company secretary Jack Penrose told

initial network was built in just five years, all within a tight budget of £77m at a time when the estimated cost of a Tube extension to Docklands was £325m.[26]

The cost savings and apparent cheapness of the DLR soon proved short lived and largely illusory. In its early years, the DLR got a regular pasting in the London *Evening Standard* as an unreliable and overcrowded 'Mickey Mouse' system, unable to cope with the large number of new commuters to Docklands that needed to use it. Expensive reconstruction and upgrading of the control systems, extensions to the Bank, and into south and east London, with better connections and new, longer trains were all necessary in the 1990s. Above all, the DLR alone was clearly inadequate to serve the new fast growing business centre at Canary Wharf, and the extension of the Jubilee line, finally completed in 1999 at much greater expense, was still essential. After a bumpy early ride the DLR became, in the early twenty-first century, one of the fastest growing and most reliable rail systems in the country. In the long run it has been a

The Times nearly a century later 'This is a private enterprise project. The first major asset the company will have is the parliamentary bill. Once we have that we expect to raise money from the increase in land values resulting from the rail transit.'

In the bullish financial atmosphere of the late 1980s, the stock market was booming, property values were rising and on the edge of Bristol building work was under way on the large new suburb of Bradley Stoke. The Avon Metro scheme looked perfectly feasible, had support from Avon County Council and secured parliamentary approval for its first route in 1989.[28]

But by late 1991, ATA was in trouble. There was growing opposition to their plans and the economic downturn made fund raising difficult. The company was wound up in 1992 with debts of £3.8m.

Private finance alone was clearly not the most promising way forward for light rail schemes, but the idea of securing a substantial private sector contribution to new public transport projects did not go away. It had become lodged in Treasury thinking and the policies of both Conservative and later New Labour national politicians, slowing down the completion of new capital projects from the Channel Tunnel and High Speed One (HS1) to the Jubilee line extension (JLE) and new light rail schemes.

Manchester Metrolink
The project that eventually led to the laying of new rails in British city streets was quite different to either the Tyne & Wear Metro or the DLR, though it too was a hybrid solution to more than one urban

Looking west from Pontoon Dock station with a DLR train approaching, 2009. The roof of the O2 dome at North Greenwich is in the centre with the towers of Canary Wharf beyond. OG

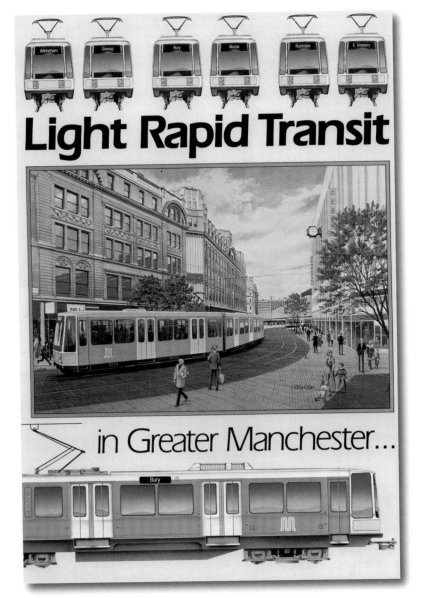

'Light Rapid Transit in Greater Manchester'. Brochure produced by the passenger transport executive in 1987 when a new light rail scheme was first proposed for Manchester. The schematic drawings showed very few wires and an almost empty city centre.

transport appeared, it was the trams that were thought to be blocking cars, vans and buses. Removing the trams after the war did not solve the problem, but passenger travel into and across the city became more difficult and inconvenient. Other public transport modes also went into decline and became less reliable as private car ownership grew. More people needed to travel to work in or across the city but could not do so easily by public transport, leading to a circle of decline. The underused and inconvenient local rail services into the city were rationalised to save money and Central station, one of the big termini, was closed but the Manchester metropolitan area's public transport remained fractured, particularly from north to south, and poorly co-ordinated.

A plan to link the existing suburban rail lines to Bury and Altrincham with a tunnel under the city centre in a scheme similar to the Tyne & Wear Metro was proposed in the 1970s, but rejected by the government as too expensive. Neither Greater Manchester Council (GMC) nor British Rail (BR) could afford it without central government support, and grants were difficult to secure and subject to strict criteria. The 'Pic-Vic' plan, which would have linked the main Piccadilly and Victoria rail stations below Manchester, was abandoned in 1977.

A cheaper urban rail system running partly on the streets was first promoted by GMC in 1984 and referred to in the council's publicity as Light Rapid Transit (LRT) or Project Light Rail. It was described as 'a cross between a tram and a train'. The plan now was a phased approach to converting a number of the city's radiating suburban rail lines to being worked by 'supertrams' which could also work on the street. It would combine segregated suburban light railway operation with a street tramway link across the city centre, where some sections would be shared with pedestrians

transport issue. This was Manchester Metrolink, which when it opened in 1992 was the first street running tramway in Britain for thirty years. Its painfully slow early gestation underlines how tortuous and complicated urban transport planning had become in late twentieth-century Britain.

Manchester had long faced issues of traffic congestion in the city centre. In the 1920s this had often been caused by horse-drawn goods wagons travelling to and from the big railway goods warehouses blocking the main city thoroughfares for electric trams. Later, as other mechanical

and other vehicles. For the UK, this was a radical concept.

In 1987, when powers and funding had been secured for the initial phase of the network to go ahead, the brand name Metrolink was introduced. Construction work by a public/private consortium began in 1990. The two heavy rail suburban lines north to Bury and south to Altrincham were converted to light rail operation, linked together across Manchester with street running between Victoria and Piccadilly stations.

The originally quoted six-week conversion programme of the former rail lines turned into a six-month delay but once operational Metrolink was a great success as the UK's first modern street-running rail system. Phase One was ceremonially opened by the Queen in July 1992. In its first year Metrolink was expected to carry 10m passengers; in fact it has exceeded that original target in every year since then. A survey in 1994 found that 10 per cent of Metrolink passengers were former car users, important evidence that light rail could encourage commuters to change their travel mode. This trend continued as Metrolink expanded, and in a later survey in 2012 it was found that around *one third* of the commuting residents of the Metropolitan Borough of Bury used Metrolink for their regular journey into Manchester.[29]

During the 1990s, the former industrial areas along the Manchester Ship Canal in Salford were designated for regeneration with a mix of commercial, housing, leisure and cultural facilities. Phase 2 of Metrolink featured a new branch to Eccles

Metrolink brought trams back to central Manchester in 1992 but with scant attention to the design impact on the streetscape. Much of the original infrastructure in the city centre now looks clunky and over-engineered, with ugly, heavy duty support columns, and intrusive boarding platforms creating unattractive clutter. OG

Three transport modes in central Manchester: tram, train and canal. This is the Deansgate-Castlefield tram/train interchange in 2010, which has since been upgraded. The original T68 trams, seen in the foreground coupled as a pair unit, were soon to be superceded. OG

First and second generation Metrolink trams at Salford Quays. The original Italian-built T68 units (left) have been replaced on all services by a fleet of Bombardier Flexity Swift trams built in Austria (right), which are quieter, roomier and more accessible. OG

running through 'Salford Quays' as the area was now renamed. It was planned on an entirely new alignment that had never been used as a railway, a mixture of private right of way, reserved track and street running like a conventional tramway. This line, adopting the same theory of 'regeneration boost' already seen with the DLR in London, was to be a key factor in the continuing development of Salford Quays and later the new Media City complex in particular. Prime Minister Tony Blair, opening the first section of the Eccles line in December 1999, praised Metrolink as 'exactly the type of scheme needed to solve the transport problems of the metropolitan areas of the country.'[30]

In 2000 officials and transport planners in Greater Manchester considered Metrolink to be a 'phenomenal success'. It was certainly a major contributor to the city region's economic and cultural resurgence long before the current buzzwords 'Northern Powerhouse' had been coined. The system had grown to 24 route miles (39km), exceeded passenger targets, reduced traffic congestion on roads running parallel to its lines and phase 2 had been mainly privately funded. Consequently, when the Government's Transport Act 2000 required all passenger transport executives (PTEs) to produce local transport plans, Manchester's top priority was an ambitious third phase of Metrolink expansion to create four more new lines in Greater Manchester. This would eventually tie in Oldham, Rochdale, Ashton, Didsbury and Manchester Airport to the growing regional light rail network.[31]

Sheffield Supertram

Before considering what happened to UK light rail in the early twenty-first century, it is worth looking at the other development that had planned to follow in Manchester's wake in the 1990s. Parliamentary approval for Britain's

second new generation light rail scheme, in urban South Yorkshire, was given in 1985, but the final go-ahead from the Government only came in 1990. The system was for Sheffield, the last English town to close its original tram system thirty years earlier in 1960. The city is much smaller than Manchester, but building a new light rail system here was a considerable challenge because of the hilly nature of parts of the urban area and the need for major new viaducts and elevated sections.

Sheffield Supertram was built by South Yorkshire Passenger Transport Executive (SYPTE) at a cost of £240m and opened in stages between 1994 and 1995. It was initially operated by South Yorkshire Supertram Ltd (SYSL), a wholly owned subsidiary company of SYPTE, but this changed with the deregulation of bus services which was taking place across the country. After earning lower than expected passenger revenue income, Supertram was sold to bus operator Stagecoach in 1997 for £1.15m. The PTE still owns the infrastructure and Stagecoach was given the contract to operate and maintain the trams on a long term-concession until

Sheffield Supertram found itself in damaging competition with newly deregulated bus services when it first opened in 1994/5. Since 1997 it has been run under contract by Stagecoach and is now co-ordinated with that company's bus operations. This view at the rail station stop in 2006 was taken just before all the trams were extensively refurbished and given a new livery. OG

A Sheffield tram carrying the later Stagecoach livery at the Park Square delta junction between the three main branches of the network, 2012. The driver is changing the points manually to switch his tram to a right turn after crossing the bowstring girder bridge from the city centre. OG

2024, integrating Supertram services with its Sheffield bus operations.

The Supertram network consists of three lines that all serve the city centre and operate on a mix of on-street tracks, reserved right of way and former railway alignment. One line runs north east from Sheffield up the formerly industrial Don Valley to the giant Meadowhall shopping centre, another northwest to Middlewood and Malin Bridge, and the third south east to Halfway and Herdings Park.

Unlike Metrolink none of the Supertram system operates over former passenger rail lines through existing stations with high platforms. This meant the rather intrusive city centre street infrastructure in Manchester, with high

ramped boarding platforms at each stop, was not required anywhere in Sheffield. Where Phase One of Metrolink seemed sometimes like an engineer's belt-and-braces practical approach with little concern for aesthetics, Supertram was more carefully designed to have minimum impact on the urban environment. Instead of thick, black support columns for the overhead wiring, for example, there are a minimal number of slim traction poles.

The fleet of German Siemens-Duewag three-car articulated trams built for Sheffield is also a more elegant and reliable design than Metrolink's original T68 trams supplied by Italian rail engineering consortium AnsaldoBreda, which had massive dodgem-car bumper units covering the couplers at either end. Manchester garnered the plaudits for its new tram system, soon inevitably described as 'iconic' of the city and regularly featured in the street scenes of TV series made on location in the area.[32] Sheffield attracts far less media interest than culturally cool Manchester, but it is fair to say that from the start Supertram set a higher standard of urban public realm design. It owed more to modern French and German practice in creating high quality infrastructure for the city, better integrated with an improved street environment. This has been emulated by later UK systems, including Metrolink's own subsequent extensions and adaptation for the second city crossing in Manchester.[33]

Writing in 1995 about the resurgence of interest in light rail for urban transport across most of Europe, a leading tramway specialist commented that British progress 'continues to be hampered by the financial stringency of the government'.[34] In the UK, proposals were then being prepared for new tramway systems to follow Manchester and Sheffield in the West Midlands (Birmingham-Wolverhampton), Leeds, south London (Croydon), Liverpool, Nottingham, Bristol, south Hampshire (Portsmouth – Fareham) and Glasgow, some of which would fail.

In late 1994 the Government announced that it was willing to provide funding for Midland Metro and Croydon Tramlink, subject to significant private sector involvement. This parsimonious approach to public transport infrastructure funding, coupled with the slow and bureaucratic authorisation process, meant that these were the only two additional light rail schemes to open in Britain by the turn of the century. Meanwhile France had already reintroduced trams to Nantes (1985), suburban Paris (1992), Rouen (1994) and Strasbourg (1994). Ironically, the futuristic low-floor cars for the

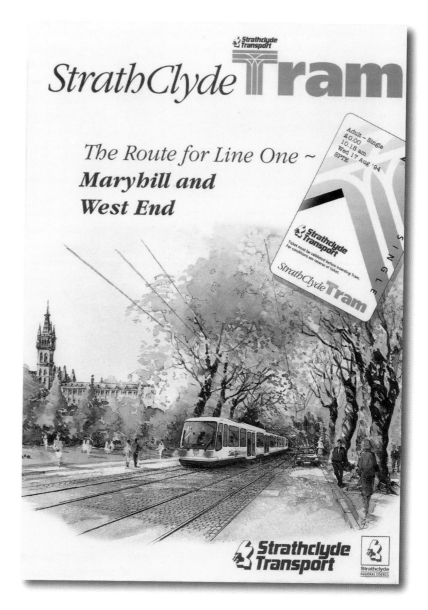

Strasbourg system were built in England by ABB in York, while all the new British systems imported their trams from continental manufacturers.[35]

Midland Metro

A century ago there was a network of electric tramways all over the industrial West Midlands and the Black Country between Birmingham and Wolverhampton, run by various council and company operators. Birmingham Corporation, which developed the largest system, replaced its last trams in 1953.[36] Throughout the area local rail services had been cut back since

Strathclyde Tram proposals promoted in a public consultation leaflet by the PTE, 1994. Plans to bring light rail back to Glasgow were abruptly abandoned soon afterwards and have not been revived. The city which once had the finest tram network in the UK now suffers from poor public transport links and still has no rail access to its airport.

The arrival point at Birmingham Snow Hill for Midland Metro trams, 2002. The extension route opened in 2016 by-passes this unwelcoming bunker of a station to run across the city centre on the streets, giving the trams much greater visibility. OG

the 1960s while road traffic had increased dramatically, making bus services less reliable. By the 1970s public transport across the region was in decline while new road building was failing to keep pace with the rise of the private car and creating swathes of bleak urban wasteland.

In the 1980s Centro, the West Midlands Passenger Transport Executive, in partnership with local authorities, decided to promote a light rail system for the West Midlands conurbation as part of its overall transport strategy. By 1993 it had obtained Parliamentary powers to build some 80km of new light rail schemes in the area. This would make it the biggest system in the country, taking WMPTE some way towards their ultimate aspiration to create a regional tramway network of about 200km. Government policy now required Centro to use what it called a DBOM package (Design, Build, Operate and Maintain) an

approach which was intended to ensure the maximum involvement of the private sector. This lengthy process, following the government's 'going for growth' strategy, meant that it was another two years before a suitable funding package was agreed and any work could begin.[37]

Altram, a consortium of developers, won the construction tender and started work on Line One in 1995. It was built mainly on the disused former Great Western Railway alignment from Birmingham Snow Hill to Wolverhampton. This passes through West Bromwich, Wednesbury and Bilston, where the tramway leaves the former rail route to run on a short street section and over a viaduct to the centre of Wolverhampton.

Midland Metro Line One opened in 1999, operated by a fleet of articulated trams built in Italy by the suppliers of Manchester's original cars. The total route length is 12.5 miles (20.1km), with eleven of the twenty-three tram stops directly replacing former and long closed railway stations. Unfortunately the trams soon proved to be too small and cramped, developing a reputation for unreliability. The overcrowding and disruption that followed may have contributed to the underperformance of Midland Metro. It has not attracted the predicted passenger numbers (still fewer than 5m passengers a year), nor led to the hoped for relief of road traffic congestion along the route.

For whatever reason, residents of the West Midlands were not leaving their cars at home and taking the tram. In contrast to Metrolink, which has grown to provide a highly visible, comprehensive and well-used transport system for Greater Manchester, Midland Metro has made painfully slow progress towards its original objectives of becoming a light rail network for a wider area. Its lack of street presence and the grim, unattractive low-level terminus at Snow Hill have not helped. Plans to extend the Birmingham end of the route on the street across the city centre to New Street station and beyond were announced in 1997, but after long delays in construction only just reached the first phase of completion and operation in 2016. A fleet of new trams for the extended tramway and their very obvious street presence in the heart of the city should at last give light rail a substantial boost in a conurbation which has been car dominated for decades.

A Metro expansion package has now been agreed under the Midlands Growth Strategy being developed by the Greater Birmingham & Solihull Local Enterprise Partnership. Centro plans to appoint a single designer and contractor to deliver ambitious extensions to the Midland Metro tramway over the next decade. This will include extended street running right across the city centre and south to Edgbaston with another line running east to Chelmsley Wood and the National Exhibition Centre/Airport/HS2 Interchange, then on to Solihull. This has an estimated cost of £470m. If this can be

delivered in the same timeframe as the first phase of HS2, projected to open in 2026, light rail should have a substantial impact across the conurbation, but Midland Metro still has a very long way to go before it can live up to its name.[38]

Wolverhampton St George's, the other end of Midland Metro Line One, with an original Italian Firema tram built in 1998 (left) and a newly delivered Alstom Citadis unit from France (right), 2014. PL Chadwick

Croydon Tramlink
In 1986 a report called *Light Rail for London* was produced jointly by London Regional Transport (LRT)[39] and British Rail. It looked at forty possible

Tracklaying for the Midland Metro outside the rebuilt New Street railway station (on the left), 2015. Work on the new tramway proceeded at a snail's pace and the short extension on the streets across the city centre from Snow Hill was not ready for another year. OG

Postcard view of East Croydon station, c1910, with two trams on the Addington route, opened in 1901 and closed in 1927.

Light Rail Study carried out by LRT with the London Borough of Croydon in 1987.

Croydon, in outer south London, was then Britain's tenth most populous town outside central London, with the greatest concentration of office space and the largest urban shopping centre in the south east. Its main transport links have always been the radial north-south links with London, rather than east-west links across the suburbs. The study found that workers and business customers came from far beyond Croydon borough and that the car was usually their automatic mode of choice for travel. The adverse environmental effects of this on quality of life, road safety, bus service reliability and access to car parking were all highlighted as issues to be addressed.

The study concluded that a light rail system could help Croydon sustain its successful development as an alternative to costly and environmentally damaging road schemes. Light rail in this area was

opportunities for conversion of existing or disused rail lines across the capital to light rail operation, as a way of increasing passenger usage and providing improved links across the city. Croydon Tramlink was to be the first and only light rail idea for London to be taken further and become a reality in the 1990s. This followed the more detailed *Croydon Area*

The same view of East Croydon station in 2009. The railway station was completely rebuilt in 1996 and trams returned four years later with the opening of the Tramlink network. OG not, like the DLR, about kick starting regeneration but about access and sustainability for a thriving suburban hub threatened by growing car traffic and congestion. Unusually, there was a consensus across the local political spectrum in Croydon, then a Conservative-led council, that public transport, and light rail in particular, had to play an increasing role in satisfying the mobility demands of local residents and employers. At this time most journeys within and across all of outer London were made by car and not public transport.[40]

After further detailed study and public consultation on prospective routes, the Croydon Tramlink Parliamentary Bill was deposited in 1991 and eventually approved in 1994. It was to be a Public Finance Initiative (PFI) with LRT and Croydon Council as joint promoters and a consortium of private companies running the concession to design, build, operate and maintain the new system. Tramtrack Croydon Ltd (TCL), who won the contract, was a partnership comprising FirstGroup, Bombardier (who built the trams), Sir Robert McAlpine and Amey (who built the system) Royal Bank of Scotland and 3i (who arranged the finance).

Tramlink utilises former rail corridors for almost half its length, with some completely new alignments and street running in central Croydon. There are three main branches and a spur, all running east and west out of the town and across the borough. Three of these terminate with interchanges to suburban rail lines at Wimbledon (also on the Underground), Elmers End (the spur) and Beckenham Junction, while the fourth gives a first rail link to New Addington with its large, isolated housing estates developed from the 1960s but with only buses as public transport.

Main construction began in 1997 and was completed by 1999 when all twenty-four trams required were delivered on

schedule. The articulated units, with their 76 per cent low-floor interiors providing a high level of accessibility, were built in Vienna by Bombardier to a proven, reliable design already used in Cologne, Germany, since 1995. From the start of the, project it was made clear that all technical aspects should be tried and tested in order to keep costs within a tight budget, and this was successfully achieved.

Tramlink opened in May 2000, just as Transport for London (TfL) took over from LRT as the capital's transport authority. Within weeks the trams were carrying 50-60,000 riders a day, increasing by 2-3 per cent each month. In the system's first year of operation, with around 16m passengers, the number of town centre shoppers in Croydon was up by 11 per cent and the use of car parks down by 6 per cent. Up to 25 per cent of riders surveyed said that they had previously used cars for their journey, more than double the modal shift that planners had predicted in three years. Tramlink was having exactly the impact on local travel in outer London that had been hoped for, but much faster.

In 2008 TfL purchased Tramlink from TCL, and it is now operated as a concession by FirstGroup. The system has remained extremely well used, reaching 32.3 million passengers in 2014/15, the

North End, Croydon, with one of the last London Transport trams heading for Thornton Heath, c1949. This is one of the principal shopping streets in the town centre and is now free of all traffic. Tramlink now crosses at this point in one direction, running from right to left on George Street.
LTM/TfL

A Tramlink unit passing the historic almshouses of Whitgift Hospital on George Street, Croydon, 2010. OG

third busiest light rail network in the UK behind the Tyne & Wear Metro and the DLR. Remarkably, Tramlink's 28km of routes in one part of suburban south London currently carries more passengers than Metrolink's 77km network across much of Greater Manchester, though light rail use in Manchester is growing twice as fast and will soon overtake it if current trends continue.[41]

Tramlink has added new high-capacity German Stadler trams to its fleet, built a second platform at Wimbledon and improved service frequency to meet growing demand. Despite its success there have been no route extensions, nor has light rail been introduced to other parts of Greater London, although both were considered by TfL. A West London Tram scheme was announced by the then Mayor of London, Ken Livingstone, in 2002. It would have run along the congested Uxbridge Road through the western suburbs from Uxbridge to Shepherd's Bush, following exactly the same path as the original London United tram route opened a century earlier. It was forecast that the tramway would carry 50m passengers a year and based on the experience of Tramlink it was anticipated that nearly 20 per cent of them would have switched from using a car to the tram for their journey.

West London Tram proved to be a contentious proposal, with public opinion along the route more or less divided on the issue. Several consultation exercises and opinion polls reported contradictory results of narrow majorities for and against the tram. Supporters of the scheme saw trams as environmentally friendly and a more effective solution to traffic congestion on the narrow Uxbridge Road corridor than buses. Opponents expressed the view that street running trams on the whole route would actually increase congestion because other traffic would simply be displaced from the A40 on to side roads, particularly in Ealing. All three local councils along the route opposed the scheme and in 2007 the project was postponed indefinitely by TfL.

A second light rail scheme proposed by TfL would have brought trams back to the streets of inner London. Cross River Tram was planned to run on a 16km north-south route from Camden Town via Holborn, over Waterloo Bridge with split branches to Brixton and Peckham. Its main benefit would have been south of the river where it could relieve overcrowding on the Northern and Victoria Underground lines and improve public transport in the Peckham area, which has no Tube and relies largely on buses. Southwark Council backed the tram plan as a regeneration benefit to some deprived parts of south-east London, but funding was not available to take this forward in 2007. When Boris Johnson succeeded Livingstone as mayor in 2008, Cross River Tram was removed from TfL's next ten-year business plan. In his foreword to the plan the Mayor announced that although the scheme had 'much merit' he could not justify further expenditure on it. 'I believe the £19m we are due to spend on its development would be better spent on improving existing public transport capacity.'

Dublin Luas

The demise of the urban electric tram in Ireland followed a similar course and timescale to British cities. The Dublin United Tramways Company (DUTC)

began replacing its trams with buses in 1938. At that time the DUTC was still an independent company outside municipal control, and the decision to abandon the city's trams was a purely financial one. Buses were cheaper to run and it appeared to be the only way that the company could remain profitable in the face of competition.

During the war a Transport Bill was introduced to establish a national transport corporation for the Republic of Ireland. The CIE took over both the DUTC and the country's railway companies in 1945. By 1949 the rest of the Dublin city tram system had gone, although the separate Hill of Howth Tramway nearby, also now run by CIE, lingered on for another ten years. The only other remaining urban system on the island, the Belfast network in Northern Ireland, had closed in 1954.[42]

For over thirty years peaks of modest prosperity alternated with troughs of deep depression in Ireland. But even during better economic times successive governments resisted every proposal to invest in public transport infrastructure. The CIE was already losing money in the 1950s, and under strong government pressure to reduce costs, began to close

The Tramlink network has not been extended, but in 2011 TfL was able to order additional trams to improve service frequency. German-based Stadler Rail have supplied ten of their latest Variobahn trams, a design already being delivered to a new system in Bergen, Norway. The first Variobahn unit entered service in 2012. TfL

The Dublin Luas Red Line terminus and interchange at Connolly station, opened in 2004. The Alstom Citadis articulated trams on this line were all extended in 2007 from three to five-section cars to cope with rapidly growing passenger demand. Each unit can carry 80 people seated plus 276 standing. OG

some local rail lines in Dublin as well and replace these too with buses. Public transport services continued to decline, but politicians remained firmly wedded to road building as a strategy.

Eventually, after commissioning an external review from transport consultants AM Vorhees, the CIE published a plan for a system of rapid transit rail lines for Dublin in the 1970s. This never came to fruition and nearly all transport spending in the eighties was on new motorways. Planning in Dublin was in a mess, with no consistent leadership either from the city council or the government. As Donal Murray, a writer who grew up in the city at this time has put it 'By the 1990s it was painfully obvious that the city of Dublin was gradually choking with motor traffic, and that things would only get worse if nothing was done.'[43]

The idea of a light rail system for the city resurfaced, following similar routes to the proposed 1970's scheme. The 1996 Dublin Light Rail Act created the legal framework to move forward, but a change of government in the following year proved disastrous to the project. Vested political interests ensured that yet another

report recommended fundamental changes which set the scheme back and dramatically increased costs.

Light rail became a political football for a while as the option of a tunnel under central Dublin was considered. Eventually, the government decided to go ahead with two physically separate tram routes. Line A (later the Red Line) would run east-west from Connolly Station through Dublin's Northside, then over the River Liffey and southwest to Tallaght and Saggart. Line B (later the Green Line) would be from St Stephen's Green through the south of the city via Sandyford to Bride's Glen. This mostly follows the route of the old Harcourt Street railway line, closed in 1958 to save money. According to some accounts the path of the former railway was 'reserved for possible re-use' although this seems unlikely as most of the bridges had been immediately dismantled. Rebuilding the infrastructure for the Green Line, and the installation of a spectacular cable-stayed suspension bridge near Dundrum,[44] was very expensive and the decision to separate the routes meant that two depots were required, one for each line. Fortunately the cost of the Red Line, much of which is street-running, was offset by EU funding of €82.5m.

Dublin's light rail system was named 'Luas' (the Irish language word for speed) and responsibility for developing it was transferred from CIE to a new government body, the Railway Procurement Agency (RPA). Construction work began in 2001, with Ansaldo of Italy and MVM getting the contract to build the system. Maintenance and operation was to be by Veolia Transport Ireland (formerly known as Connex) with articulated low-floor Citadis trams manufactured in La Rochelle by French multinational Alstom. Construction delays pushed the original launch date back by a year, but both lines were opened

A Dublin tram crossing the River Liffey on the Luas Red Line, 2012. The historic Sean Heuston Bridge, originally called the King's Bridge when it opened in 1821, was renovated and strengthened in 2003 to take the weight of trams. OG

in 2004. The total cost of the original Red and Green lines was €728m. Work is now under way to link the Red and Green lines with the BX line. This will run through the city centre from St Stephens Green and on to Broombridge, opening in 2017.

When Luas was being planned it was highly controversial, often dismissed in the Irish media as a white elephant that would be a burden on the taxpayer and which would make no difference to traffic congestion. In fact Dublin's commuters took to Luas immediately, and a significant number of them were former weekday car users. Luas also broke even and started to be operationally profitable sooner than had been expected. Claims of a negative effect on city centre businesses have also been completely disproved. By 2007, three years after the opening of the first two lines, some 28.4m journeys a year were being made on Luas. There were soon calls for further light rail schemes in Ireland but the world financial crisis in 2008 and the subsequent recession, which

was particularly serious in Ireland, led to the cancellation or postponement of nearly all big infrastructure projects.

Nottingham Express Transit
Construction work on the Nottingham Express Transit (NET) project began in June 2000, one month after the opening of

Riding a Luas tram in Dublin, 2012. The design of the moquette seating fabric includes well known features of the city such as the Ha'penny Bridge (right). OG

Market Street, Nottingham, from Old Market Square, c1910. The city's first-generation electric trams shown here were replaced by motor and trolleybuses between 1927 and 1936.

Market St & Queen Victoria Statue, Nottingham.

Twenty-first century revival at the same location. A Nottingham Express Transit (NET) tram entering Old Market Square in 2005. The five section articulated cars were the first 100 per cent low-floor trams in Britain, built locally in the UK to a design developed by ABB Transportation (Adtranz), whose Derby factory was taken over by Bombardier before construction began. OG

Tramlink in Croydon. NET was the first new tramway to be authorised by the Labour Government elected in 1997, which was determined to improve local transport around the country. The government set out ambitious targets to reduce car use in urban areas and under the Transport Act 2000 required all passenger transport authorities to produce a plan which would address environmental and access needs. At the time there were up to twenty-five new tramway schemes in preparation around the country.

By the time the first phase of NET opened four years later in March 2004, all but one of the other new light rail schemes had been turned down, cancelled or abandoned. There was a policy shift in the new Department for Transport (DfT) from support for tramways to dismissing them nearly everywhere in favour of buses. This was largely because of cost and an apparent failure to offer 'value for money' under government scrutiny. NET became not only the first new UK tramway to open in the first decade of the twenty-first century but also the last. The minister who launched NET in 2004, alongside the Sheriff of Nottingham, was Alastair Darling, who as Secretary of State for Transport presided over several tram project cancellations. Ironically, the only new tramway scheme that did survive was for Edinburgh, which Darling represented as an MP at Westminster.

Scotland was beyond the DfT's remit after devolution and the creation of a separate Scottish Parliament in 1999.

Nottingham's plans to create a light rail system began in the late 1980s when the city and county councils worked in partnership with Nottingham Development Enterprise (NDE), a private sector body charged with promoting regeneration. They needed a project that could help with the restructuring of the local economy and reverse growing social problems. The old employment base of the area was withering, with remaining local coal mines and breweries closing and other traditional industries such as Raleigh Cycles and Imperial Tobacco winding down. The city's ageing shopping malls, built in the city centre in the 1970s, faced competition from newer out of town retail centres in Sheffield and Leicester that were more accessible by car. Nottingham needed to attract new employers and improve access from outside and within the city, both to the centre and to the business parks and university beyond it. The city's existing park-and-ride system using buses, introduced in the early 1970s, was already proving inadequate and did not encourage enough people out of their cars.

The hope was that light rail could provide a step change towards achieving the future vision for Nottingham, but it was to take sixteen years from conception to the opening of the first line. The councils and NDE created Greater Nottingham Rapid Transit to handle preparatory processes, including developing the public-private partnership underpinning NET's delivery. A private Bill was set before parliament in 1991 and after a lengthy process, the Greater Nottingham Light Rapid Transit Act was given Royal Assent in 1994.

This was only the first milestone. Pat Armstrong, the original NET project director, has described the next five years

as the most difficult, during which his team had to maintain local commitment and enthusiasm while convincing successive Transport Ministers of the scheme's worth. There was a significant change of national government in May 1997 from Conservative to Labour and with local government reorganisation in the same year Nottingham City became a unitary authority taking on transportation responsibility, including the NET team. Looking back on the prolonged evolution of NET after his retirement in 2012, Armstrong recalled that:

On many occasions…people said we would not succeed. Much time was spent waiting for decisions while thinking what more we could do to provide the convincing case and ensure the project structure remained consistent with a rapidly changing finance environment…The period also saw the adoption by Government of the Private Finance Initiative (PFI), creating substantial additional work to significantly alter contractual documents and bidding arrangements. This involved

Transport Secretary Alastair Darling at the official opening of NET in 2004. At the time he had just rejected all but one of the new UK tram proposals as being 'poor value for money'. The exception that went ahead was Edinburgh, authorised by the Scottish Parliament, which became the most costly and controversial project of them all. Nottingham City Council/Daljit Phullar

A civilised city environment: people and trams but no cars in Waverley Street, just five minutes' walk from the centre of Nottingham, December 2014. A well-used park and ride service is linked to the NET trams. At present no other urban area in Britain looks set to follow this example of progressive and integrated transport planning. OG

NET required an additional fleet of larger trams for its Phase 2 expansion and followed Dublin Luas in selecting Alstom Citadis units. These are the first three new trams to arrive at the Wilkinson Street depot in Nottingham from Alstom's Barcelona factory in 2013.

www.neilhoylephotography.com

groundbreaking process development, closely shadowed by HM Treasury officials keen to see NET as a pathfinder project for local government involvement in PFI.[45]

At £200m NET was then the largest local authority PFI project and contractually extremely complex. By the time the Government, local authority and private

sector partners were all formally signed up, and construction work could begin on Phase One, over 200 agreements, schedules and related documents had been drawn up.

It was this exhaustive (and no doubt exhausting) planning and financial process rather than physical construction difficulties that delayed NET's initial completion. However, it can also be argued that this meticulous preparation and management, along with unusually positive partnership working by all involved with the project, was largely responsible for NET becoming the only new tram system in the UK to be an instant success in every respect. Whilst others are only gradually starting to carry the numbers of passengers that was hoped for, NET has exceeded the most optimistic predictions and did so from the start.

In its first ten years from 2004 to 2014 it provided some 90m passenger journeys. NET Line One has underpinned widespread economic and social benefits for the city, and this supported the case for extending the system south and south

west of the city centre. Phase Two has been developed as a second PFI scheme, further complicated by the financial crash of 2008, another change of national government in 2010 and the need to part fund the expansion locally through a Workplace Parking Levy (WPL). Nottingham is the first and so far only city in the UK to use such a scheme, which places a levy on city employers who provide eleven or more parking places, a bold approach to public transport funding which no other local authority seems willing to adopt.

Phase Two construction work began in 2012 and although subject to some months' delay, both new lines to Clifton and Chilwell opened in August 2015, doubling the size of the NET system. This means that over 30 per cent of Greater Nottingham's population now live within 800m of a tram stop, the only urban area in the UK where this is the case. Some of the city's largest employers, including the Queen's Medical Centre, the University of Nottingham's main campus, the ng2 business park and many other workplaces, to which around 55,000 employees commute, will benefit.

Edinburgh Trams
Edinburgh is the only other UK city to build and open a new tramway in the twenty-first century, but it has been the opposite of Nottingham's success story. A big infrastructure project is rarely trouble free, but the saga of Edinburgh Trams has been particularly fraught mainly, it would seem, through poor contract specification and project management. At the time of writing it is subject to a full public inquiry in Scotland to determine just how and

The long awaited extensions doubled the size of the NET system. Trams now run beyond the original Nottingham Station terminus over two new branches to park and ride stops at Clifton South and Toton Lane. Here two of the new Citadis trams cross at the station stop on opening day in August 2015.

Nottingham City Council/Tracey Whitefoot

Edinburgh's last traditional double-deck tram decorated for the final run, November 1956.

why it went so badly wrong and almost led to the project's cancellation.

Edinburgh's first generation electric tramways were closed down in 1956. Since then public transport in the city and the surrounding Lothian area has consisted of buses and a limited network of commuter rail lines. Proposals for a new light rail network were first made in the 1990s at a time when many other UK cities were considering light rail after the reappearance of trams in Manchester and Sheffield. On 4 June 1999 an optimistic headline in the *Herald* newspaper announced confidently to Scotland 'Capital on track to see return of the trams'. Nobody imagined at this stage that the return would take another fifteen years to achieve, fifty-seven years after trams had last been seen on Princes Street and at far greater cost than any other UK tram project.

By 2001 plans for a network of three routes were being drawn up as a public/private partnership led by Edinburgh City Council, who established an arms-length company, Transport Initiatives Edinburgh (TIE), to project manage the construction. All three routes were to pass through the city centre, one circling the northern suburbs, the other two radial lines running west to

Newbridge and south to Newcraighall. Two bills to reintroduce a tram network were passed by the Scottish Parliament in March 2006, but funding the entire network was deemed impossible. Line 3, to be paid for by a proposed Edinburgh congestion charge, was dropped when the congestion charge idea was defeated in a referendum.

By 2007 the tram scheme had already become a political football in the Scottish Parliament, but a report by Audit Scotland commissioned by the Scottish Government confirmed that the cost projections were sound. Edinburgh Council approved the final business case and TIE signed contracts with private design and build consortium BSC, made up of Bilfinger Berger and Siemens for network construction and Spanish rolling stock builder CAF for the trams. When work began in 2008 the total cost was estimated at £521m.

Contractual disputes arose between TIE and BSC soon after construction had begun, with street closures and disruption extending for months as work was suspended and track laying delayed. Wrangles descended into legal disputes and costs rose dramatically, estimated at £770m by June 2011. Earlier in the year Scotland's First Minister, Alex Salmond, had told the *Sunday Herald* newspaper that 'as soon as they dug up Edinburgh it was a recipe for disaster.' He said he regretted the tram project and would rather have seen the money spent on a fleet of eco-buses built in Falkirk (home of Scottish bus builders Alexander Dennis) than the far more costly trams imported from Spain.

Edinburgh Council decided to disband TIE and appoint consultants Turner Townsend instead to manage the project. A proposal to scrap the whole scheme was rejected, but after much acrimony it was eventually agreed with the Scottish Government to save money by cutting the network back to a single

route from Edinburgh Airport to York Place in the centre, but no line north of the city to Leith.

From late 2012 work continued mostly on schedule. Fewer trams would now be required to operate the shorter route, but it was already too late to reduce the order with CAF for twenty-seven Urbos 3 trams. Only seventeen of the 42.8m long articulated trams were now needed to run a full service but no other UK system was able to take the ten spare units delivered from Spain in 2012. Tram testing along the full route started at the end of 2013 and Edinburgh Tram was finally opened to passengers without ceremony on 31 May 2014. With extra interest payments factored in, the cost of the line was by then expected to exceed £1 billion.

Around 4.92m passenger journeys were made on Edinburgh Trams during its first year of operation, some 370,000 ahead of the pre-launch target. The tramway achieved 99 per cent service reliability and a 95 per cent overall customer satisfaction rating in a UK-wide survey by Passenger Focus. The figures reflect an excellent operation, but it is quite a limited service, mainly providing travellers and visitors with a convenient link between the city centre and Edinburgh Airport.

Edinburgh Trams will only meet its original objective of providing a useful

The first of Edinburgh's new trams to be seen on Princes Street has a night time trial run in December 2013. The much delayed public service began without ceremony six months later. Peter Stubbs/www.edinphoto.org.uk

Princes Street, Edinburgh, seen from the Scott Monument, c1930. Jenners department store is on the left and the giant North British Hotel (now the Balmoral) looms above Waverley station to the right. There are thirteen double-deck trams and just one bus in this postcard view.

The same view in 2014 with the cityscape almost unchanged some seventy-five years on. One of the newly operational CAF trams is turning on to Princes Street, heading west towards Edinburgh Airport. OG

An Edinburgh tram ready to leave St Andrew Square in the city centre, December 2015. The first eighteen months' operation had been a great success, but a funding mechanism for the planned northern extension to Leith has yet to be agreed. OG

The spacious and accessible interior of an Edinburgh tram, 2014. Modern electric trams offer a smoother, more comfortable ride than buses and no emissions to pollute the urban environment. OG

everyday service for city residents and commuters if the tramway is extended out to Leith as originally intended. Edinburgh City Council remains determined to achieve this, but it is still not clear how the extension will be funded given the disastrous handling of the initial scheme. Looming over everything is the public enquiry into what went so badly wrong in 2008-12. One of the Edinburgh Tram inquiry's terms of reference is 'to report to the Scottish Ministers making recommendations as to how major tram and light rail projects of a similar nature might avoid such failures in future'.[46]

Where to next?

The light rail renaissance in the UK and Irish Republic has been modest but steady. There are now ten systems in operation, seven of them opened since 1992. The latest official figures from the Department for Transport (for England only, excluding Scotland and Dublin LUAS) record just under 240m passenger journeys by light rail in 2013-14, nearly half of them made on London's DLR. As a proportion of all journeys made by public transport in Great Britain, this amounts to just under 3

Strasbourg, home of the European Parliament, opened a new tramway in 1994. Its original futuristic low-floor Eurotrams were designed and partly manufactured on the Continent but final assembly was in Britain when ABB took over the former British Rail carriage works in York. The company collapsed and the works closed in 1996, partly through a lack of UK orders.

per cent. It looks like a tiny figure, but bald statistics only tell a partial story and the numbers are growing steadily. Taken as a whole, and compared to the total for bus, rail and the London Underground, they are small but in every area where they are now operating, trams are having a significant and growing impact.

Inevitably, people complain about and are inconvenienced by engineering and building work during the construction phase, but passenger focus surveys invariably indicate high satisfaction rates once new lines and systems open. They are never white elephants or a waste of taxpayers' money. Recent developments in Manchester and Nottingham have been particularly successful, both integrated with local suburban passenger rail lines, and Birmingham's street running is now

coming on stream. The first tram/train operation in the UK will begin soon between Sheffield and Rotherham. In London the heavily used DLR and upgraded Tramlink system are both now firmly plugged into a wider, integrated rail and bus network, though no further light rail schemes are currently planned for the capital.

It is very clear that given the option the vast majority of passengers much prefer trams to buses, and that light rail is both popular with the public and can attract drivers out of their cars in towns and cities. In Europe trams are a vital feature of smaller historic cities like Freiburg (Germany), Padua (Italy) and Strasbourg (France). There they are considered an essential part of a sustainable urban transport mix which encourages cycling

and walking but discourages use of the private car by providing a convenient and environmentally sound alternative.[47] Buses alone cannot do this and do not mix with city centre pedestrian streets nor, as yet, offer highly efficient and pollution-free public transport. Trams can deliver the practical benefits of speed, cleanliness and reliability, but also a much more intangible quality as a marker of civic pride, an almost forgotten concept in the UK. They are a positive asset to any town or urban area.

It is much more difficult to make a persuasive case for light rail with the politicians who make the decisions on future projects. Tramways are expensive, long term capital projects and a single poorly managed scheme that runs over budget can have a damaging impact on public and political perception. In difficult economic times it is always easier to argue for cheaper or watered down options such as guided busways to tackle urban transport issues, though these are likely to be short term and inadequate solutions.

Proposed light rail schemes in the UK have often been treated as one-off schemes, micro-managed against flawed financial and cost-benefit projections. Many local projects were cancelled or rejected by the Department for Transport in the years before the financial crisis of 2008. Some of these may have been the victims of Government cuts and rationing rather than failing to meet specific authorisation criteria. New projects are now even harder to promote in a period of continued financial austerity. There are no longer any start-

Blackpool, the great tramway survivor in the UK, has been fully modernised and upgraded in the twenty-first century. One of the new fleet of Bombardier Flexity Swift trams heads south from the Tower on the first day of operation, 4 April 2012. The much loved heritage trams have been retained to provide a supplementary service. OG

Brave new Birmingham. A computer generated image showing a tram outside the Town Hall on the next modest extension of Metro Line 1 from New Street to Centenary Square. This is not scheduled to open before 2020. Centro

up tramways on the horizon anywhere in the UK, and the complexity of planning and financing light rail projects under current conditions does not encourage new development.

Investment in trams should really be considered as part of an integrated public transport policy and in association with land use planning in urban and surrounding areas. Unfortunately neither of these has been applied across the UK in the last seventy years. There is no easy balance between the modern expectation of complete personal mobility through a private car with the demand for universal access and mass transit in towns and cities for all. Light rail can play an important role in strategic planning, but rarely does. With only a few exceptions, coherent land use and transport strategies have never

been effectively combined across the UK's city regions.[48]

The limited number of successful light rail projects completed since the 1980s has owed more to fortuitous local circumstances and robust individual public/private partnerships than any national policy. Having abolished all regional economic and planning mechanisms outside London in 2010, the UK Government is now looking to Local Enterprise Partnerships to take plans forward and encourage regional economic growth around the country. As transport planner Peter Headicar has suggested in a recent paper for the Independent Transport Commission (ITC), this will be a challenge because of the 'fractured array of public and private bodies with transport responsibilities'. Unless already weakened

local authorities either combine or work in effective partnership across their borders, the new 'localist' regime 'will only further inhibit the planning and delivery of integrated spatial strategies'.[49]

With light rail it seems that every case in Britain over the last twenty-five years has been different. There is certainly no such thing as UK best practice yet and very little seems to be learned and applied from elsewhere. This is despite the wealth of examples from European towns and cities whose transport and planning is much admired in Britain but rarely emulated. A great deal of public consultation goes on, particularly from local councils, but this can seem like tokenism leading to stalemate when a project is shelved through lack of resources. Public transport bodies and local authorities have generally shown poor leadership, and failed to work in partnership with the private sector to achieve practical results. Projects are often poorly managed, badly delayed and run over budget. Perhaps this is not surprising when our planning systems and financial restrictions require almost superhuman and long term tenacity to see a project through from vision to achievement. The Government's announcement in October 2015 of a new independent National Infrastructure Commission to review and advise on future policy and capital projects is a welcome development. However, it has been met with an understandable degree of cynicism about its likely impact. The commission is purely advisory and will have no budget or powers to implement any recommendations it eventually comes up with. Whatever the long term benefits of investment in light rail, an uncertain roller-coaster ride for tramways seems likely to continue into the foreseeable future.

A vision of St Giles in the historic centre of Oxford, pedestrianised and served by modern trams. Part of Oxfordshire County Council's public consultation on future transport strategy in 2015. Despite its obvious benefits, a light rail scheme is a highly unlikely outcome under current economic conditions.

Oxfordshire County Council

TIMELINE OF TRAMWAY HISTORY
IN BRITAIN AND IRELAND

1807 First horse-drawn passenger rail service in UK opens on the Swansea and Oystermouth Tramroad in South Wales.

1860 First horse-drawn street railway in UK, promoted by G.F. Train, opens in Birkenhead.

1861-2 Train opens three tramways in London, all closed down within months.

1863 Landport & Southsea Tramway in Portsmouth is the first to open along a street with Parliamentary authority.

1870 First permanent street tramways open in London and Liverpool.

Wolverton and Stony Stratford steam tram, first operated 1887.

Sheffield horse tram first introduced on the Attercliffe route 1873.

1870 Tramways Act sets rules and procedure for authorising street tramways in UK.

1872 First urban horse tramways open in Ireland, in Dublin, Belfast and Cork.

1876 First regular use of steam power on a rural roadside tram line, the Wantage Tramway in Berkshire.

1877 First regular use of steam power on an urban street tramway, the Vale of Clyde line in Govan, near Glasgow.

1883 Volk's electric railway, 'the first public electric conveyance in the UK', opens on Brighton Beach but with no street running.

1883 First electric line in Ireland opens, the Giant's Causeway, Portrush and Bush Valley Tramway, using third rail power supply.

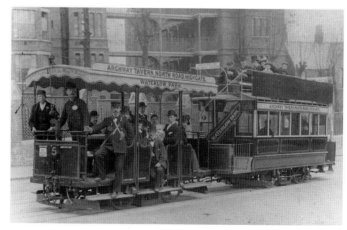

Highgate Hill cable tramway, north London, opened 1884. LTM/TfL

1884 First cable tramway in Europe opens up Highgate Hill, London.

1885 First electric street tramway in England opens in Blackpool, using conduit power supply.

1888 First cable tramway in Scotland opens in Edinburgh.

1891 First overhead electric street tramway in UK opens at Roundhay Park, Leeds.

1893 First electrification of a steam tramway in the UK in Walsall, Staffordshire.

1893 Manx Electric Railway opens, now the oldest operational roadside electric tramway.

1895 First electric tram line opens in Bristol, planned by James Clifton Robinson. Bristol becomes the first major UK city to be electrified, and by a private company, not the local authority.

1896 First electric street tramway in Ireland from Dublin city boundary to Dalkey, opened by a private company, again planned by Clifton Robinson.

1898 Glasgow and Liverpool are the first two big city local authorities in the UK to open their own electric tramways. This municipal route to electrification is used in most urban areas of the UK over the next fifteen years, with relatively few company-run electric tramways opening in Britain and Ireland.

1901 First electric lines in Greater London opened by London United Tramways Company, running west of the LCC boundary from Shepherds Bush into Middlesex.

Opening of the first LCC electric tram route, south London 1903.

1903 First electric route of the London County Council (LCC) opened by Prince of Wales from Westminster Bridge to Tooting in south London.

1911 First UK trolleybus services open in Bradford and Leeds on same day.

1914-18 First World War.

1915 Glasgow Corporation employs first women tram conductors in UK as a wartime expedient, followed by female tram drivers from 1916.

1917 Isle of Sheppey system in Sheerness, Kent, is the first electric tramway in UK to close.

1920s UK tramways reach their maximum size and use, but some of the smaller systems across the country are replaced by motor buses or trolleybuses, including Ipswich, Keighley, Lincoln, Camborne & Redruth and Wolverhampton.

1926 Last horse tram service in mainland England closes, on the seafront at Morecambe.

1931 First replacement of trams with trolleybuses on London United system in south-west London.

1931 Royal Commission recommends replacement of tramways across the country.

1933 Creation of London Passenger Transport Board (LPTB), which soon announces a major programme to replace its inherited trams with new trolleybuses.

1930s Several towns start tram replacement, including Brighton, Bristol, Carlisle, Cork, Halifax, Nottingham, Newport, Portsmouth, Hull and Leicester.

1939-45 Second World War.

1945-50 Many cities complete tram closures started before the war, including Dublin, Cardiff, Newcastle, Bradford, Southampton, Manchester & Newcastle.

New RT type diesel bus passing one of the trams it replaced on Southwark Bridge, London 1951.

1952 Last tram in London, once the UK's largest system.

1953 Last tram in Birmingham.

1954 Last tram in Belfast.

1956 Llandudno & Colwyn Bay line closes, the last privately run street tramway in the UK.

1956 Last tram in Edinburgh.

1957 Last tram in Liverpool.

1957 Last horse tram service in Ireland, the Fintona 'van', closes.

1959 Last tram in Leeds.

1959 Last electric tramway in Ireland, the Hill of Howth line near Dublin, closes.

1960 Last tram in Sheffield.

1960 Last electric tramway in Wales, the Swansea & Mumbles Railway, closes.

A Glasgow Cunarder, the last double deck tram design in the UK.

1962 Last tramway in Scotland, the once extensive Glasgow Corporation system, the final major city network in the UK, closes.

1962-92 Blackpool has the only regular year-round, street-running public tramway service in the UK during this thirty-year period. The Manx Electric Railway continued to run a seasonal service on its roadside inter-urban tramway and the Douglas horse trams also continue seasonal operation.

1964 First electric service at the Tramway Museum, Crich, later to become the National Tramway Museum.

1972 Last trolleybus system in UK closes, in Bradford.

1980 Tyne & Wear Metro opens, a cross between light and heavy rail, and entirely off-road.

1987 Docklands Light Railway (DLR) opens in London, an entirely off-road and fully automated system.

1992 Manchester Metrolink opens, first new light rail system in UK with some street running, initially only across Manchester city centre.

1994 Sheffield Supertram system opens, with extensive street running.

1999 Midland Metro opens between Birmingham and Wolverhampton, mainly on old railway alignments with short street running.

2000 Croydon Tramlink opens, the return of street running trams in London, though only across Croydon town centre.

Light rail returns to Ireland. A Dublin Luas tram in 2012. OG

2004 Luas system opens in Dublin, the first new light rail operation in Ireland.

2004 Nottingham Express Transit (NET) light rail system opens.

2012 Blackpool system is upgraded with new European-style trams for daily operation but retains its heritage tram fleet for special weekend and seasonal services.

2014 Edinburgh Tram opens, first new light rail line in Scotland.

2015-17 Significant extensions and/or improvements to light rail systems in Nottingham, Manchester, Birmingham, Dublin, Blackpool, Sheffield and London scheduled to open, but no new tramways likely to be authorised.

FURTHER READING

There are detailed histories available of most individual tramways and networks in Britain and Ireland. Many of them concentrate heavily on the technicalities of rolling stock and service provision, which can obscure the much wider significance of light rail and its contribution to our increasingly urban world. Relatively few studies look more widely at the changing social, financial and political environment in which tramways have operated over the last 150 years, and their potential role in our urban futures. The case for investing in light rail infrastructure for our cities as an essential part of the UK's forward planning is clear but still barely recognised by politicians, planners or indeed the general public. The references listed here are the secondary sources I found most helpful when researching this book, but the list is by no means exhaustive.

I have not gone back to primary sources such as company records and council minutes. The trade journal *Tramway & Railway World* is an invaluable source for the early electric period from c1900 to 1940 and a complete reference set is available for consultation at the London Transport Museum Library **www.ltmuseum.co.uk** and in the John Price Memorial Library at the National Tramway Museum, Crich **www.tramway.co.uk**. For recent and current developments see *Tramways & Urban Transit* (formerly *Modern Tramway*), the monthly journal of the Light Rail Transit Association (LRTA). **www.lrta.org**. A wide range of tramway publications is available from the LRTA and Tramway & Light Railway Society (TLRS), while specialist transport publishers like Adam Gordon, the Oakwood Press and the Middleton Press have extensive backlists. Secondhand books and journals are now easily available through online sources.

John B. Appleby *Bristol's Trams Remembered* (J.B. Appleby 1969)

Philip Bagwell & Peter Lyth *Transport in Britain 1750-2000, From Canal Lock to Gridlock* (Hambledon & London 2002)

T.C. Barker & Michael Robbins *A History of London Transport* Vols 1&2 (George Allen & Unwin 1974 & 1976)

Wingate H. Bett & John C. Gillham *Great British Tramway Networks* (LRTL 1957)

A. Winstan Bond *The British Tram, History's Orphan* (TLRS 1980)

Alan W. Brotchie *The Twilight Years of the Edinburgh Tram* (Adam Gordon 2001)

R.J. Buckley *A History of Tramways from Horse to Rapid Transit* (David & Charles 1975)

Richard Buckley *Sheffield Trams Past and Present* (Stenlake Publishing 2008)

Richard Buckley *Leeds Trams 1871-1959* (Stenlake Publishing 2011)

John Carlson & Neil Mortson *Sunderland Transport* (The History Press 2009)

Ernest F. Carter *Trams and Tramways* (Foyles Handbooks 1961)

Terence Cooper (ed) *The Wheels Used to Talk To Us: A London Tramwayman Remembers* (Sheaf Publishing 1977)

Michael Corcoran *Through Streets Broad and Narrow, A History of Dublin Trams* (Ian Allan 2008)

R.T. Coxon *Roads & Rails of Birmingham 1900-1939* (Ian Allan 1979)

Peter Davey *Bristol's Tramways* (Middleton Press 1995)

John R. Day *London's Trams and Trolleybuses* (London Transport 1977)

Colin Divall & Winstan Bond (eds) *Suburbanizing the Masses: Public Transport and Urban Development in Historical Perspective* (Ashgate 2003)

Norman Ellis *Trams Around Dewsbury & Wakefield* (Wharncliffe Books 2004)

David Foley *The Bloomsday Trams* (David Foley 2009)

Peter Fox, Paul Jackson & Roger Benton *Tram to Supertram, An Old Friend Returns to the Streets of*

Sheffield (Platform 5 1995)

Colin Garratt *The Golden Years of British Trams* (Milepost 92½ in association with the National Tramway Museum 1995)

John B. Gent & John H. Meredith *Croydon's Tramways* (Middleton Press 1999)

Denis Gill *Tramcar Treasury* (George Allen & Unwin 1963)

David Gladwin *Britain's Traditional Tramways* (Brewin Books 2004)

Edward Gray *Salford's Tramways* Parts One & Two (Foxline Publishing 1997/1999)

E. Jackson-Stevens *100 Years of British Electric Tramways* (David & Charles 1985)

Chas C. Hall *Sheffield Transport* (Transport Publishing Company 1977)

Robert J. Harley *LCC Electric Tramways* (Capital Transport 2002)

Robert J. Harley *London United Electric Tramways* (Capital Transport 2010)

Robert J. Harley *North London Trams* (Capital Transport 2008)

Robert J. Harley *London Tramway Twilight 1949-1952* (Capital Transport 2000)

David Harvey *Birmingham Before the Electric Tram* (Amberley Publishing 2013)

David Harvey *Birmingham in the age of the tram 1933-53* Vols 1-3 (Silver Link Publishing 2003)

George S. Hearse *Tramways of the City of Carlisle* (George S. Hearse 1962)

Peter Hesketh *Trams in the North West* (Ian Allan 1995)

S.H. Pearce Higgins *The Wantage Tramway* (The Abbey Press 1958)

Martin Higginson (ed) *Tramway London. Background to the abandonment of London's trams 1931-1952* (LRTA/Birkbeck College 1993)

J.B. Horne & T.B. Maund *Liverpool Transport* Vols 1-4 (Senior Publications/Transport Publishing Company/LRTA 1982 onwards)

D.L.G. Hunter *Edinburgh's Transport, The Early Years* (Mercat Press 1992)

W.G.S. Hyde *The Manchester, Bury, Rochdale & Oldham Steam Tramway* (Transport Publishing Company 1979)

J. Joyce *Tramway Heyday* (Ian Allan 1974)

J. Joyce *Tramway Twilight* (Ian Allan 1962)

J. Joyce *Trolleybus Trails, A Survey of British Trolleybus Systems* (Ian Allan 1963)

J. Joyce *Roads and Rails of Tyne and Wear* (Ian Allan 1985)

'Kennington' *London County Council Tramways Handbook* (TLRS 1977)

James Kilroy *Irish Trams* (Colourpoint 1996)

J.S. King *Bradford Corporation Tramways* (Venture Publications 1998)

Charles Klapper *The Golden Age of Tramways* (Routledge & Kegan Paul 1961)

Martin Langley & Edwina Small *The Trams of Plymouth, A 73 Years Story* (Ex-Libris Press 1990)

Charles E. Lee *The Swansea & Mumbles Railway* (Oakwood Press 1954)

Stephen Lockwood *Trams Across the Wear: Remembering Sunderland's Electric Trams* (Adam Gordon 2009)

Colin G. Maggs *The Bath Tramways* (Oakwood Press 1992)

Barry M. Marsden *Nottinghamshire & Derbyshire Tramway* (Middleton Press 2005)

T.B. Maund & M. Jenkins *The Tramways of Birkenhead and Wallasey* (LRTA 1987)

Mike Maybin *A nostalgic look at Belfast Trams since 1945* (Silver Link Publishing 1994)

John P. McKay *Tramways and Trolleys, The Rise of Urban Mass Transport in Europe* (Princeton University Press 1976)

James Millington *UK Light Rail and Tram Museum Guide 2015* (Train Crazy Publishing 2015)

Donal Murray *Tracks of the City, An Introduction to the Railways, Tramways and Metro of Dublin* (Colourpoint Books 2014)

Julia Neville *Exeter and the Trams 1882-1931* (Exeter Civic Society 2010)

Charles A. Oakley *The Last Tram* (Glasgow Corporation 1962)

E.R. Oakley *The British Horse Tram Era* (Nemo Productions 1978)

E.R. Oakley *London County Council Tramways Vols 1&2* (London Tramways History Group/TLRS/LRTA 1989 & 1991)

Nicholas Owen *History of the British Trolleybus* (David & Charles 1974)

Steve Palmer *Blackpool, 125 Years by Tram* (Tramroad House 2010)

Brian Patton *The Development of the Modern Tram* (Adam Gordon 2006)

Alan Pearce, Brian Hardy & Colin Stannard

Docklands Light Railway Official Handbook (Capital Transport 2006)

R. Stuart Pilcher *Road Passenger Transport* (Pitman 1937)

M.F. Powell *Light Rail & Guided Transit* (Natula Publications 1997)

Edwin A. Pratt *A History of Inland Transport and Communication* (David & Charles Reprint 1970 of 1912 original)

J.H. Price *A Source Book of Trams* (Ward Lock 1980)

Struan Jno. T. Robertson *The Glasgow Horse Tramways* (The Scottish Tramway & Transport Society 2000)

'Rodinglea' *The Tramways of East London* (TLRS/LRTL 1967)

Bob Rowe *UK Tram and Light Rail Systems* (Venture Publications 2009)

R.W. Rush *Horse Trams of the British Isles* (Oakwood Press 2004)

Robert Schwandl *Tram Atlas Britain and Ireland* (Robert Schwandl Verlag 2015)

Bill Simpson *The Brill Tramway* (Oxford Publishing Co 1985)

Geoffrey Skelsey *Nottingham's New Trams, The NET Success Story* (LRTA 2007)

C.S. Smeeton *The London United Tramways* Vols 1&2 (LRTA/TLRS 1994/2000)

C.S.Smeeton *The Metropolitan Electric Tramways* Vols 1&2 (LRTA/TLRS 1984/1986)

J. Soper *Leeds Transport* Vols 1-5 (Leeds Transport Historical Society 1985 onwards)

S.A. Staddon *The Tramways of Sunderland* (The Advertiser Press Limited 1964)

John R. Stevens & Alan W. Brotchie *Pioneers of the Street Railway in the USA, Street Tramways in the UK ...and elsewhere* (Stenlake Publishing 2014)

Michael Steward, John Gent & Colin Stannard *Tramlink Official Handbook* (Capital Transport 2000)

Ian G. McM. Stewart *The Glasgow Tramcar* (Scottish Tramway & Transport Society 1983)

Michael Taplin *Light Rail in Europe* (Capital Transport 1995)

Michael Taplin & Michael Russell *Trams in Western Europe* (Capital Transport 2002)

Michael Taplin & Michael Russell *Trams in Eastern Europe* (Capital Transport 2003)

Peter Tuffrey *Doncaster's Electric Transport* (Amberley 2010)

Keith Turner *Directory of British Tramways* Vols 1-3 (Tempus/History Press 2007-10)

Keith Turner, Shirley Smith & Paul Smith *The Directory of British Tram Depots* (Oxford Publishing Company 2001)

Andrew Turton *Horse-Drawn Transport in Leeds* (The History Press 2015)

David Voice *The Age of the Horse Tram* (Adam Gordon 2009)

Michael H. Waller & Peter Waller *British & Irish Tramway Systems since 1945* (Ian Allan 1992)

Peter Waller *Glory Days: British Trams* (Ian Allan 2003)

Peter Waller *Trams of the British Isles 1945-1962* (Nostalgia Road/Crecy Publishing 2013)

Peter Waller *Regional Tramways: Scotland* (Pen & Sword 2016)

Peter Waller *Regional Tramways: Yorkshire and North East England* (Pen & Sword 2016)

J.S. Webb *Black Country Tramways* Vols 1&2 (J.S. Webb 1974/76)

H.A. Whitcombe *History of the Steam Tram* (Oakwood Press 1954)

Stewart Williams (ed) *Vintage Buses & Trams in South Wales* (Stewart Williams 1975)

D.W. Willoughby & E.R. Oakley *London Transport Tramways Handbook* (Nemo Productions 1972)

Frank E. Wilson *British Tramway Accidents* (Adam Gordon 2006)

Geoffrey Wilson *London United Tramways, A History 1894-1933* (George Allen & Unwin 1971)

R.J.S. Wiseman *Classic Tramcars* (Ian Allan 1986)

Ian Yearsley & Philip Groves *The Manchester Tramways* (Transport Publishing Co 1991)

Ian Yearsley *Tramway Museum Story* (Tramway Museum Society 2005)

Photomontage poster by Maurice Beck for the Underground Group, 1932, promoting the 'record of service' for their London tramway operations in 1931. There were matching posters for their bus and Underground services. The images feature the newly introduced LUT trolleybuses (left) and the latest Feltham trams (upper right) used on both the LUT and MET networks. London Transport took over in 1933 and announced plans to replace all the capital's trams with trolleybuses. LTM/TfL

CHAPTER NOTES

Chapter 1

1 See Charles E. Lee's classic history of the line *The Swansea & Mumbles Railway* (1954).

2 Lee quotes from Miss Spence's *Summer Excursions*, an account of her travels in England and Wales, published in 1809.

3 See John H. White Jr, *Horsecars, Cable Cars and Omnibuses* (1974), which reproduces more than 100 photographs of Stephenson products from an album presented to the Smithsonian Museum in 1888. By the 1890s, the Stephenson Company was in decline and J.G. Brill took over as the leading US streetcar builders in the electric era.

4 Charles Dickens *American Notes*, Chapter 6 (1842).

5 See John R. Stevens *Pioneers of the Street Railway in the USA* (Stenlake Publishing, 2014), whose extensive research counters some of the repeated misconceptions about early passenger tramways.

6 George Francis Train *My Life in Many States and in Foreign Lands*, 1902, p259. Train dictated the book when he was seventy-four, two years before his death in 1904. It was republished in 1991 by Adam Gordon from an original copy apparently presented by Citizen Train to James Clifton Robinson, 'The Tramway King', who opened the first electric tramway in London. It is a fascinating though highly unreliable memoir.

7 *My Life in Many States*, p260-1.

8 'Haworth's Patent Perambulating Principle' is described on the website of the Greater Manchester Museum of Transport.

9 *Report of the Banquet given by George Francis Train Esq of Boston US to Inaugurate the Opening of the first street Railway in Europe at Birkenhead, August 30 1860 with Opinions of the Press on the Subject of Street Railways*. The original pamphlet was reported, printed and published by Lee and Nightingale, Liverpool, 1860, but clearly produced on Train's behalf. A limited edition reprint was published by Adam Gordon in 2004.

10 See Alan W. Brotchie *Pioneers of Street Tramways in the UK*, section 2 of the joint publication with Stevens (Stenlake Publishing, 2014).

11 T.C. Barker and Michael Robbins *A History of London Transport Vol 1 The Nineteenth Century*, p181.

12 Herbert Bright *Remarks on Street Tramways Applied to London and its Suburbs* (1868), p8.

13 Figures quoted by Barker and Robbins, op cit, p196.

14 *Herapath's Railway Journal*, 19 January 1884.

15 See Walter McGrath, *The Tramways of Cork*, The Tramway Review Vol 2, issue 12, 1953.

16 See Michael Corcoran's history of Dublin trams *Through Streets Broad and Narrow* (2008).

17 See J.B. Horne and T.B. Maund, *Liverpool Transport Volume 1 1830-1900* (2nd edition, 1995).

18 See Andrew Turton, *Horse-drawn Transport in Leeds: William Turton, Corn Merchant and Tramway Entrepreneur* (2015).

19 Figures from Charles Klapper, *The Golden Age of Tramways* (1961), p37, who has taken them from the contemporary *Duncan's Tramway Manual*, which he says are not comprehensive.

20 *Trams & Buses of the Great Cities in the 1880s*,

reprinted with added illustrations by the Omnibus Society, c2000. Original text from *The Railway & Tramway Express*, 1884/5.

21 Struan Jno. T. Robertson, *The Glasgow Horse Tramways* (2000), p68.

22 Figures from Barker & Robbins Vol One, p285.

23 See W.J. Gordon, *The Horse World of London* (1893, reprinted 1971).

24 See Stevens & Brotchie op cit and David Voice, *The Age of the Horse Tram* (2009). Section 2 of Voice's book has details of all known manufacturers of horsecars used in the British Isles.

25 See *The Manchester horse tram* (2008) a Tramfare special publication, **www.tramways.freeserve.co.uk**

26 For an entertaining and well-illustrated account of the Fintona tram see Anthony Burges *Horseshoes and Trolleypoles* (2008).

27 For a brief history and description of recent operation see Norman Johnston *Douglas Horse Trams in colour* (1995). At the time of writing (early 2016), the future of the horse tramway remains uncertain.

Chapter 2

1 Michael Corcoran *Through Streets Broad and Narrow, A History of Dublin's Trams* (2008).

2 J.H. Price *A Source Book of Trams* (1980), p24.

3 H. Osborne O'Hagan *Leaves from my Life* (1929).

4 For a detailed case study of the largest steam tram system in Britain see W.G.S. Hyde *The Manchester, Bury, Rochdale & Oldham Steam Tramway* (1979).

5 See George W. Hilton *The Cable Car in America* (1971) and Robert C. Post *Street Railways and the Growth of Los Angeles* (1989).

6 See D.L.G. Hunter *Edinburgh's Transport, The Early Years* (1992) for a detailed account of the city's complex and disputed original tramway development. It almost makes the painful problems that have surrounded the planning and construction of Edinburgh's twenty-first century tram system look simple and straightforward.

7 See S.V. Fay (intro) *The Matlock Steep Gradient Tramway* (1972), a reprint by the Arkwright Society of the original 1893 opening souvenir booklet.

8 See F.K. Pearson *Cable Tram Days* (1977), a booklet published by the Douglas Cable Car Group who had just completed the restoration of cable car 72/73 in time for the line's centenary in 1976.

9 See *An Illustrated Guide to the Funicular Railways of Great Britain*, Heritage Railway Association (2015).

10 Quoted in S.H. Pearce Higgins *The Wantage Tramway* (1958), p46. Chapter 4 includes an interesting contemporary account of the compressed air trials in 1880.

Chapter 3

1 Quotation and description from Chris O'Brien's website **www.edinburghtrams.info**

2 See Alan A. Jackson *Volk's Railways Brighton* (1992).

3 Quotation and reference from R.J. Buckley *History of Tramways from Horse to Rapid Transit* (1975), p48.

4 Quotations and description from Brian Turner and Steve Palmer *The Blackpool Story* (1976).

5 See William D. Middleton & William D. Middleton 3rd *Frank Julian Sprague, Electrical Inventor and Engineer* (2009), Chapter 4.

6 George W. Hilton *Transport Technology and the Urban Pattern*, Journal of Contemporary History 4 (1969), p126.

7 Figures from US Transportation census, quoted by John P McKay *Tramways and Trolleys, The Rise of Urban Mass Transport in Europe* (1976), p50.

8 Information from Keith Turner *Directory of British Tramways Vol 2* (2009), p97.

9 See the *Manx Electric Railway Official Guide* by Gordon N. Kiveton & Andrew A Scarffe (revised ed1994).

10 A. Reckenzaun, commenting on Edward Hopkinson's paper *Electrical Railways: The City & South London Railway*, Proceedings of the Institution of Civil Engineers 112, 1893, p235.

11 See Kenneth T. Jackson *Crabgrass Frontier: The Suburbanization of the United States* (1985).

12 T.C. Barker *Urban Transport* in Freeman & Aldcroft (eds) *Transport in Victorian Britain* (1988), p157.

13 Quoted by I.S. Bishop *A History of Bristol's Trams, The City & Kingswood Line* (1995), p12.

14 See John B. Appleby *Bristol's Trams Remembered* (1969), p16-18.

15 Quoted by I.S. Bishop, p10.

16 See D.G. Tucker *The Beginnings of Electricity Supply in Bristol 1889-1902, Journal of Bristol Industrial Archaeology Society Vol 5* (1972).

17 Michael Corcoran *Through Streets Broad and Narrow* (2008), p33.

18 All of Ireland was part of the UK at this time. The Irish Free State was not created until 1922, following the War of Independence (1919-22). The IFS, effectively a British dominion, was replaced by the fully independent state of Eire (Ireland) in 1937. Ulster, Northern Ireland, has remained within the UK.

19 Quoted by Corcoran, p45, whose masterly account of the tortuous evolution of the Dublin system is acknowledged as my principal source for this section.

20 Trams play a significant background role in Joyce's seminal work *Ulysses*. The action within the novel takes place across Dublin on a single day, June 16 1904, the date on which Joyce met the love of his life, Nora Barnacle. Joyce started writing *Ulysses* ten years later when living abroad, but for him Dublin and its trams were forever frozen in 1904. See David Foley, *The Bloomsday Trams* (2009) for an exploration of the background.

21 Corcoran again is particularly good at examining and explaining the unique social context of Dublin's trams. See especially pp80-90.

22 Reported in *Electrical Engineering* 15 June 1895, p747.

23 Quoted in *Electrical Engineering* 18 August 1896, p195.

24 McKay, pp182-3.

25 Frederic C. Howe *The British City: The Beginnings of Democracy* (1907).

26 See David Daiches *Glasgow* (1976), p147-153.

27 For a concise account of Liverpool's electrification see T.B. Maund *Shutting the Stable Door: The Transformation of City Transport in Liverpool* in *Archive, the Quarterly Journal for British Industrial and Transport History Issues 25* (March 2000) *and 26* (June 2000).

28 Account and quote from J.B. Horne & T.B. Maund *Liverpool Transport Vol 1* (1995), p124.

29 This is a simplification of a complex story. For a detailed account see *Horne & Maund Vol 2*.

30 Frederic C. Howe *European Cities at Work* (1913), pp284-286.

31 The electric tramways of Plymouth are a case in point. There were four independent networks

operated by three different companies serving the adjacent towns of Plymouth, Stonehouse and Devonport. The merger of the 'Three Towns' into the new borough of Plymouth in 1914 led to the three tram companies being taken over by the new Plymouth Corporation and merged into a single council run network.

32 See *Tramways and Electric Railways in the Nineteenth Century, Cassier's Electric Railway Number 1899*, limited edition reprint by Adam Gordon, 1992.

33 Figures from E. Jackson-Stevens *100 Years of British Electric Tramways* (1985), p36.

34 Quoted by Edwin A. Pratt in *A History of Inland Transport & Communication* (1912), p459.

35 Baker's report quoted in Robert J. Harley *LCC Electric Tramways* (2002), p11.

36 Dr Kennedy was a former professor of engineering at University College London but had no practical experience of electric tramways.

37 Harley Chapter 2, pp10-25, is a good account of the LCC's painfully slow and flawed progress with tramway electrification.

38 Klapper *The Golden Age of Tramways*, p77.

39 Taken from the *Yorkshire Telegraph and Star*, 14 December 1907.

40 For an account of Robinson's adroit planning of London's first electric tramway see T.C. Barker & Michael Robbins *A History of London Transport Vol 2* (1974), p31-34.

41 Opening guest list and quotations from Geoffrey Wilson *London United Tramways* (1971), Chapter 5.

42 Figures from Barker & Robbins Vol 2, p98.

43 Quoted from her husband's personal papers by Lucy Masterman in *CFG Masterman, A Biography* (1939), p82-3.

44 Figures from T.C. Barker *Urban Transport* p158 and Ian Yearsley & Philip Groves *The Manchester Tramways* (1991), p67.

45 See Winstan Bond *The British Tram, History's Orphan* (1980), a superb and concise overview of the first hundred years of electric traction given as the Walter Gratwicke Memorial lecture at the Science Museum in 1979.

46 Details of first-class trams from Horne & Maund, Vol 2, p24-27.

47 The Subway was fully opened in 1908 but could only be used by single-deck cars. It was rebuilt in 1930/31 to take double deck trams and was used almost until the end of London's trams in 1952. The northern entrance ramp, complete with conduit track, can still be seen in Southampton Row.

48 Life on the LCCT is well described in the recollections of former motorman Stan Collins in Terence Cooper (ed) *The Wheels Used To Talk To Us* (1977). Collins started working on the LCC trams in the 1920s. The change pit procedure is shown clearly in the BTF film *The Elephant Will Never Forget* (1953).

49 Figures quoted by McKay, p192-3, from US *Census Transportation Business 1890* and Manchester Tramways Department *The Passenger Transportation Problem* (1914).

50 *Keighley News* early 1904 quoted in J.S. King *Keighley Corporation Transport* (1964), p20.

51 Quoted from McKay, p219, where he reproduces a fascinating star-shaped time-zone map of tram travel in Greater Manchester prepared for a corporation report in 1914.

52 See *Electric Edwardians, The Films of Mitchell & Kenyon*, and the BBC TV series *The Lost World of Mitchell & Kenyon*, both available on DVD from the BFI.

53 Details from Robert J. Harley *London United Tramways* (2010), p18.

Chapter 4

1 Quotation and information from Nicholas Owen *History of the British Trolleybus* (1974), Chapter One, pp17-34.

2 Edwin A. Pratt *A History of Inland Transport and Communication* (1912), p465-6.

3 Quoted by Gordon R. Urquhart in *Along Great Western Road, An Illustrated History of Glasgow's West End* (2000), p86.

4 Research for the story of Eliza Orr, who became a First World War tram conductor and driver in Glasgow, included on Glasgow's War website **www.firstworldwarglasgow.co.uk**.

5 Quoted by Charles A. Oakley in *The Last Tram* (1962), p65. Oakley's book is a superb history of Glasgow's trams commissioned by the Corporation Transport Department to mark the end of the city's trams in 1962.

6 Quoted by Roger Benton in *Women in Tramways in World War 1, Roads & Road Transport History Association Journal, August 2014*.

7 Chesterfield recollections from Dennis Gill *On the Trams* (1986), p78.

8 Extract from D.H. Lawrence *Tickets Please* (1919).

9 See Barry M. Marsden *The Nottinghamshire & Derbyshire Tramway* (2005) for some fascinating wartime photographs of this eccentric system which appears to confirm some of D.H. Lawrence's observations. These include a female conductor called Emla, a Belgian refugee who had a reputation for quelling troublesome passengers with a blow from her ticket rack, and another clippie wearing a Royal Artillery cap badge. Marsden also reproduces a studio shot of conductress Annie Bronson who could well have been the model for Lawrence's fictional character, Annie Stone.

10 Information from Gill *On the Trams*, p75.

11 Tram bombing incidents recorded in Ian Castle's *London 1914-17: The Zeppelin Menace* (2008) p74 and *London 1917-18: The bomber blitz* (2010). p40.

12 Details of the Walsall attack from the *Express & Star* website **www.expressandstar.com/millennium/ 1900/1900-1924/1916.html**.

13 Information from *On the Trams*. p78.

14 C. Playne *Britain holds on 1917, 1918* (1933). p44.

15 Notes on the Sheerness system from Keith Turner *The Directory of British Tramways* (1996), p129.

16 Recollections from his youth by E. Jackson-Stevens in *100 Years of British Electric Tramways* (1985).

17 For the full, sorry story of the B&ALR see P.M. White & J.M. Storer *Sixpenny Switchback, A Journey in Photographs Along the Burton & Ashby Light Railways* (1983). As described here, a B&ALR tram that survived as a garden pavilion was restored fifty years after the 1927 closure and shipped to the USA in 1980 to work on a heritage tramway in Detroit. The heritage tramway eventually closed in 2003. B&ALR tram no. 14 was put up for sale in 2014, secured by British purchasers and returned to the UK in 2015. It is now housed at the privately owned Statfold Barn Railway near Tamworth, not far from Burton, where it last ran on the B&ALR over eighty years ago. The curious tale of the well-travelled tram continues.

18 These early closures are just a few selected examples. For comprehensive details of openings and closures, see Keith Turner's *Directory*, from which these have been taken.

19 On UK tramcar design and construction see J.H. Price A *Source Book of Trams* (1980), *The Brush Electrical Engineering Company Ltd & its Tramcars* (1976) and *The Dick, Kerr Story* (1993); also David Voice *British Tramcar Manufacturers: British Westinghouse and Metropolitan-Vickers* (2008).

20 Royal Commission on Transport *The Co-ordination and Development of Transport* (1931), para 368.

21 See discussion of the Royal Commission Report by Martin Higginson and Oliver Green in Higginson(ed) *Tramway London, background to the abandonment of London's trams 1931-1952* (1993).

22 Ian Yearsley and Philip Groves *The Manchester Tramways* (1991), p104-5.

23 See Pilcher's book *Road Passenger Transport* (1937), a confident and detailed guide to the management and planning of a road passenger transport operation, including the relative merits of trams, buses and trolleybuses. It is based on his own experience as Tramways Manager in Manchester and Edinburgh, his previous post until 1929. But see also Yearsley's critical but carefully balanced assessment of Pilcher's policies in *The Manchester Tramways*, Appendix 5, pp292-3.

24 For full details of Luff's makeover plans see John Woodman *Municipal Transport in Transition, Blackpool 1932-1940* (2011) and Steve Palmer *Blackpool 125 Years by Tram* (2010). Luff included new buses, coaches *and* trams in his plans, giving the whole of Blackpool's public transport system an unusually consistent modern corporate identity that was applied to the whole vehicle fleet, buildings, shelters and publicity. It was almost the equivalent, on a much smaller scale, of Frank Pick's design strategy for the Underground and London Transport.

25 See Vanessa Toulmin *Blackpool Pleasure Beach* (2011).

26 This was LCC experimental tramcar no.1, nicknamed 'Bluebird' because of its distinctive original colour scheme. It remained the only one of its kind and is now preserved at the National Tramway Museum, Crich.

27 Details from Neil Cossons and Martin Jenkins *Liverpool, Seaport City* (2011), pp79-82.

28 See Chas C. Hall *Sheffield Transport* (1977), p240-251. Newcastle 114, one of the redundant trams bought by Sheffield in 1941 to replace vehicles damaged by wartime bombing, was a remarkable survivor. After refurbishment, it ran for another ten years as Sheffield 317 before the body ended up as a farm shed near Scunthorpe. It was acquired by Beamish Museum in the 1980s, returned to its original 1901 appearance in a nine-year restoration project, and fitted to a truck and motors sourced from Oporto, Portugal. Since 1996 the tram has seen regular passenger service on the museum tramway and a full repaint in 2015 (see Beamish Transport Online **www.beamishtransportonline.co.uk**).

29 See Ian G. McM Stewart's exasperated account of this in *The Glasgow Tramcar* (1994), p123.

30 J. Joyce *Tramway Twilight* (1962), p11. A 'Pilcher' is the last new tramcar design for Manchester built in the Corporation workshops at Hyde Road between 1930 and 1932, and named after General Manager R.J.S. Pilcher, who later recommended progressively replacing the trams in 1934.

31 For the full story see J. Joyce *'Operation Tramaway', The End of London's Trams 1950-1952* (1987).

32 *The Elephant Will Never Forget* (1953) directed by John Krish for British Transport Films, is available on DVD from the BFI.

Chapter 5

1 J. Joyce *Tramway Twilight*, p33.

2 See Ian G. McM Stewart *The Glasgow Tramcar* (1994), p178. Stewart's book is the definitive detailed history of the Glasgow tram as a vehicle from the first electric car in 1897, to the final Coplawhill product in 1952. This was 'Cunarder' no. 1392, the last all-new double-deck tramcar constructed in Britain. It was in service for just ten years and has been on static museum display for over fifty, currently in Glasgow's Riverside Museum.

3 *Tramway Twilight* is the source of most information in this section.

4 To this day trams remain *the* focus of nostalgic folk history in Glasgow. For a humorous take on this

from a Glaswegian who rode the caurs every day in their final years see Allan Morrison *Last Tram tae Auchenshuggle* (2011).

5 For a comprehensive and well-illustrated account of Glasgow's final years see G.H.E. Twidale & R.F. Mack *A Nostalgic Look at Glasgow Trams since 1950* (1988).

6 The 1-mile Eastbourne Tramway was transferred to Devon in 1970, re-laid and extended over the trackbed of the former Seaton branch line, closed by BR in 1966.

7 Joyce *Tramway Twilight*, p92.

8 Glasgow Transport Museum was transferred to the larger Kelvin Hall in 1987, which in turn was replaced by the purpose-built Riverside Museum, which was opened in 2011. The remaining Coplawhill works and depot buildings were adapted to house the Tramway arts centre.

9 These were a standard London County Council E/1 and a smaller West Ham Corporation car, both dating from 1910. The WH car is now on display in the London Transport Museum at Covent Garden; the E/1 is in the LTM Depot at Acton.

10 Information from Geoff Creese *Leicester and its Trams, Tramscape and Townscape 1903-1949* (2006), p50.

11 Another Portstewart steam tram locomotive is preserved in the Ulster Museum. Hull did have similar steam trams but they were built by a different company in Leeds, Greens not Kitsons. The Ryde horsecar has no connection with Hull at all and does not resemble the trams used in the city, but it is thought to be the oldest existing horsecar in the UK. If Sheppard had not acquired the tram in the 1930s, it would probably not survive today. Presumably no museum on the Isle of Wight was interested in preserving it at the time.

12 Information from Hull Museum's website and the *Guide to The Transport Museum* (1968) by Hull Museum Director John Bartlett.

13 Denis Dunstone *For the Love of Trains, The Story of British Tram and Railway Preservation* (2007), p65-69.

14 Ian A. Yearsley *Tramway Museum Story* (2005), p5.

15 See Geoff Price *Llandudno & Colwyn Bay Trams since 1945* for the full story.

16 The Albion Depot, which houses the Black Country Museum's trams, is a genuine Victorian structure recovered from Handsworth, near the West Bromwich Albion football ground. It was built in the 1880s for horse trams and raised in height to accommodate electric trams in the 1900s.

17 See Keith Turner, Shirley Smith and Paul Smith *The Directory of British Tram Depots* (2001).

18 See **www.loftco.net**. Tramshed is due to open in its new guise in 2016.

19 The Kelham Island Museum is housed in the former power station building of Sheffield Corporation Tramways, the impressive administrative offices of Leeds Corporation Tramways have been converted into a Malmaison Hotel and the striking Bristol Tramways generating station at Counterslip, which ceased operation in 1941 after wartime bombing, is due to be turned into luxury city centre apartments.

20 Designed by the LCC Architects Department under Vincent Harris. Described by Bridget Cherry & Nikolaus Pevsner in *The Buildings of England: London 4* (1998) as 'blind brick walls with rusticated Baroque entrance aedicules, inspired by Dance's Newgate Gaol' which had just been demolished in 1902.

21 C. Oakley *The Last Tram*, p124.

22 See Michael Taplin *Light Rail in Europe* (1995) for a comprehensive summary of tramway development in the first fifty years after the Second World War.

23 For a fascinating account of the difference in urban transit policies between the US and Germany in the 1950s and 60s see Jan L. Logemann *Trams or*

Tailfins: Public and Private Prosperity in Postwar West Germany and the United States (2012).

24 See John Gruber & Brian Solomon *Streetcars of America* (2014) for a useful introduction to the history of streetcars in the US and Canada, including new developments, trolley museums and urban historic lines.

25 See J. Joyce *Roads and Rails of Tyne & Wear 1900-1980* (1985), p133-144. DfT figures recorded 38.1m journeys on the Metro in 2014/15, a 6.7 per cent rise over 2013/14 and the highest increase on a UK light rail system outside London.

26 For the full story of the DLR See Alan Pearce, Brian Hardy & Colin Stannard *DLR Official Handbook* (2006).

27 Mea culpa. The concluding words on the DLR from Oliver Green *The London Underground, an illustrated history* (1987). This was the official view promoted at the time by London Regional Transport (LRT), the London Docklands Development Corporation (LDDC), and the Government, joint partners in the project.

28 Account and quotation from Eugene Byrne *Unbuilt Bristol, the city that might have been 1750-2050* (2013), p94-98.

29 Figures from Transport for Greater Manchester *Greater Manchester Growth and Reform Plan:Transport Strategy and Investment Plan* (March 2014).

30 See Barry Worthington *The Metrolink Companion* (2014) for an account of the system's complex evolution since the 1980s and a knowledgeable Mancunian's guide to using Metrolink to explore the city's cultural and economic regeneration.

31 See *21 Years of Metrolink*, a Tramways & Urban Transit special publication (2013).

32 A glimpse of a tram became an immediate signifier that a UK tv drama was set in gritty Manchester or Salford. In December 2010 this culminated in the famous tram crash episode of *Coronation Street*, in which a Metrolink tram toppled off the viaduct on to the street. Or, as the *Mail Online* headline put it, 'Carnage on the cobbles as tram crash brings devastation and death to Weatherfield on soap's 50th anniversary!'

33 St Peter's Square in central Manchester, for example, has been carefully and completely redesigned around the new tram station opening in 2017, whereas at Piccadilly the busy shared tram and bus station still looks like the ugly and chaotic urban space it was twenty-five years earlier when trams were reintroduced.

34 Taplin *Light Rail in Europe*, p138.

35 For a full description see David Haydock *Strasbourg's Futuristic Tramway in Light Rail Review 6* (1994).

36 See W.H. Bett & J.C. Gillham *The Tramways of the West Midlands* (Networks updated edition 2000).

37 The frustrating process of getting Midland Metro started is described by Bob Tarr, Director General of West Midlands PTE, in *Light Rail Review 4* (1992).

38 See *Tramways and Urban Transit*, June 2013.

39 London Transport was renamed London Regional Transport in 1984 when it was transferred from GLC to direct government control. LRT was replaced by Transport for London in 2000.

40 Background information from Michael Steward, John Gent & Colin Stannard *Tramlink Official Handbook* (2000).

41 Official DfT Light Rail and Tram Statistics for England 2014/15, released 9 June 2015.

42 For the demise of Dublin's trams see Corcoran *Through Streets Broad and Narrow*, pp119-139.

43 Donal Murray *Tracks of the City* (2014) p77. Murray's book is an excellent introduction to Dublin's railways, tramways and metro, and a gratefully acknowledged source for this section.

44 This is the William Dargan Bridge at Taney Cross, named in honour of a pioneering Irish railway engineer of the 1800s.

45 See Armstrong's contribution to *Ten Years of Nottingham Express Transit* (Tramways & Urban Transit 2014).

46 For updates and results see the inquiry website **www.edinburghtraminquiry.org**.

47 See *Oxford Transport Strategy Consultation Response* by Alan Baxter & Associates for Oxford

City Council (April 2015). Co-operation and joint planning between Oxfordshire County Council, Oxford City Council and national authorities like the Department for Transport and Network Rail has been almost non-existant for years.

48 For an example of long term urban transport and planning inadequacy, look at Bristol, bizarrely awarded European Green Capital status in 2015.

49 Peter Headicar *Traffic and Towns: the next 50 years*, ITC Occasional Paper no. 6 (January 2015).

Laying new tram track in the centre of Birmingham for the extension of the Midland Metro, 2014. Centro

Opening day of the new tram stop at Rochdale railway station outside St John the Baptist Catholic Church, February 2013. The Metrolink line was then extended into Rochdale Town Centre, providing a new tram service to Manchester via Oldham from March 2014. Jza84

Rails in the road, 1936. Trams, buses and other traffic at the busy intersection outside Vauxhall station. London Transport had just started its tram replacement programme, which because of the war was not completed until 1952. LTM/TfL

Rails in the road, 2016. Trams were back on some of the streets of south London from 2000. This scene at East Croydon station shows one of the original Tramlink units heading for West Croydon (right) and a newly delivered Stadler tram on a special tour of the system (centre). OG

INDEX